CONTENTS

◆ HOW TO PLAY 6

◆ WALKTHROUGH 20

◆ REFERENCE & ANALYSIS 108

◆ EXTRAS 136

VERTICAL TAB

The vertical tab on the right-hand margin of each double-page spread is a navigational tool designed to help you find your way around the guide. The top section lists the individual chapters, while the lower section highlights the part of the chapter you are currently reading.

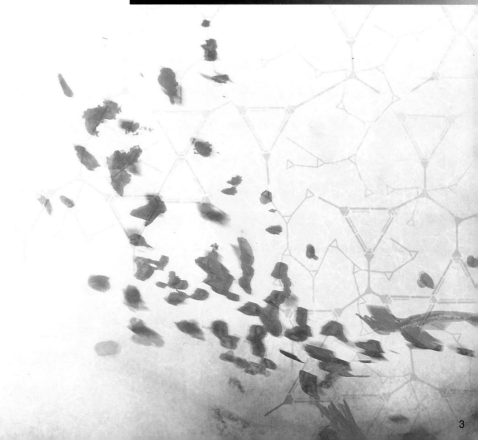

FOREWORD

Roughly five hundred years ago, western civilization underwent a seismic shift, and it has never looked back. Our ancestors "rediscovered" the importance of human beings, and put man back at the center of the universe. This inspired a tsunami of new ideas, and asked all to rethink how things actually worked. The changes were immense; it was as if humanity was reborn. It was the Renaissance. We still feel the aftershocks today.

When I first envisioned the *Assassin's Creed* universe, I knew a sequel would be required for it all to make sense, for it to complete its true grandeur. *Assassin's Creed II* had to take place in a very special setting – and where better than the Renaissance?

In order to best reflect the period, we built the story around the life of an Italian. But a life is more than an anecdote, it is a vast web of details, encounters and complex intrigues. Making sense of all of this can be overwhelming and in true Renaissance style, we have arranged an order to our universe and present it here in this book.

This official guide is the best possible tool to experience *Assassin's Creed II* to its fullest, covering everything from first steps to its deepest secrets. I hope that it will help you discover, play and complete the entire game.

Patrice Désilets
Creative Director

HOW TO PLAY | 01

ASSASSIN'S CREED II IS A HUGE ADVENTURE WITH MANY UNIQUE FEATURES. IN THIS SHORT OPENING CHAPTER WE AIM TO PROVIDE NEW PLAYERS WITH A SOLID UNDERSTANDING OF KEY GAMEPLAY CONCEPTS, INCLUDING PLAYING CONTROLS, COMBAT, AND FREE RUNNING.

COMMANDS

PLAYSTATION 3

XBOX 360

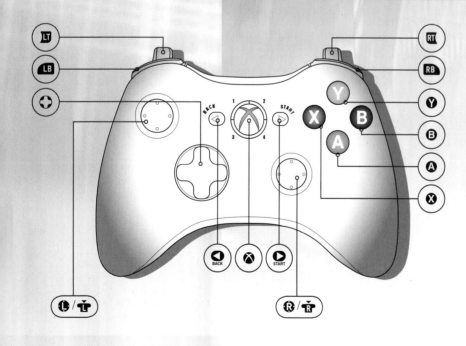

COMMANDS LIST

This is not an exhaustive list of default controls and commands for Assassin's Creed II, but simply a handy recap of all functions available during the opening stages of the game. We will introduce all additional features (and there are many) during the Walkthrough chapter. Note that you can find a moves overview in the Reference & Analysis chapter.

COMMANDS

ONSCREEN DISPLAY

BASIC MOVES

FREE RUNNING & CLIMBING

COMBAT

ESSENTIAL CONCEPTS

PS3	XBOX 360	GUIDE DESCRIPTION	COMMANDS
L	L	Movement Stick	Used to direct all forms of movement; also used to specify blocking angle in combat.
R	R	Camera Stick	Camera control; can also be employed to switch between targets during combat.
✛	✛	Quick Inventory Buttons	Instantly select the weapon in the corresponding direction of the Weapon Selector radial menu.
✕	A	Legs Button	Used in conjunction with the High Profile Button to sprint, start climbing, and perform free running actions. Also used to pickpocket people in "low profile" mode.
◎	B	Empty Hand Button	Provides many contextual commands, such as gently pushing pedestrians aside, barging people out of the way (hold button), releasing or grasping for a hand-hold while climbing, opening doors, and looting corpses (hold button).
△	Y	Head Button	Principally used for interaction and the Eagle Vision power (hold button); use it to speak with appropriate NPCs.
□	X	Weapon Hand Button	Attack target; press again as your weapon is about to make contact with the enemy (and repeat) to perform a combo attack.
R1	RT	High Profile Button	Switches to "high profile" mode, enabling more expansive and dramatic actions when combined with other buttons. On its own, it causes Ezio (or Desmond) to run when the Movement Stick is held, or block/deflect during combat.
R2	RB	Weapon Selector Button	Hold button to open a radial menu for weapon and item selection.
L1	LT	Target Lock Button	Activates Fight Mode when aggressors are nearby; otherwise fixes the game camera to the nearest individual in the direction faced.
L2	LB	Contextual Camera Button	Hold to fix the game camera to a point of interest when an onscreen prompt appears.
L3	L	First-Person Button	Toggles first-person camera. Clicking the stick again exits first-person view.
R3	R	Center Camera Button	Center camera in the direction that Ezio or Desmond is currently facing.
START	START	Pause Button	Enter the pause menu.
SELECT	BACK	Map Button	Enter the map screen; can also be used to access database entries when an onscreen prompt appears.

BUTTON DESCRIPTIONS

With Assassin's Creed II being played across three distinct formats, we have chosen generic terms to refer to buttons, keys, sticks and triggers that apply to each platform. These "guide descriptions" follow the terminology used by the game itself, and will be easy for any player to recognize – even those who have opted to adjust the default layout.

PC CONTROLS

As there is no standardized controller for the PC, we obviously can't offer a button commands diagram for the PC version of the game. We highly recommend that PC users invest in an Xbox 360 Controller for Windows, which is the easiest way to enjoy the game in the way that the Assassin's Creed II development team intended.

ONSCREEN DISPLAY

1   **Notoriety Level** – This icon depicts Ezio's current reputation on a linear scale. Certain deeds and activities (particularly tangling with the local soldiery, mistreating citizens, and acting in a suspicious or alarming manner) can cause it to fill in a clockwise progression. Once Ezio reaches the "Notorious" status, it becomes more difficult for him to walk the streets anonymously until he becomes "Incognito" again. We discuss this system in much greater depth in the Walkthrough chapter (see page 33).

2   **Health Meter** – This acts as a health gauge. Once it reaches zero, you will be sent back to the last checkpoint reached.

3   **Controls HUD** – This is a map of the face buttons on your controller (or relevant keyboard commands for PC users), with the displayed functions updated as they change based on Ezio's current position and proximity to points of interactivity. For example, it will let you know when Ezio can use a light push to navigate crowds of civilians, or alert you when he is sufficiently close to a target to perform a stealth kill with the Hidden Blade.

4   **Equipment** – Ezio's currently selected weapon or item is shown here.

5   **Currency** – Ezio's current funds (known as florins), used initially to buy items and services.

6   **Mini-Map** – See text opposite.

7   **Compass** – A simple yet effective navigational aid, this pointer always faces north.

8   **Social Status Indicator (SSI)** – By default, the outer edge of the Mini-Map is white. This will change to red when Ezio is in danger (usually when pursued by or actively fighting opponents), and green if he is completely safe while hiding. Animated SSI icons also appear whenever individuals (particularly guards) are paying close attention to Ezio. We cover this in greater detail on pages 19 and 29.

9   **Distance Meter** – This useful numerical display gives you an indication of how far you have to travel to the next active waypoint.

USING THE MINI-MAP

The map in the bottom right-hand corner of the display is an invaluable tool. While it does not plot direct routes for you, the information that it provides makes it surprisingly easy to navigate sprawling urban expanses.

◆ Most of the information on the Mini-Map for a given area is displayed only after you "unfog" it by synchronizing with Ezio's world by climbing a lofty viewpoint in the vicinity.

◆ Once you've "unfogged" the Mini-Map, a good starting point is to recognize the subtle yet intuitive color-coding system it employs. Orthodox paths (such as streets and alleys) are a darker gray than the buildings that surround them, while noteworthy destinations (particularly large structures that dominate skylines or have a specific plot purpose) are displayed in dark gray.

◆ Destinations or points of interactivity are marked by icons. A flashing exclamation mark, for example, denotes a mission start point.

◆ Potential aggressors (particularly city guards) are represented by red circles. If these are at a different elevation to Ezio (as with, say, a bowman stationed on a rooftop as he walks below) the red circle will appear faded. Note that this fading system applies to most icons.

◆ Some markers are contextual, and will only appear when relevant to your current situation. For example, nearby hiding spots (blue circles) only appear if you are being pursued or engaged by opponents.

◆ Certain icons (such as shops) will shrink and fade out of view as you move away from them. Mission objectives or starting points are always shown.

COMMANDS

ONSCREEN DISPLAY

BASIC MOVES

FREE RUNNING & CLIMBING

COMBAT

ESSENTIAL CONCEPTS

PAUSE MENU

Most of the options in the Assassin's Creed II Animus Desktop are self-explanatory, but a few warrant at least a brief introduction.

◆ DNA offers statistics on your progress so far in all areas, from plot missions to optional undertakings. You can also use this screen to locate and replay activities that you have already completed.

◆ The Inventory menu is where you can equip capes and find out about weapon stats and item status.

◆ For those keen to keep abreast of story developments, the Database is where all information acquired during Ezio's adventures is stored.

BASIC MOVES

Assassin's Creed II introduces its many features gradually, incrementally rewarding players with new abilities, weapons and assorted diversions as they progress through its story. It's no great secret to reveal that the Ezio Auditore we meet at the start of the tale is very different than the man he becomes over the course of the game.

Attempting to document and explain even a quarter of his many (potential) talents here would be hugely confusing and hard to digest, which is why we have sensibly opted to introduce and analyze most gameplay features in the relevant sections of the Walkthrough chapter. In this early section of the guide, then, we focus specifically on fundamental gameplay commands and concepts, offering advice that complements the information provided by the early in-game tutorials and your game manual.

WALKING

DESCRIPTION	XBOX 360	PS3
Movement Stick	**L**	**L**

A purposeful stride that won't attract undue attention. Suitable for situations where Ezio needs to trail a target, move in close without causing alarm, or pass patrolling soldiers without arousing their curiosity.

◆ Use the analog functionality of the Movement Stick to reduce Ezio's pace. This can be useful when attempting to match a companion's stride pattern or when blending into the crowd to evade prospective aggressors.

◆ If potential enemies are close to Ezio, walking causes the Social Status Indicator to change color at the slowest possible rate.

GENTLE PUSH

DESCRIPTION	XBOX 360	PS3
Hold Movement Stick, press/hold Empty Hand Button	Hold **L**, press/hold **B**	Hold **L**, press/hold **○**

A command available when Ezio is moving at walking speed. This can help him to stride through crowds with greater ease by casually easing civilians out of his path.

◆ Walking directly into a pedestrian will still slow Ezio down – you'll need to aim for fairly peripheral contact.

◆ Unlike the Tackle move, the Gentle Push action is deemed socially acceptable. If Ezio is Incognito, he can even use it to glide through a group of patrolling militiamen without arousing their ire or curiosity.

RUNNING

DESCRIPTION	XBOX 360	PS3
Hold Movement Stick + High Profile Button	Hold **L** + **RT**	Hold **L** + **R1**

Faster than walking, slower than a full sprint, this movement speed is suitable for navigating all but the busiest city streets.

◆ Use this movement speed to move quickly yet safely through less crowded areas. Slow down to walking pace to pass through large groups of civilians.

◆ Collisions with individual passers-by while running will usually cause Ezio to stumble very briefly, but without impeding his forward momentum by a great degree. Barging into crowds, however, will usually cause him to tumble awkwardly.

◆ At his basic running speed, Ezio will automatically vault low obstacles as he encounters them. He will also hop onto (and run along) walls and other architectural features, though he will not actively climb or jump from any real degree of height in this movement mode.

◆ Colliding with potential aggressors (such as soldiers) is unwise. At best, they will stop to berate him; at worst, they may draw their weapons and attack him.

◆ If would-be aggressors are watching for Ezio, running while in their line of sight will cause the Social Status Indicator to fill at an increased rate. It's prudent to slow to a walk, and pay them a wide berth.

TACKLING

DESCRIPTION	XBOX 360	PS3
Hold Movement Stick + High Profile Button + Empty Hand Button	Hold 🄻 + 🆁🆃 + 🅱	Hold 🄻 + R1 + ⭕

This command replaces Gentle Push whenever Ezio is running or sprinting. Hold the button to make him drop a shoulder to barge people out of his path.

◆ This move will usually knock individuals aside with no huge loss of momentum. It's also a good way to knock fleeing targets from their feet.

◆ If speed is of the essence, this can be employed to cannonball through larger groups of civilians. The trick is to aim for the areas where their ranks are thinnest.

SPRINTING

DESCRIPTION	XBOX 360	PS3
Hold Movement Stick + High Profile Button + Legs Button	Hold 🄻 + 🆁🆃 + 🅰	Hold 🄻 + R1 + ✖

The Sprint command is actually the same as the Free Running one; for the purposes of this introduction, we focus on the first application alone. Should you direct Ezio towards buildings or other obstructions while sprinting at ground level, he will automatically attempt to climb or leap.

◆ Collisions with pedestrians while sprinting will usually cause Ezio to fall or stagger backwards. Even if you have several assailants chasing you down, it's sensible to use it in sparsely populated streets, and slow down for busy thoroughfares.

◆ Be very cautious when close to ledges: Ezio will happily leap into rivers and vault railings and balustrades while sprinting. Try to regulate your pace to prevent this.

◆ You can use the Tackle function while sprinting, but it will cause Ezio to slow to his basic running pace for as long as the button is held.

SWIMMING

	DESCRIPTION	XBOX 360	PS3
Swimming	Movement Stick	🄻	🄻
Fast Swimming/ Climbing Out	Movement Stick + High Profile Button + Legs Button	🄻 + 🆁🆃 + 🅰	🄻 + R1 + ✖
Diving	Hold Movement Stick + High Profile Button + Legs Button to jump, then press Legs Button	Hold 🄻 + 🆁🆃 + 🅰 to jump, then press 🅰	Hold 🄻 + R1 + ✖ to jump, then press ✖

The Animus 2.0 software allows for the full simulation of swimming, which means that Ezio can navigate through water and use it as a hiding place.

◆ Once you're used to moving on land at various speeds, the basic swimming controls are entirely intuitive. Climbing out is as simple as initiating a climb in Free Running mode once you reach a suitable surface.

◆ Use the Dive command to send Ezio under the surface of the water to conceal him from view – but only for a limited time. Note that hiding under bridges is also a good way to escape less diligent foes.

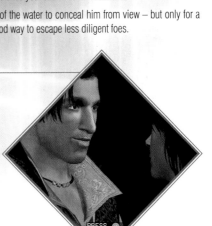

CAMERA AND CUTSCENE INTERACTION

	DESCRIPTION	XBOX 360	PS3
Contextual Camera	Contextual Camera Button	🄻🅱	L2
Center View	Center Camera Button	🆁̇	R3
Cutscene Interaction	Follow onscreen button prompts as they appear.		

Though little coaching should be required for the Assassin's Creed II camera functions, there are still a few facts that are useful to know.

◆ Use Center View to immediately restore the game camera to a position directly behind Ezio.

◆ An onscreen prompt appears in the top right-hand corner whenever you can use the Contextual Camera Button. It usually draws your attention to a specific point of interest, or locks your view while strolling with a companion.

◆ Certain cutscenes contain button prompts that enable you to influence the way that the cinematic sequence plays out. Simply tap them when specified, but be quick – there is a time limit.

PRESS

HOW TO PLAY

WALKTHROUGH

REFERENCE & ANALYSIS

EXTRAS

COMMANDS

ONSCREEN DISPLAY

BASIC MOVES

FREE RUNNING & CLIMBING

COMBAT

ESSENTIAL CONCEPTS

13

FREE RUNNING & CLIMBING

FREE RUNNING & CLIMBING

DESCRIPTION	XBOX 360	PS3
Hold Movement Stick + High Profile Button + Legs Button	Hold **L** + **RT** + **A**	Hold **L** + **R1** + **X**

Ezio will automatically attempt to climb or jump if he makes contact with a suitable surface or ledge in Free Running mode. As scaling walls and leaping across rooftops are two quite distinct disciplines, we'll examine them separately. Naturally, the best way to get to grips with the fluid and intuitive movement system used in Assassin's Creed II is to practice; the advice we offer here is designed purely to accelerate the learning curve.

CLIMBING TIPS

In Free Running mode, Ezio will automatically attempt to grab a handhold on a wall if he makes direct contact. If a surface cannot be scaled, or the handholds you are attempting to reach are out of his grasp, Ezio will simply take a few steps up the wall and drop back.

The real challenge is to acquire the ability to appraise your immediate environment quickly, identifying all potential points of interactivity. Once you gain the ability to recognize where Ezio can and cannot climb, a glance at the surface of any given building will immediately suggest a route to its rooftop.

◆ To begin climbing, always look for features such as beams above doorways and windows, or posts sticking out of walls. Any architectural feature within reach is a potential starting point.

◆ Once Ezio grabs a surface, you can release the Legs Button if you are simply scaling a wall. The button is technically only required while free running, and moving without it minimizes the risk of unexpected leaps.

◆ Use the movement controls to direct Ezio towards available handholds. Ideally, you should also be adjusting the camera to plan your route. This will help to prevent situations where you clamber up to a dead end.

◆ If a structure you intend to scale has no obvious positions where Ezio can begin climbing, examine the surrounding buildings – there may often be a route to the top if you approach it from a higher elevation. You will encounter instances where a structure has only one face that has a suitable arrangement of features for Ezio to climb. This is where smart use of the camera will pay off.

◆ Certain rooftops may be guarded by soldiers armed with bows; watch your Mini-Map closely to spot these. The best course of action is often to avoid them entirely.

◆ If you are spotted by a rooftop archer, you should either seek to swiftly move out of sight or neutralize him. Being hit by projectiles will cause Ezio to lose his grip while climbing. If this happens, use the Grasp command (introduced shortly) to attempt to catch a ledge as Ezio falls past.

HOW TO PLAY

WALKTHROUGH

REFERENCE &
ANALYSIS

EXTRAS

COMMANDS

ONSCREEN
DISPLAY

BASIC MOVES

**FREE RUNNING
& CLIMBING**

COMBAT

ESSENTIAL
CONCEPTS

FREE RUNNING TIPS

Much like Altaïr during Desmond's first foray into the footsteps of his antecedents, Ezio is supremely agile, utterly fearless, and capable of spectacular feats of athleticism. Graduates of Assassin's Creed, then, will immediately feel comfortable with the refined yet familiar experience of free running.

Newcomers to the series should note that the art of confidently bounding from pillar to post and leaping between rooftops with consummate ease really isn't as difficult as it may initially seem. As Ezio automatically jumps, grabs and maintains his balance in Free Running mode, instances where success depends purely on precision timed button presses are rare. Instead, your role is something more akin to a navigator, where the real challenge lies in picking the most efficient route to your destination.

◆ Once you climb to a rooftop or elevated platform, note that it's not always necessary (or indeed wise) to hold the Legs Button at all times. Moving with the High Profile Button only is slower, but has the unique and useful side effect of making Ezio more conservative. He will still climb low obstacles and drop short distances, but will refrain from leaping to his doom if directed perilously close to the edge of a rooftop. An easy summary is to say that holding the High Profile Button alone puts Ezio in "low risk" mode; adding the Legs Button enables "high risk" motions.

◆ Try to think a few steps ahead. The trick isn't to focus on where Ezio is now, but where he'll be in two or three jumps.

◆ Ezio's direction is governed purely by the Movement Stick (unless Target Lock is activated), so try to acquire the habit of using the camera controls to appraise your surroundings during less eventful moments of your journey. Doing this will help you to identify potential paths or future escape routes, especially while familiarizing yourself with new environments. The Mini-Map is also highly useful. Remember that lighter shades of grey indicate higher elevations.

◆ Don't hesitate to pause to visit the area map to plan a suitable route – especially while performing a timed task. When you rely on instinct alone, it's very easy to find yourself led astray by rooftops that lead away from your destination, or abruptly end with gaps between adjacent buildings that Ezio simply can't leap over.

◆ Note that Ezio's athletic prowess will steadily (and sometimes subtly) increase during the course of the story.

DROPPING & GRASPING

DESCRIPTION	XBOX 360	PS3
Empty Hand Button	Ⓑ	Ⓞ

Scaling buildings is easy: getting back down can be a little harder. These two simple instructions share the same button, and offer the most convenient way to climb down when there are no nearby shortcuts.

◆ Press the Empty Hand Button while positioned close to a ledge to drop over the side. Ezio will automatically grab the surface. The Controls HUD in the upper right-hand area of the screen will inform you when the action is available.

◆ While hanging, a single press will cause Ezio to release his grip.

◆ When combined with the Grasp command, the Drop function can be used to make rapid descents if the situation demands it.

◆ The Grasp command is only available when Ezio is falling. If a suitable surface is within reach, he will grab it. The timing window is initially quite generous, but soon narrows as his falling velocity increases.

◆ Being hit by arrows (a regular occupational hazard) will cause Ezio to lose his grip while climbing. Tap the Grasp Button to grab an available hand-hold as he falls.

JUMPING (FROM LEDGE)

DESCRIPTION	XBOX 360	PS3
Movement Stick + High Profile Button + Legs Button	Ⓛ + RT + Ⓐ	Ⓛ + R1 + Ⓧ

When Ezio is hanging from a ledge, the Jump command enables you to perform a vertical or horizontal leap, or kick back off the current wall to reach an adjacent structure.

◆ When climbing, only use this move if absolutely necessary. If there are available handholds to move in a specified direction, Ezio will find them; if he stops abruptly, it may be that you need to adjust your position slightly, or pick an alternative route. Jumping at the wrong moment may cause him to leap into thin air, with obvious consequences.

◆ Remember to direct these leaps carefully with the movement controls.

COMBAT COMMANDS & TECHNIQUES

TARGET LOCK/ACTIVATING FIGHT MODE

DESCRIPTION	XBOX 360	PS3
Target Lock Button	LT	L1

Ezio eventually acquires a dazzling array of weapons and combat techniques, but no amount of raw power or finesse will compensate for a poor understanding of the Target Lock command and related Fight Mode system.

◆ By default, Target Lock acts as a "toggle", but you can change this to "hold" mode in the pause menu if you prefer.

◆ Press Target Lock to fix Ezio's view to the nearest target in the direction he is currently facing. The camera will focus on this individual until you manually specify otherwise, the person is disabled, or Ezio's line of sight to the target is broken. Outside active combat, this is useful for tracking an individual through busy crowds, and focusing on a specific NPC when you intend to interact with them.

◆ While locked to a target, all actions (such as combat moves) will be directed at the highlighted individual.

◆ When Ezio is confronted by assailants, press the Target Lock Button to enter Fight Mode. Once this is engaged, he will automatically face and target the nearest opponent in the direction he is facing, and all movements will be made in relation to that individual's position. Use the Camera Stick to switch between targets, but bear in mind that your proximity to a combatant has a bearing – changes only occur if an enemy is sufficiently close.

◆ The Fight Mode targeting system becomes second nature with a little dedication, so it's worth engaging in a few practice brawls to get a better feel for it. Instead of wading in with fists flailing, concentrate solely on blocking incoming attacks at first, then aim to systematically pick and beat each opponent in turn.

ESCAPING A FIGHT

DESCRIPTION	XBOX 360	PS3
Hold High Profile Button + Legs Button	Hold RT + A	Hold R1 + X

When the odds are against you, discretion is *always* the better part of valor. With the default configuration, holding the High Profile and Legs Buttons will, after a short delay, enable you to cleanly exit Fight Mode primed for a swift departure.

◆ When you engage multiple enemies, it's a good idea to maneuver Ezio into a good position before you attempt to escape. He will kick straight into Free Running mode while the buttons are held, so finding a large gap or scalable surface will enable you to bid farewell in the most perfunctory manner possible.

HOW TO PLAY

WALKTHROUGH

REFERENCE &
ANALYSIS

EXTRAS

COMMANDS

ONSCREEN
DISPLAY

BASIC MOVES

FREE RUNNING
& CLIMBING

COMBAT

ESSENTIAL
CONCEPTS

ATTACKING

DESCRIPTION	XBOX 360	PS3
Weapon Hand Button	✗	□

At the start of Assassin's Creed II, Ezio is a reasonably accomplished pugilist. In this section we focus on tips that apply when he is using his default fists, leaving later weapons and abilities (such as sword use) to the appropriate sections of the Walkthrough chapter.

◆ Ezio's attacks are aimed at a highlighted individual if you have Target Lock engaged; if not, Ezio will attack in the direction he is currently facing. We strongly advise that you always use Target Lock to enter Fight Mode, even if fighting a solitary opponent.

◆ Pressing the Weapon Hand Button once will cause Ezio to throw a punch towards an assailant; press it again with the right timing to perform combination attacks.

◆ Though Ezio can land many blows in sequence, note that combos provide other aggressors with the opportunity to lash out. When fighting multiple enemies, watch their movements and be ready to halt your onslaught by quickly switching to the blocking pose.

◆ Opponents are often less likely to block assaults after they attempt a hit or, if you have good timing, you can strike at the moment they begin an attack.

◆ Try to identify and disable weaker or injured opponents first. The fewer fists or weapons you face, the easier it will become to defend. Fighting against multiple aggressors becomes more fluid and varied once Ezio learns the art of effective counter-attacking and disarming, among many other talents that are discussed thoroughly in the Walkthough chapter as you acquire them.

BLOCKING/DEFLECTING

DESCRIPTION	XBOX 360	PS3
Hold High Profile Button	Hold RT	Hold R1

Blocking is the backbone of the Assassin's Creed II combat system. Inefficient use of attacks might lead to rather protracted battles, but poor use of blocking techniques will cause fights to end both abruptly and unhappily. As with the Target Lock system, this is a technique that all players should be prepared to practice.

◆ Holding the blocking pose enables Ezio to deflect all blows directed to the front of his body.

◆ If Ezio is attacked from behind, quickly press the Movement Stick in the direction of the incoming assault to block it. Most fights involve more than one opponent, so it's shrewd to work on mastering this ability from an early stage.

◆ A solid defense is more than a matter of quick responses. You need to think tactically, constantly maneuvering Ezio into better positions as his opponents attempt to surround him. You should try to evaluate the situation at every moment, as no position is unassailable. With a wall at Ezio's back, he can face his assailants and block their attacks with greater ease – but with the attendant drawback of being boxed in. Equally, taking up position in a narrow alleyway is sometimes a clever move (unless opponents manage to get behind you), as is disengaging to climb to a more defensible position (until a crunching blow sends Ezio plummeting from a rooftop).

◆ Watch assailants closely, evaluating their intentions in order to judge when best to strike, defend or dodge. A feint by one soldier may be the cue for another to strike; pursuing a single aggressor may embolden one of his companions. Identifying enemy behaviors will enable you to dispatch opponents quickly while sustaining a minimum of damage.

ESSENTIAL GAME CONCEPTS

Before you start playing Assassin's Creed II, it's worth taking a moment to learn a handful of useful things about the game world. Once inside the Animus many players will feel the urge to cause a little mischief, just to see what happens. The following pointers should help them to understand the events that may ensue, or sights they may see.

HIGH PROFILE/LOW PROFILE

Like its predecessor, Assassin's Creed II divides physical actions into two categories: "low profile" and "high profile". There is a clear common-sense divide between the two categories. Strolling through the streets, gently pushing other citizens aside as you travel to a destination will rarely attract unwarranted attention. Scaling a wall, leaping across rooftops and engaging in any form of physical confrontation, however, will all have the effect of drawing eyes towards Ezio.

MISSION STRUCTURE

Most missions offer flexibility in terms of how you achieve specified goals; within the parameters of each challenge, there is not necessarily a right or wrong way to proceed. Unless expressly or implicitly forbidden, you can often pick your own routes, use the degree of stealth or force that satisfies you most, and generally feel free to experiment. You will find that you are steered almost exclusively towards plot-oriented missions during the early stages of the story, but the horizons of the game world soon expand with the steady introduction of optional sub-missions and countless other distractions.

EMPTY HEALTH METER

The Health Meter positioned in the upper left-hand area of the screen acts as a classic health meter. When this is reduced to zero (principally due to combat injuries or damage sustained through falling), you will be returned to the last stored checkpoint. Assassin's Creed II employs an autosave system to record your progress after each mission or side-quest, and is generally very scrupulous in the way that it divides its main challenges into manageable chunks.

SOCIAL BEHAVIOR

Though Assassin's Creed II is packed with combat encounters, subtlety and restraint are vital attributes in many circumstances. Try to avoid unusual or socially unacceptable behavior if there is a high chance that it may be detected by anyone who might react to it. Ducking into a side alley to scale a wall to reach the rooftops is more prudent than clambering up a house on a main street as a group of local militiamen stroll by. You should also note that killing innocent civilians (even accidentally) will soon cause Desmond to desynchronize from his ancestor's world. Later in the game, the introduction of the "Notoriety" system (see page 33) penalizes many potential indiscretions. Trust us when we say that it pays to get into good habits quickly.

ESCAPING

Although early missions don't pit you against the local soldiery, some players may accidentally (or playfully) provoke a violent response. The best plan of action is to escape. To achieve that, flee from your pursuers until you comfortably break their direct line of sight with Ezio; the ring surrounding the Mini-Map will change from red to yellow to let you know when this happens. You should then aim to use the nearest hiding spot until your new friends move on. These hiding spots are marked as blue circles on the Mini-Map, and include piles of straw (both inside carts and loose on the ground), benches, wells and rooftop shelters. If you're feeling ambitious, leaping over a bridge into the river is a stylish way to evade a vicious beating.

HOW TO PLAY

WALKTHROUGH

REFERENCE &
ANALYSIS

EXTRAS

COMMANDS

ONSCREEN
DISPLAY

BASIC MOVES

FREE RUNNING
& CLIMBING

COMBAT

ESSENTIAL
CONCEPTS

▌SOCIAL STATUS INDICATOR ▬▬

Watch out for Social Status Indicator icons when you pass potential adversaries (such as guards). When the icon fills with yellow, Ezio is arousing their curiosity; as it fills with red, they will actively approach and examine him. Once fully red, they will attack. You can avoid this by paying would-be aggressors a wide berth, walking rather than running when they are close, and just generally doing little to attract unnecessary attention.

▌MAP EXPLORATION ▬▬

Use the in-game map to plan approximate routes to optional objectives or while sightseeing; you can even set a waypoint to follow if it helps. Your first instinct may be to explore Florence, but you should note that not all areas of the city are available from the very start. Attempting to push through into areas that have yet to be unlocked will cause Desmond to desynchronize, which will send you back to a previous checkpoint.

WALKTHROUGH | 02

WITH OVER 100 INDIVIDUAL MISSIONS TO FINISH AND MANY OTHER ASSORTED DIVERSIONS, COMPLETING ASSASSIN'S CREED II IS NO TRIVIAL UNDERTAKING. WHETHER YOU STRIVE FOR NOTHING LESS THAN 100% COMPLETION, OR SIMPLY NEED OCCASIONAL GUIDANCE DURING TRICKY STORY MISSIONS, THIS CHAPTER HAS EVERYTHING YOU NEED.

USER INSTRUCTIONS

Before you go any further, take a few seconds to familiarize yourself with the structure and systems used in the Walkthrough chapter with this simple illustrated guide.

A **Overview maps** – Whenever you have access to a new region in the game, you will find a corresponding overview map in the guide. Each of these provides a top-down view of the entire location, with lines marking the borders of individual districts within larger cities. To avoid potential spoilers, and because practically all collectibles and points of interest already appear on the in-game maps, our maps are designed purely as an aid to easy navigation, with annotations used only to document notable landmarks, viewpoints and Codex Pages (see "Walkthrough Maps: Legend" text box) – the latter being a special collectible required to complete the game. We cover other items of note in the Extras chapter.

B **Left-hand pages: main walkthrough** – The main walkthrough guides you through every main Memory (for which, read: mission) in the story. It has been written to offer just the right amount of knowledge required to successfully complete all missions, but without giving too much away. We abhor needless story spoilers, so rest assured that we do our utmost to avoid unnecessary plot references throughout the chapter.

C **Right-hand pages: analysis, tactics and points of interest** – The right-hand page of each walkthrough spread focuses on tactics, trivia, feature introductions and step-by-step guidance for larger or more complicated gameplay sections.

D **Secondary Memories** – Where applicable, the walkthrough for each game Sequence ends with a section dedicated to optional pursuits that are available at that point in time. Though not required to complete the game, we nonetheless strongly recommend that you browse these pages to learn about the many enjoyable side-quests and distractions available in Assassin's Creed II.

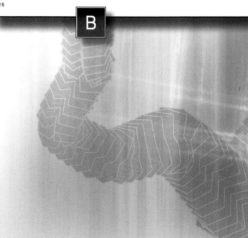

PRESENT 01

ABSTERGO ESCAPE

Follow Lucy's instructions and onscreen prompts as applicable, and you shouldn't encounter any difficulties. While in the Abstergo laboratory, press the Head Button to activate Eagle Vision if you would like to study the cryptic messages encountered at the end of Assassin's Creed. Once you reach your destination, you can speak to each member of the Brotherhood support team before you climb into the Animus.

SEQUENCE 01

MEMORIES 01-04

These four short missions introduce us to Ezio and the city of Florence, and act as gentle tutorials.

BOYS WILL BE BOYS: The brawl has two distinct stages. Once hostilities commence, focus only on the members of Vieri's mob who attack Ezio directly before attending to the others. When the second wave arrives, move to a defensible position and focus on blocking, using short combos until you face fewer aggressors. Remember to keep Ezio in Fight Mode at all times – press the Target Lock Button to activate it when necessary.

YOU SHOULD SEE THE OTHER GUY: This is simply an introduction to free running. Follow Federico's lead to reach the doctor.

SIBLING RIVALRY: Rather than take Federico's route to the finish line, you can instead run into an alley on the left-hand side of the church. Climb up by the first door on the right (Fig. 1) to gain a massive advantage.

NIGHT CAP: It's a short jog to Christina's window after the Leap of Faith, but try not to disturb any of Vieri's men as you travel there. During Ezio's escape, take to the rooftops to lose the chasing mob with ease.

MEMORIES 05-09

These five missions involve errands and favors for different members of the Auditore family. Unless you stir up a commotion, the city guard will leave you to your own devices. Pazzi henchmen, by contrast, should be carefully avoided.

PAPERBOY: Groups of the hostile Pazzi are wandering the streets, so the quickest way to reach your destination is to stay above them. It's not a bad time to practice combat against weaker opponents if you feel so inclined, though.

BEAT A CHEAT: You can pummel Duccio in any way you please, but strictly speaking this is a tutorial on the use of the Grab function and related assaults.

PETRUCCIO'S SECRET: The time allocation is generous, so you should have no difficulties reaching each feather by following the waypoints. Completing this mission unlocks collectible feathers throughout the game world. We'll tell you more about this optional objective shortly.

FRIEND OF THE FAMILY: A simple two-stage journey – no advice required.

SPECIAL DELIVERY: The best way to avoid complications is to stick to the rooftops on route to each delivery – only one of which necessitates a return to street level (Fig. 2) – and during the return to the Auditore household.

26

B

**USER
INSTRUCTIONS**

MAP: FLORENCE

PRESENT 01

SEQUENCE 01

SEQUENCE 02

MAP: TUSCANY

SEQUENCE 03

SEQUENCE 04

SEQUENCE 05

MAP: ROMAGNA

SEQUENCE 06

PRESENT 02

MAP: VENICE

SEQUENCE 07

SEQUENCE 08

SEQUENCE 09

SEQUENCE 10

SEQUENCE 11

SEQUENCE 14

PRESENT 03

FLORENCE

EAGLE VISION

Hold the Head Button to activate Eagle Vision, the preternatural ability shared by Ezio and Desmond to perceive hidden information in the surrounding environment, and discern the motives or purpose of any individual they scrutinize. Unlike Assassin's Creed you can move freely while using Eagle Vision, but with the drawbacks of having your view distance impaired and losing all HUD elements while it remains active.

The color scheme used for citizens once inside the Animus is very simple: red for potential enemies (Fig. 3), white for people who Ezio can interact with (to obtain missions, for example), blue for allies, and gold for anyone with a purpose specific to a current mission (such as an assassination target, or person under escort). Other points of interest (including hiding spots or collectibles, more on that later) are usually highlighted by white contours.

climb), but you should note that uncovering the map confers the following additional benefits:

- ◆ Other nearby landmarks will be revealed on the city map and Mini-Map, enabling you to further expand the visible area.
- ◆ Once they become available, optional objectives, stores and other points of interest will also be marked on all synchronized zones.
- ◆ Surrounding hiding spots are revealed, and will appear on your Mini-Map whenever Ezio is being pursued. Being able to see the outline of streets and buildings makes it easier to plan routes in order to lose persistent enemies during chases.

LOOTING & CURRENCY

Though not entirely pertinent at this point in the story, Ezio can accumulate money through his exploits and invest it in a wide variety of weapons, armor, items and services. The currency used is the *florin*, abbreviated as "*f*", with Ezio's current total displayed in the lower left-hand corner of the screen.

Florins are awarded for completing certain missions and optional objectives, but can eventually be acquired through various forms of theft. The first of these, looting bodies, is introduced at the end of the brawl on the Ponte Vecchio. The sums acquired through rooting through the pockets of the dead or unconscious are usually small, but ultimately add up during the course of the game. Naturally, this kind of behavior is both callous and criminal, so it's something that should only be attempted if there are no witnesses of note to see it -- particularly those carrying weapons.

Ezio can also obtain florins by opening treasure chests hidden throughout the game world, generally located inside building interiors. As there are so few ways to invest your wealth at this point, we'll return to the subject later in the walkthrough.

VIEWPOINTS & SYNCHRONIZING

Both main map and Mini-Map are covered in a gray fog during the first few missions, but you can uncover sections of each region by "synchronizing" with the environment from lofty vantage points. We refer to these as landmarks or viewpoints. The concept is introduced at the start of the Night Cap mission (before Ezio visits Cristina) with a mandatory example, but it soon becomes your sole responsibility to seek out these special locations.

Viewpoints appear as an eagle symbol on maps (both in-game and throughout this guide), so they're far from difficult to locate. The actual position where you can synchronize is always marked by the presence of an eagle circling or resting on a special perch (Fig. 4).

The importance of synchronizing will soon become apparent once you start to explore. Scaling landmarks is never a chore (the views alone are worth the

GRAB ATTACKS

The Boys Will Be Boys and Beat a Cheat missions introduce the Grab command. Once Ezio has seized an opponent by his collar, refer to the command HUD in the top-right hand corner to pick your favored attack. You can build combinations of up to three blows before the target is knocked to the ground, with each assault delivering equal damage.

Tactically, the "throw" option is the most interesting. Hurling an enemy at his peers will stagger them momentarily; when fighting on rooftops or near rivers and guardrails, throwing an assailant over the side is a rapid way to disable them.

LEAP OF FAITH

Ezio can make a rapid return to street level by leaping from areas of rooftop marked by pigeons and their droppings, or by diving from synchronization perches (Fig. 5). He will always land safely (usually in a pile of straw), which makes this a useful way to escape and hide from enemies.

WALKTHROUGH MAPS: LEGEND

The two main icons used on our maps are the same as those used in the game, ensuring instant identification.

ICON	REPRESENTS
◈	Viewpoint
◇	Codex Pages

SEQUENCE 07: SECONDARY MEMORIES

ASSASSINATION CONTRACTS

EQUIPMENT UPGRADES

TEMPLAR LAIR: OVER BEAMS, UNDER STONE

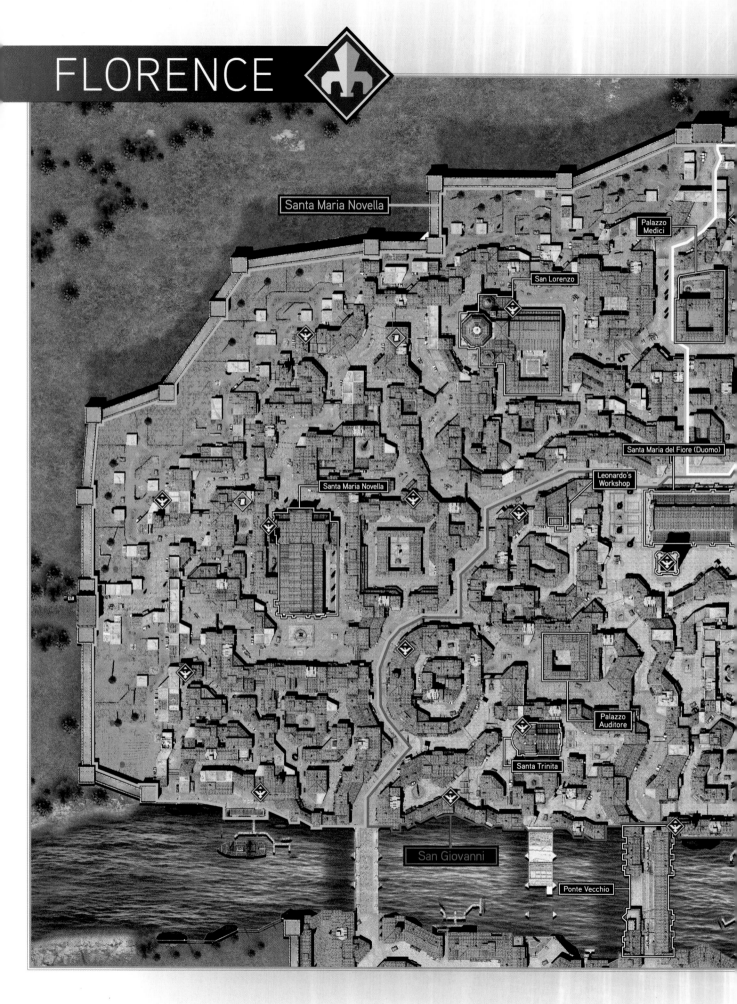

FLORENCE

Santa Maria Novella

Palazzo Medici

San Lorenzo

Santa Maria del Fiore (Duomo)

Leonardo's Workshop

Santa Maria Novella

Palazzo Auditore

Santa Trinita

San Giovanni

Ponte Vecchio

Ospedale degli
Innocenti

San Marco

Apennine Mountains & Romagna (Forlì)

Monteriggioni (Villa Auditore)

Tuscany (San Gimignano)

Santa
Croce

Palazzo della
Signoria

Please note that collectible items do not appear on this map to avoid potential spoilers. You can find them
on dedicated maps in the Secrets section of the Extras chapter.

USER
INSTRUCTIONS

MAP: FLORENCE

PRESENT 01

SEQUENCE 01

SEQUENCE 02

MAP: TUSCANY

SEQUENCE 03

SEQUENCE 04

SEQUENCE 05

MAP: ROMAGNA

SEQUENCE 06

PRESENT 02

MAP: VENICE

SEQUENCE 07

SEQUENCE 08

SEQUENCE 09

SEQUENCE 10

SEQUENCE 11

SEQUENCE 14

PRESENT 03

PRESENT 01

ABSTERGO ESCAPE

Follow Lucy's instructions and onscreen prompts as applicable, and you shouldn't encounter any difficulties. While in the Abstergo laboratory, press the Head Button to activate Eagle Vision if you would like to study the cryptic messages encountered at the end of Assassin's Creed. Once you reach your destination, you can speak to each member of the Brotherhood support team before you climb into the Animus.

SEQUENCE 01

MEMORIES 01-04

These four short missions introduce us to Ezio and the city of Florence, and act as gentle tutorials.

BOYS WILL BE BOYS: The brawl has two distinct stages. Once hostilities commence, focus only on the members of Vieri's mob who attack Ezio directly before attending to the others. When the second wave arrives, move to a defensible position and focus on blocking, using short combos until you face fewer aggressors. Remember to keep Ezio in Fight Mode at all times – press the Target Lock Button to activate it when necessary.

YOU SHOULD SEE THE OTHER GUY: This is simply an introduction to free running. Follow Federico's lead to reach the doctor.

SIBLING RIVALRY: Rather than take Federico's route to the finish line, you can instead run into an alley on the left-hand side of the church. Climb up by the first door on the right (Fig. 1) to gain a massive advantage.

NIGHT CAP: It's a short jog to Christina's window after the Leap of Faith, but try not to disturb any of Vieri's men as you travel there. During Ezio's escape, take to the rooftops to lose the chasing mob with ease.

MEMORIES 05-09

These five missions involve errands and favors for different members of the Auditore family. Unless you stir up a commotion, the city guard will leave you to your own devices. Pazzi henchmen, by contrast, should be carefully avoided.

PAPERBOY: Groups of the hostile Pazzi are wandering the streets, so the quickest way to reach your destination is to stay above them. It's not a bad time to practice combat against weaker opponents if you feel so inclined, though.

BEAT A CHEAT: You can pummel Duccio in any way you please, but strictly speaking this is a tutorial on the use of the Grab function and related assaults.

PETRUCCIO'S SECRET: The time allocation is generous, so you should have no difficulty reaching each feather by following the waypoints. Completing this mission unlocks collectible feathers throughout the game world. We'll tell you more about this optional objective shortly.

FRIEND OF THE FAMILY: A simple two-stage journey – no advice required.

SPECIAL DELIVERY: The best way to avoid complications is to stick to the rooftops en route to each delivery – only one of which necessitates a return to street level (Fig. 2) – and during the return to the Auditore household.

01

02

EAGLE VISION

Hold the Head Button to activate Eagle Vision, the preternatural ability shared by Ezio and Desmond to perceive hidden information in the surrounding environment, and discern the motives or purpose of any individual they scrutinize. Unlike Assassin's Creed you can move freely while using Eagle Vision, but with the drawback of having your view distance impaired and losing all HUD elements while it remains active.

The color scheme used for citizens once inside the Animus is very simple: red for potential enemies (Fig. 3), white for people who Ezio can interact with (to obtain missions, for example), blue for allies, and gold for anyone with a purpose specific to a current mission (such as an assassination target, or person under escort). Other points of interest (including hiding spots or collectibles, more on that later) are usually highlighted by white contours.

03

LOOTING & CURRENCY

Though not entirely pertinent at this point in the story, Ezio can accumulate money through his exploits and invest it in a wide variety of weapons, armor, items and services. The currency used is the *florin*, abbreviated as "*f*", with Ezio's current total displayed in the lower left-hand corner of the screen.

Florins are awarded for completing certain missions and optional objectives, but can eventually be acquired through various forms of theft. The first of these, looting bodies, is introduced at the end of the brawl on the Ponte Vecchio. The sums acquired through rooting through the pockets of the dead or unconscious are usually small, but ultimately add up during the course of the game. Naturally, this kind of behavior is both callous and criminal, so it's something that should only be attempted if there are no witnesses of note to see it – particularly those carrying weapons.

Ezio can also obtain florins by opening treasure chests hidden throughout the game world, generally located inside building interiors. As there are so few ways to invest your wealth at this point, we'll return to the subject later in the walkthrough.

VIEWPOINTS & SYNCHRONIZING

Both main map and Mini-Map are covered in a gray fog during the first few missions, but you can uncover sections of each region by "synchronizing" with the environment from lofty vantage points. We refer to these as landmarks or viewpoints. The concept is introduced at the start of the Night Cap mission (before Ezio visits Christina) with a mandatory example, but it soon becomes your sole responsibility to seek out these special locations.

Viewpoints appear as an eagle symbol on maps (both in-game and throughout this guide), so they're far from difficult to locate. The actual position where you can synchronize is always marked by the presence of an eagle circling or resting on a special perch (Fig. 4).

The importance of synchronizing will soon become apparent once you start to explore. Scaling landmarks is never a chore (the views alone are worth the

climb), but you should note that uncovering the map confers the following additional benefits:

◆ Other nearby landmarks will be revealed on the city map and Mini-Map, enabling you to further expand the visible area.

◆ Once they become available, optional objectives, stores and other points of interest will also be marked on all synchronized zones.

◆ Surrounding hiding spots are revealed, and will appear on your Mini-Map whenever Ezio is being pursued. Being able to see the outline of streets and buildings makes it easier to plan routes in order to lose persistent enemies during chases.

PRESS ◯ to SYNCHRONIZE.

04

GRAB ATTACKS

The Boys Will Be Boys and Beat a Cheat missions introduce the Grab command. Once Ezio has seized an opponent by his collar, refer to the command HUD in the top right-hand corner to pick your favored attack. You can build combinations of up to three blows before the target is knocked to the ground, with each assault delivering equal damage.

Tactically, the "throw" option is the most interesting. Hurling an enemy at his peers will stagger them momentarily; when fighting on rooftops or near rivers and guardrails, throwing an assailant over the side is a rapid way to disable them.

LEAP OF FAITH

Ezio can make a rapid return to street level by leaping from areas of rooftop marked by pigeons and their droppings, or by diving from synchronization perches (Fig. 5). He will always land safely (usually in a pile of straw), which makes this a useful way to escape and hide from enemies.

05

USER INSTRUCTIONS

MAP: FLORENCE

PRESENT 01

SEQUENCE 01

SEQUENCE 02

MAP: TUSCANY

SEQUENCE 03

SEQUENCE 04

SEQUENCE 05

MAP: ROMAGNA

SEQUENCE 06

PRESENT 02

MAP: VENICE

SEQUENCE 07

SEQUENCE 08

SEQUENCE 09

SEQUENCE 10

SEQUENCE 11

SEQUENCE 14

PRESENT 03

▌MEMORY 10▐

JAIL BIRD: Climb the north wall of the Palazzo della Signoria – look for a door next to an archway. When you reach the first rooftop guards, wait out of sight until both move away from your position, then quickly climb the nearby scaffold. The second pair of sentries below the tower where Giovanni is imprisoned are a little harder to evade, so don't climb to the higher level just yet. Instead, use the gray ledge to traverse around to the south face of the building (Fig. 6), observing their patrol routes as you move. Take refuge in the pile of straw, then wait for the best moment to dash out and begin climbing the tower via the stonework above the doorway.

06

If you are detected, the Grab move is your best attack – try to throw the guards into breakable items (such as barrels or wooden platforms) for an instant knockout, or simply hurl them over the parapet. Don't forget to climb to the top and synchronize at the viewpoint above before you return to the streets.

▌MEMORY 11▐

FAMILY HEIRLOOM: Ready your sword before you leave the hidden room, then be ready to block when attacked. Weapon-based hits drain the Health Meter rapidly, so try to get a feel for your opponents before you commit to lunges of your own and keep your combos short. The Grab command is a powerful tool here – both for quick finishing moves, and for temporarily disabling a target.

You may be attacked by other would-be executioners as you run to the waypoint marker, so travelling via the rooftops will help you to enjoy a less eventful journey. Even so, a further pair of hostiles will intercept you before you can reach Uberto Alberti's residence (Fig. 7). You must be anonymous to meet with Alberti so you'll have to fight them first.

07

▌MEMORY 12▐

LAST MAN STANDING: Don't even think about fighting. As soon as the mission begins, sprint away from the surrounding guards. Once you establish a little distance (or, ideally, a couple of corners) between you and the pursuing mob to break their line of sight, you can either dive into a hiding place, or head for higher ground.

Ezio's fugitive status makes the journey to the first mission of Sequence 02 more difficult than most. Pick your route carefully, taking detours to avoid any guards you encounter.

SOCIAL STATUS INDICATOR

Be watchful for the Social Status Indicator (SSI). These appear above all potential adversaries whenever there is a danger that they might recognize Ezio (Fig. 8). If the individuals in question are currently off-screen, the icons are displayed at the border of the display in a position that indicates their approximate position.

08

◆ There are three stages: detection (yellow), investigation (yellow and red), and full alert (red). These broadly correspond to the color code used for the Mini-Map's outer ring, as shown in the nearby table.

◆ During the detection phase, the SSI arrow will gradually fill with yellow as prospective aggressors become aware of Ezio's presence. In order to avoid the next stage, avoid all high-profile actions (such as running or climbing). Slow down to a stroll and try to stay as far away as possible. If it's a group of patrolling guards, you could also stop at a safe range and wait for them to pass.

◆ The transition from detection phase to investigation phase is marked by a distinctive sound effect. Enemies will now follow Ezio, watching him intently, with the icon steadily filling with red as their suspicions are confirmed. Your initial reaction may be to break into a run, but this is the worst thing you can do. Instead, stay calm and continue walking away. Look for any route that will enable you to break the line of sight between enemies and Ezio, then – and only then – make a dash for safety or a nearby hiding spot.

◆ Avoiding unnecessary combat encounters becomes much easier once Ezio acquires the vital Blending ability.

MINI-MAP: OUTER RING COLOR CODE

COLOR	DESCRIPTION
White	Ezio's default state
Green	Ezio is hidden
Red	Ezio is in open conflict
Yellow	Ezio is in open conflict, but his enemies cannot see him
Blue	Ezio is hiding, but his enemies are still searching for him

ROOFTOP ARCHERS

The Jail Bird mission will probably mark your first encounter with guards stationed on rooftops. They are faster to react unfavorably to Ezio's presence than many other enemies, so you'll need to quickly break the line of sight to avoid conflict when they spot him. Fortunately, being detected by a rooftop guard will generally not cause a full alert – only the individual(s) in question will attack. Their first reaction once combat begins is to use their bows (Fig. 9). A direct arrow hit will cause Ezio to lose his grip while climbing, or stumble when free running. At close range, they will draw swords and attack like any other enemy. Archers are relatively uncommon during the early stages of the story.

09

TRICKS & TRIVIA

◆ When enemies are pursuing Ezio, distance can work just as well as any hiding place. Comfortably escape the boundaries of the yellow "investigation circle" on the Mini-Map without alerting other hostiles, and the city alert will end. If you're looking for hiding spots, don't forget that these are marked as blue circles on the Mini-Map, and include piles of straw, herbs or leaves (both inside carts and loose on the ground), benches, wells and rooftop shelters.

◆ Note that certain enemies can throw objects at Ezio while he climbs; a direct hit will cause him to lose his grip and fall. If a chasing pack is close behind, it's sensible to look for free running opportunities that quickly lead to higher ground, rather than slower and more involved ascents.

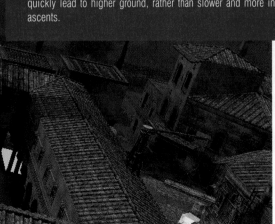

HOW TO PLAY

WALKTHROUGH

REFERENCE & ANALYSIS

EXTRAS

USER INSTRUCTIONS

MAP: FLORENCE

PRESENT 01

SEQUENCE 01

SEQUENCE 02

MAP: TUSCANY

SEQUENCE 03

SEQUENCE 04

SEQUENCE 05

MAP: ROMAGNA

SEQUENCE 06

PRESENT 02

MAP: VENICE

SEQUENCE 07

SEQUENCE 08

SEQUENCE 09

SEQUENCE 10

SEQUENCE 11

SEQUENCE 14

PRESENT 03

SEQUENCE 02

MEMORY 01

FITTING IN: During the Blending tutorial, stand inside the boundaries of stationary groups while you wait for suitable collections of pedestrians to pass (Fig. 1). Try not to fall too far behind Paola, though as a general rule it's advisable to wait for a party heading in the required direction. When Paola teaches Ezio about pickpocketing, alternate between the areas just outside the two courtyard entrances to avoid detection between attempts.

01

MEMORY 02

ACE UP MY SLEEVE: Feel free to hire a group of Courtesans to simplify the journey to Da Vinci if money is no object. When the time comes to put the newly acquired hidden blade to good use, use common sense to judge the best moment to strike (Fig. 2), but don't take too long or else you might be detected.

MEMORY 03

JUDGE, JURY, EXECUTIONER: After reaching the first waypoint take a moment to appraise the square below, particularly the route taken by the majority of pedestrians; this is the path you need to follow. The entrance to the exhibition is at the south-east of the Santa Croce building, so drop down and blend into a group heading in that direction. There is a group of Courtesans that you can hire once you turn the corner to the left, but those seeking to conserve florins can skulk into a group close to the entrance, then wait for a party to head inside (Fig. 3).

Move carefully through the crowds until you get close to Uberto. There are boxes close to Ezio once the assassination is complete. Immediately climb these after the cutscene and scale the wall to reach the rooftop, though be ready to evade the archers stationed there. A little purposeful free running should lead to a swift and undemanding escape.

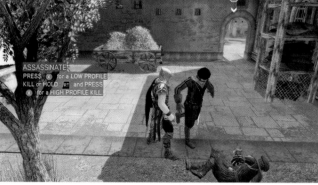

02

03

ASSASSINATIONS

Acquiring the Hidden Blade enables Ezio to perform instant assassinations. Executions performed by pressing the Weapon Hand Button alone are accomplished with a high degree of subtlety, and may go entirely unnoticed for a few moments. Holding the High Profile Button enables faster, further and more expressive takedowns (Fig. 5), but these will be witnessed by all in range. The targeting system discriminates wisely, but it's still good practice to use the Target Lock function before you strike – especially if your intended quarry is surrounded by guards.

As a general rule of thumb for now, the Hidden Blade only works against opponents who are not in active combat; alert enemies with weapons drawn will resist Ezio's attacks. That said, there is a short period at the start of a fight where most opponents will still be vulnerable to this one-hit kill – a quirk that can be exploited whenever violence is imminent and unavoidable.

05

USER INSTRUCTIONS

MAP: FLORENCE

PRESENT 01

SEQUENCE 01

SEQUENCE 02

MAP: TUSCANY

SEQUENCE 03

SEQUENCE 04

SEQUENCE 05

MAP: ROMAGNA

SEQUENCE 06

PRESENT 02

MAP: VENICE

SEQUENCE 07

SEQUENCE 08

SEQUENCE 09

SEQUENCE 10

SEQUENCE 11

SEQUENCE 14

PRESENT 03

BLENDING

Blending occurs automatically whenever Ezio is in close proximity to (but ideally in the midst of) a group of three or more citizens standing or walking together. This indispensible ability is painless to learn, and you will soon find that the invisibility it confers makes the process of avoiding Ezio's enemies much less time consuming. The following tips should complement the practice you experienced during the Fitting In mission.

04

◆ Blending with a group will immediately make Ezio disappear from view (Fig. 4). Any level of yellow "suspicion" will swiftly drain from the Social Status Indicator of nearby enemies. If a guard is actively focusing on Ezio (red/yellow SSI), he may still move in to investigate. In these instances, it's better to enter a group only after (however briefly) breaking the direct line of sight.

◆ Ezio cannot Blend when the Mini-Map's outer ring is red. However, once it turns yellow, any party of citizens essentially becomes a mobile hiding spot.

◆ Interestingly, there is a short but strategically significant "grace period" whenever you exit a group, a short delay before nearby enemies will begin to detect Ezio. This makes it possible to make seamless transitions between suitable parties of citizens. An advanced technique is to quickly Blend, then exit and exploit this feature to safely pass hostiles standing in an area where there are no pedestrians without fully arousing their suspicions.

HIRING COURTESANS

Press the Head Button to hire a group of Courtesans. The ladies will walk in formation around Ezio (unless instructed to stop), providing a highly convenient Blending opportunity. There is a twist, though: individual ladies will peel off to consort with guards as you pass them, departing the group permanently. If required, you can order them to perform this manually – just target a guard, then tap the Head Button. The instruction creates a stationary distraction that doesn't lead the guards away but holds their line of sight.

▌MEMORY 04 ▌

LAYING LOW: This mission introduces the Notoriety mini-game, where Ezio must perform certain tasks to reduce his current level of infamy and return to Incognito status.

The objective here is to completely empty the gauge in the top left-hand corner (Fig. 6). Removing Posters is the least risky option, though killing corrupt Officials offers an excellent training opportunity for a handful of vital skills (including guard evasion, Blending, and assassination techniques). See "Notoriety" on the page to your right for further details.

06

▌MEMORY 05 ▌

ARRIVEDERCI: If you have outstanding business in Florence, attend to it before you begin this mission. With Ezio's Notoriety level reduced to zero, the journey to the city limits should be uneventful. Use the new Throw Money ability (Fig. 7) to divert attention elsewhere should you encounter any problems, especially Harassers (see page 49). To cross the city gate, you will need to hire Courtesans and use them to keep the guards busy while you quietly leave Florence.

07

08

09

10

NOTORIETY

Unless story-related conditions specify otherwise, Ezio is "Incognito" by default. In this state, members of the local militia will not react to his presence unless he provokes them. Most indiscretions will elicit no sterner response than a curt rebuke, though assault, murder and theft will obviously inspire immediate aggression.

Ezio is Notorious for the first three missions of Sequence 02, with the fourth introducing the means by which he can return to Incognito. Being Notorious means that guards will actively look for him, with the Social Status Indicator revealing their level of suspicion whenever he encounters them.

From Memory 05 onwards, socially unacceptable or overtly conspicuous actions cause the Notoriety gauge in the top left-hand corner of the screen to fill at a rate determined by the severity of each transgression. Once it is completely red, two things happen: Ezio becomes Notorious, and icons for Posters, Heralds and corrupt Officials appear on the game map. You can only restore Ezio to Incognito by completely removing his Notoriety level. The system has the interesting effect of encouraging discretion and restraint. Behave like an assassin, avoiding unnecessary conflict or attention, and this sub-game will be an occasional distraction. Stalk the streets with villainous intent, though, and it will act as a frequent reprimand.

WAYS TO REDUCE NOTORIETY

MINI-MAP ICON	CONDITION	ADVICE
	Removing Posters	Perhaps the easiest way to reduce the Notoriety level, as Posters are plentiful and are often found above street level (Fig. 8). However, the mere 25% reduction each Poster provides can make it a little too labor intensive on its own.
	Bribing Heralds	Offers a 50% drop in Notoriety, but some will baulk at the expense (Fig. 9).
	Assassinating corrupt Officials	Leads to a huge 75% Notoriety reduction, but you'll need to hunt them carefully (Fig. 10). They will flee if they see Ezio, and are hard to track while avoiding guards.

TRICKS & TRIVIA

◆ Pickpocketing may seem like a simple recipe for easy money, but the attendant Notoriety penalty for indiscriminate use means that it's best used sparingly. Ideally, try to perform it in areas where you can quickly Blend to evade detection.

◆ Dead or unconscious victims can be concealed in hiding spots, which proves useful in areas where you would like discrete takedowns to remain that way. On busy city streets, though, it's usually prudent to just move on and put distance between Ezio and the scene of the crime.

HOW TO PLAY

WALKTHROUGH

REFERENCE & ANALYSIS

EXTRAS

USER INSTRUCTIONS

MAP: FLORENCE

PRESENT 01

SEQUENCE 01

SEQUENCE 02

MAP: TUSCANY

SEQUENCE 03

SEQUENCE 04

SEQUENCE 05

MAP: ROMAGNA

SEQUENCE 06

PRESENT 02

MAP: VENICE

SEQUENCE 07

SEQUENCE 08

SEQUENCE 09

SEQUENCE 10

SEQUENCE 11

SEQUENCE 14

PRESENT 03

SEQUENCES 01 & 02: SECONDARY MEMORIES

FREE MISSIONS: INTRODUCTION

Free Missions are optional Memories that provide small, self-contained challenges that can be completed whenever you are ready to tackle them. They are gradually unlocked as you complete main story objectives, though you will also need to synchronize at available viewpoints to have their start locations marked on the in-game maps.

For now, there are three types of Free Mission:

◆ **Beat Up Events:** Generally the easiest Free Mission type. After consulting with an aggrieved citizen, you must travel to a waypoint marker, identify a target with Eagle Vision, then pummel them into submission. Killing the target is strictly prohibited, even if they attack Ezio with a weapon.

◆ **Courier Assignments:** These involve rapid travel to one or more waypoints to deliver letters within strict time limits.

◆ **Races:** Timed expeditions through numerous waypoint gates that are designed to test your free running and navigational skills. These can be tough to beat at first, but this is part of the fun. Refining your route to shave valuable seconds from your time is the secret to winning, so don't be too disheartened if your initial attempts are less than convincing.

Completing Free Missions leads to a monetary reward. This is initially small, but gradually increases as you complete Sequences. There is one final Free Mission type – Assassination Contracts – but these do not yet appear in the game world.

FREE MISSIONS

A WOMAN SCORNED (BEAT UP)	
Location:	West of Palazzo Auditore in the San Giovanni district.
Advice:	The errant husband can be found in a courtyard not far to the south of the starting position. Administer a succession of blows until he cowers in fear to complete the Memory.

CASANOVA (COURIER)	
Location:	A short walk to the south of the Palazzo Auditore entrance.
Special Conditions:	Deliver the two letters before the time expires; both recipients are guarded by individuals who will attack Ezio if their suspicion level (represented by the Social Status Indicator) is maxed out by standing in their line of sight.
Advice:	The recipient to the southeast is standing on a balcony, with two guards gazing balefully at would-be suitors strolling below. Scale the south wall of the building (you will need to start climbing to either side of the bench beneath, then traverse to the left or right as applicable), then speak to her and leave quickly before her guardians can react. The second woman can be found inside a courtyard with a group of men standing guard at its only entrance. Climb onto the roof, then quietly drop down and converse with her to complete the delivery.

FLORENTINE SPRINT (RACE)	
Location:	By the Palazzo Della Signoria in the San Giovanni district.
Special Conditions:	Run through all gates within the allotted time limit.
Advice:	Don't hurry on your first attempt – just aim to complete the course at a steady pace, with the process of learning the route your principle concern. When you reach the penultimate gate (it's on top of a chimney), just keep moving forward to perform a Leap of Faith to a pile of leaves directly below. If you find the course too difficult at this stage of the game, it may be a good idea to return to it at the end of Sequence 04. We won't spoil surprises by telling you why this will help, but trust us when we say that it *will* be easier.

CODEX PAGES

By now, you will have noticed a number of "scroll" icons dotted around the available areas of Florence. These mark the locations of Philosophical Codex pages. There are 16 of these located throughout the game world (on top of those obtained during the main storyline), and all of them must be collected before you can begin the final Sequence. For this reason, it's a good idea to start looking for them now. As a fringe benefit, every fourth one you find confers the bonus of an extra permanent square on Ezio's Health Meter.

◆ To reveal the location of Philosophical Codex pages on the in-game maps, you must first synchronize at viewpoints.

◆ Philosophical Codex pages are (with the exception of four collected during a main story mission) always hidden inside Banks with groups of guards stationed outside. Once you have killed the soldiers you can walk inside and retrieve the page from the chest.

◆ Every time you have collected four pages, visit Leonardo at his workshop – look for the ⓛ icon on the map. After Leonardo has decoded them, Ezio will receive the Health Meter bonus.

◆ You can visit the Database menu to read text on each Codex page once they have been translated.

There are two special "collectibles" hidden throughout the Assassin's Creed II game world: Feathers and Glyphs.

01

◆ **Feathers** (Fig. 1) are usually found on rooftops or placed on walls and, though small, are surrounded by a distinctive visual effect that makes them easy to see from surprisingly large distances.

There are 100 Feathers in total, distributed evenly throughout the locales that Ezio visits during the course of the story. You cannot collect them all until the penultimate Sequence.

While you will stumble across many while engaged in other tasks, we strongly advise that you leave the process of collecting Feathers until you have completed the main story Memories. By then you will have acquired abilities and equipment that will make the process of finding them much easier. This does mean that you miss out on a couple of rewards (given at 50% and 100% completion) until after the final credits, but we would advise that this is a small price to pay for an easier hunt once Ezio has full command of all possible upgrades.

◆ **Glyphs** (Fig. 2) are fewer in number than Feathers (there are only 20 in total), and are much easier to locate. They are always positioned on the surface of notable buildings, and are "collected" by scanning them with Eagle Vision at close range. All Database entries for structures that have a Glyph are marked by a special HUD icon (Fig. 3). You cannot find all Glyphs until much later in the game.

02

Collecting a Glyph unlocks puzzles in a Database menu entitled "The Truth". Completing all 20 leads to the reward of a video that has a huge bearing on the Assassin's Creed story. However, as with Feathers, collecting Glyphs and solving their associated puzzles is a task best left until after the final credits. Without spoiling any surprises, we can confidently state that Glyph-related mysteries may not make a great deal of sense until then…

LA ROSA COLTA

03

BORGIA COURIERS

While strolling through the streets of Florence (and other locales you have yet to visit), you will periodically stumble across a Borgia Courier (Fig. 4). These are randomly encountered when you are not actively playing a Memory, and will exclaim their horror and flee the moment they cast eyes on Ezio. As capable free runners, they will usually head for the rooftops. Once out of sight, they will disappear within a short period of time.

This behavior may seem rather bizarre, but they have their reasons: Borgia Couriers carry reasonably large sums of currency. If you can catch up with one and knock him off his feet (ideally with the Tackle technique), Ezio will obtain an instant bonus of 1,500 *f* – a fairly sizable sum for the effort involved at this stage of the story. The catch, of course, is that guards will view this as reprehensible behavior, and will attack should they witness the robbery. You should also do your utmost not to kill the courier, as doing so will result in an instant +50% penalty to Ezio's Notoriety level.

04

HOW TO PLAY

WALKTHROUGH

REFERENCE & ANALYSIS

EXTRAS

USER INSTRUCTIONS

MAP: FLORENCE

PRESENT 01

SEQUENCE 01

SEQUENCE 02

MAP: TUSCANY

SEQUENCE 03

SEQUENCE 04

SEQUENCE 05

MAP: ROMAGNA

SEQUENCE 06

PRESENT 02

MAP: VENICE

SEQUENCE 07

SEQUENCE 08

SEQUENCE 09

SEQUENCE 10

SEQUENCE 11

SEQUENCE 14

PRESENT 03

MONTERIGGIONI

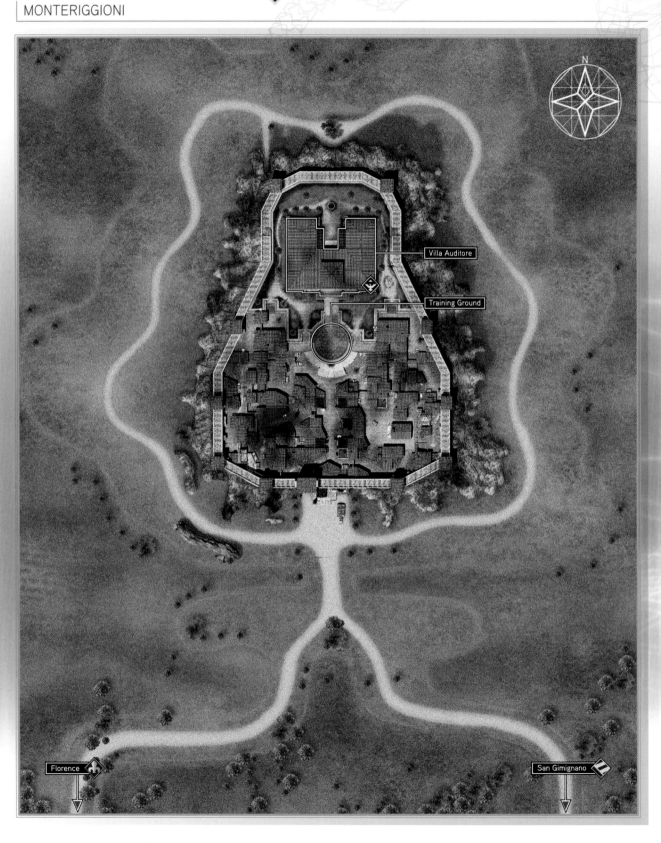

Villa Auditore

Training Ground

Florence

San Gimignano

SAN GIMIGNANO

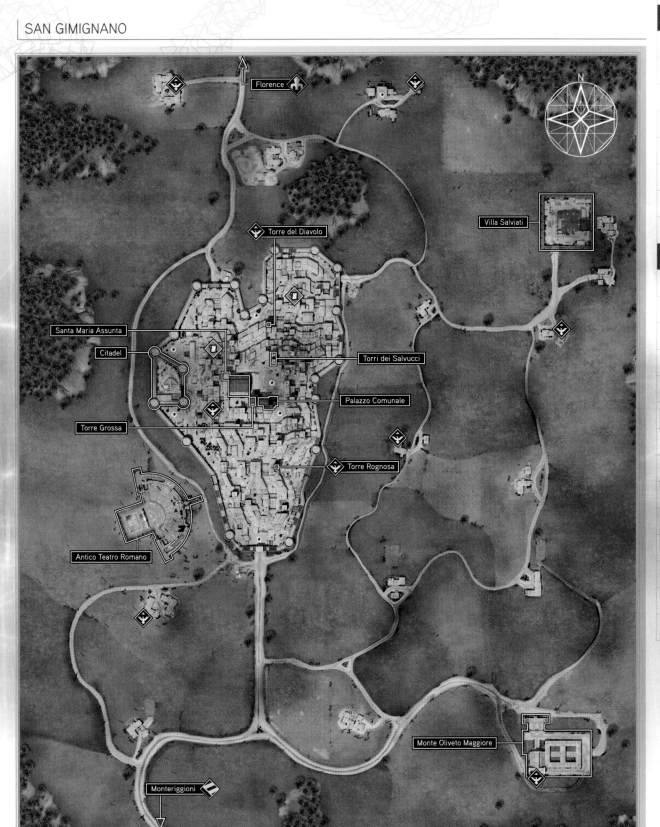

USER
INSTRUCTIONS

MAP: FLORENCE

PRESENT 01

SEQUENCE 01

SEQUENCE 02

MAP: TUSCANY

SEQUENCE 03

SEQUENCE 04

SEQUENCE 05

MAP: ROMAGNA

SEQUENCE 06

PRESENT 02

MAP: VENICE

SEQUENCE 07

SEQUENCE 08

SEQUENCE 09

SEQUENCE 10

SEQUENCE 11

SEQUENCE 14

PRESENT 03

Please note that collectible items do not appear on this map to avoid potential spoilers. You can find them on dedicated maps in the Secrets section of the Extras chapter.

SEQUENCE

▌MEMORY 01

ROADSIDE ASSISTANCE: The ambush offers an opportunity to engage in open combat (Fig. 1) – something that you'll experience more often from this point onward. Ensure that Maria and Claudia are not attacked, and this conflagration will be brief. If you do not have a sword, Mario will throw you one when the second stage of the battle begins.

01

▌MEMORY 02

CASA DOLCE CASA: After an eventful introduction (and one truly brazen gaming in-joke), the stroll with Mario through Monteriggioni is rather less eventful. The primary purpose of this Memory is to introduce the process of buying from storekeepers (Fig. 2). Mario provides Ezio with the necessary funds; simply complete the shopping list to finish the mission.

02

▌MEMORY 03

PRACTICE MAKES PERFECT: This sparring session introduces essential combat abilities, with the staple Counter Kill being the most noteworthy. Execute each move as specified to proceed to the next. The conclusion is a training battle against Mario (Fig. 3). He may be stronger and more aggressive than opponents you have faced so far, but employing your new stock of techniques is the trick to beating him. Travel to Mario's office to conclude the Memory once the fight is over, then go to Maria's room.

Ezio can return to the Training Ground to practice available combat skills at any time once Memory 03 is complete. If you feel that you don't have the hang of techniques learned to date, we strongly advise that you return here before departing for San Gimignano. Once you are ready, grab a horse from outside the town gates, then follow the waypoint markers to reach your next objective.

03

04

05

USER
INSTRUCTIONS

MAP: FLORENCE

PRESENT 01

SEQUENCE 01

SEQUENCE 02

MAP: TUSCANY

SEQUENCE 03

SEQUENCE 04

SEQUENCE 05

MAP: ROMAGNA

SEQUENCE 06

PRESENT 02

MAP: VENICE

SEQUENCE 07

SEQUENCE 08

SEQUENCE 09

SEQUENCE 10

SEQUENCE 11

SEQUENCE 14

PRESENT 03

ARMOR

Purchasing armor is the most convenient way to increase Ezio's overall endurance – and, therefore, your ability to fight against ever more powerful opponents.

The Leather armor acquired by Ezio in Memory 02 provides an entirely new block on the Health Meter, raising your total health. However, this should not be regarded as a permanent, inviolable upgrade. General wear and tear sustained during battles will eventually cause armor elements to break; when this happens, Ezio loses any additional Health Squares that they provide. This is represented by the appearance of a new icon that replaces the affected gauge units (Fig. 4).

Visit the Armor section of the Inventory screen to study the current status of Ezio's protective gear. When the percentage is low, you should visit a nearby Blacksmith to commission repairs. Note that the separate Resistance rating simply reveals how sturdy armor is, with lower grades tending to require more frequent maintenance. For this reason, you should invest florins in new types whenever they become available.

COUNTER KILL

The training sessions at the Villa Auditore furnish Ezio with vital combat abilities. The Counter Kill (Fig. 5) is a talent that you should work on perfecting straight away. Without it, battles against multiple opponents will be both protracted and far more dangerous.

◆ With a weapon equipped, hold the High Profile Button and tap the Weapon Hand Button as an opponent attempts to attack Ezio to perform a Counter Kill. Against most enemies you face, precise timing will lead to an instant-death slice or stab. Ezio is invulnerable for a short period while the animation is played.

◆ Stronger opponents will resist Ezio's attempts to perform a Counter Kill. Reduce their health by other means before you attempt to use it. In battles where you face several adversaries, it's usually sensible to concentrate on dispatching rank and file assailants with this move before you turn your attention to more capable warriors.

◆ Ezio can only use Counter Kills against opponents wielding two-handed weapons (such as spears and hammers) if he is using a weapon of the same class, or the Hidden Blade (though the timing is harder with the latter).

◆ Though not immediately apparent, the Taunt and Counter Kill abilities are related. Provoking an enemy will often inspire an immediate attack – which, naturally, can be addressed with a well-timed Counter Kill. Repeated use of Taunts increases the aggressiveness of your foes, which is tactically useful when they are adopting a more defensive fight strategy.

TRICKS & TRIVIA

◆ Though their wares are currently limited, check back with merchants fairly regularly to shop for new equipment, weapons and other items of note.

◆ Carrying Medicine enables you to restore the Health Meter whenever you need. All you have to do is press left with the Quick Inventory Buttons. This will automatically use the item without changing your equipped weapon.

◆ Each weapon is graded in a handful of categories, with each one offering bonuses in combat. Though your options are limited for now, it makes sense to acquire arms that complement your fighting style.

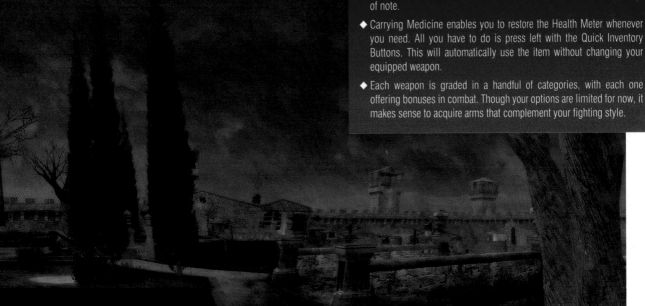

▌MEMORY 04 ▐

WHAT GOES AROUND: Use the Throwing Knives supplied by Mario to kill the archers situated on the town wall and surrounding buildings. Don't forget to acquire a Target Lock before you use them, as Ezio's supply is limited (Fig. 6). This first step accomplished, activate the mechanism to open the gate for Mario and his cohorts to enter. After the cutscene, use your Mercenaries to defeat your targets and accompany you to the next waypoint. Offer assistance to Mario, then head towards Vieri's location; your best bet is to use the rooftops for a safe and fast journey. Once the cinematic interlude ends, it's time for revenge…

06

▌MEMORY 05 ▐

A CHANGE OF PLANS: Read the letter (via the Database option on the Animus Desktop) and follow the successive waypoints until you synchronize on the roof of the villa to reveal four Codex Pages to collect from chests situated in and around Monteriggioni. Three are in the town itself; the last one is not far outside the walls, behind a small building (Fig. 7). Once you're done, speak in turn to Claudia, to the architect, and finally to Mario to learn about the Assassin Sanctuary. Your next destination is Florence.

07

USER
INSTRUCTIONS

MAP: FLORENCE

PRESENT 01

SEQUENCE 01

SEQUENCE 02

MAP: TUSCANY

SEQUENCE 03

SEQUENCE 04

SEQUENCE 05

MAP: ROMAGNA

SEQUENCE 06

PRESENT 02

MAP: VENICE

SEQUENCE 07

SEQUENCE 08

SEQUENCE 09

SEQUENCE 10

SEQUENCE 11

SEQUENCE 14

PRESENT 03

HIRING MERCENARIES

Like Courtesans, Mercenaries are hired in groups of four. They can be employed whenever you need a little extra muscle for a fight, attacking automatically when Ezio enters combat, or should you need to create a loud and violent distraction.

Press the Head Button to hire Mercenaries; the same button is used to instruct them to follow or wait on Ezio's command once they have accepted his coins. If you lock on to a viable target, pressing the Head Button will instruct the group to attack the highlighted individual and their nearby allies (Fig. 8). When you order Mercenaries to launch an assault, Ezio will not be subject to the wrath of enemies unless you do something to attract their attention. This clearly has many applications, but principle among these is the ability to rid yourself of prospective aggressors without tarnishing Ezio's reputation or apparel. From soldiers blocking your path to a mission objective, to guards standing watch over Treasures or Codex Pages, any potential aggressor is a viable target.

08

CODEX PAGES

Though some may shy away from the labor of collecting Feathers, Codex Pages offer more palpable and immediate rewards.

◆ Collecting all Codex pages is a mandatory step in order to be able to finish the game.

◆ Mario teaches Ezio about Codex Pages at the end of Sequence 03. Some provide new weapons, or upgrades for existing equipment; others offer Health bonuses.

◆ Though certain Codex Pages are awarded as milestone rewards, synchronizing at viewpoints makes optional parts appear within the unfogged zone if they are present. These are often watched by guards who will not take kindly to Ezio's presence.

◆ Codex Pages have no effect until they are deciphered by Leonardo Da Vinci.

◆ Four "Philosophical Codex" sections will permanently add a new square to the Health Meter.

◆ Once deciphered, Codex Pages have to be placed on the wall in Mario's office at Villa Auditore, and are linked to a larger mystery. This is revealed through progression in the main story, so we'll keep you up to date with important developments as they occur.

09

TREASURES

Ezio departs Monteriggioni to explore an expanded area of Florence packed with new opportunities, so this seems like a timely moment to discuss Treasures. If you need funds to finance your exploits, locating these hidden caches of currency is a worthwhile endeavor.

◆ Treasures are always contained within chests (Fig. 9), and are immediately converted into florins. The sums you receive are higher than through pickpocketing or looting.

◆ It's possible to stumble across Treasure Chests quite accidentally, though you can also visit Art Merchants to buy documents that mark the locations of all Treasures in a district on your area map. These Treasure maps can only be bought for your current locale – so Art Merchants in Florence will only sell Florentine maps.

◆ There are no maps for chests found in secret locations, or inside Villa Auditore.

TRICKS & TRIVIA

◆ Throwing Knives are only instantly fatal against enemies during the first half of the game. As guards become stronger later on, you will need to use two or three Knives to kill them.

◆ Opponents facing away from Ezio can sometimes be stabbed for one-hit kills. This is something that you can exploit profitably in brawls where he is accompanied (or temporarily supported) by allies.

SEQUENCE 03: SECONDARY MEMORIES

FREE MISSIONS

✉ WEDDING BELLS ARE RINGING (COURIER)

Location:	On the main street leading into the center of town when you enter the south gate in San Gimignano.
Special Conditions:	Complete the journey before the time expires.
Advice:	Two minutes is a highly generous time allocation – your destination, as a quick glance at the map will reveal, is a church in the northeast of the city. As long as Ezio's Notoriety level isn't at maximum, you could jog there and still have plenty of seconds to spare.

◆ SAN GIMIGNANO DASH (RACE)

Location:	On top of a wall tower in the north of San Gimignano.
Special Conditions:	Reach the final gate before the time expires.
Advice:	It's not the route that makes this Race difficult, but the level of precision required to reach the final gate within the tight time limit. The solution is to practice until you refine the path you take – trite, but true. The most important thing to remember is that you do not have seconds to spare for dealing with archers: your only option is to sprint past and lose them. Secondly, aim to keep time spent hanging on ledges to a bare minimum – the optimal route is one where Ezio hits the ground running after the vast majority of jumps. One tip that will definitely shave seconds off your time is to complete a continuous free run sequence on the beams and poles above the path that leads to the last few gates (Fig. 1). Stick to the left-hand wall, and you'll find that it's faster than running at ground level.

01

EQUIPMENT UPGRADES

Sequence 03 marks the first occasion when Ezio can buy armor and weapons, with Blacksmiths receiving more advanced stock at the start of Sequence 04. While we recommend that you spend much of your income on upgrading Monteriggioni at this stage of the game (more on the next double page), purchasing a full set of Leather Armor is definitely a high priority. If you are flush with florins obtained through looting Treasure Chests and completing Secondary Memories, though, you could also consider purchasing a new weapon to replace your initial sword.

INTRODUCTION: VILLA AUDITORE

There are no Free Missions in Monteriggioni, but Villa Auditore is much more than a destination – it's actually a sizable side-quest in its own right. Over the following pages, we'll introduce its many rooms and features.

Weapons Room: All armaments bought by Ezio during his travels are automatically mounted on racks and displayed in this room. Approach a stand and press the Head Button to examine each class of weapon and study details on their strength in relation to his current equipment. You can also switch to different armaments here, which is a thoroughly useful feature. As Ezio automatically carries the last weapon purchased, you may encounter instances where you buy a sword less powerful than other blades in your armory or, alternatively, accidentally lose a weapon after being disarmed in a fight. In either event, a quick trip to Villa Auditore will enable you to pick up the equipment you need.

Armor Room: There are five unique armor classes that Ezio can acquire during the course of the game – four that he must buy as individual pieces from Blacksmiths, and one that comes as a complete set. These are displayed in this room; as with weapons, you can also switch between different types if you wish. The two tables are used to display scale models that are automatically placed here after Sequence 06 and Sequence 08.

HOW TO PLAY

WALKTHROUGH

REFERENCE & ANALYSIS

EXTRAS

USER INSTRUCTIONS

MAP: FLORENCE

PRESENT 01

SEQUENCE 01

SEQUENCE 02

MAP: TUSCANY

SEQUENCE 03

SEQUENCE 04

SEQUENCE 05

MAP: ROMAGNA

SEQUENCE 06

PRESENT 02

MAP: VENICE

SEQUENCE 07

SEQUENCE 08

SEQUENCE 09

SEQUENCE 10

SEQUENCE 11

SEQUENCE 14

PRESENT 03

Art Gallery: Ezio can buy Paintings from Art Merchants located in each major region visited during his adventure. These contribute to the prestige and overall value of Monteriggioni.

Workshop: This acts as the central hub for a mini-game in which you invest florins to improve Monteriggioni and Villa Auditore in order to reap long-term financial rewards. Claudia controls the town ledger, which you can view to study your progress or learn more about your current income. The Architect implements building works in the town when furnished with the requisite finance. We cover these features in much greater detail overleaf.

Maria's Room: Feathers collected from the destinations Ezio visits can be placed in the chest here, with special rewards when he reaches a landmark at 50 and the full collection at 100.

Codex Room: Once located and decoded by Leonardo, Codex pages can be placed in the special frame here. All 30 must be found for Ezio to meet a date with destiny in Sequence 14, though there is actually no pressing need to interact with the Codex Wall before then.

Attic Study: Every major target that Ezio assassinates is represented by a portrait in this room. Select each painting with the Head Button to view details on the subject.

Assassin Sanctuary: In this secret chamber, the Armor of Altaïr lies behind a secure gate. It can only be unlocked by collecting six "Seals" from special destinations located throughout the game world. We will reveal more about these later as the corresponding missions become available in the game.

Training Ground: Speak to the Trainer south of Villa Auditore to learn new techniques or practice existing commands. Any abilities not yet available are written in gray. Of particular interest is the Special Moves category, where you can play a tutorial for the Throw Dirt ability. Once you have sufficient florins to spare, you can also buy the (entirely optional) Flying Knives, Smash and Sweep special techniques. The in-game messages and prompts will explain the necessary button commands, and you are free to repeat the practice sessions once an ability has been acquired. The Flying Knives technique can prove genuinely useful in certain specific circumstances. If you only purchase one of the three special techniques, this should be your choice.

INTRODUCTION: MONTERIGGIONI UPGRADES

The Workshop inside Villa Auditore is the location of an important mini-game where you can spend florins to renovate buildings and facilities, and open (or improve) new shops in Monteriggioni. When you first speak to Claudia to look at the ledger (Fig. 2), you will discover that your Villa Auditore income is under 200*f* – a total that may, on face value (or lack thereof) lead you to believe that the sums available are rather trivial.

Don't be discouraged. The amount of florins awarded at each 20-minute interval is exactly 10% of Monteriggioni's overall value, which is extremely low right now. This is Ezio's "Chest Income", which can be collected by interacting with the glowing chest behind Claudia (Fig. 3), or via the ledger interface. However, as Claudia explains during the cutscene that introduces the side-quest, there is a limit to the amount of currency that can accumulate in the Villa coffers. This "Maximum Chest Capacity" is, of course, a feature designed to prevent players from simply leaving the game running overnight to amass a fortune.

Both Chest Income and Maximum Chest Capacity can be increased by making progress in four different categories. We'll now take a look at each of these in turn.

1. SHOPS

There are two stores open for business when you first enter Monteriggioni (a Blacksmith and a Doctor), but you can open a further three (Fig. 4) and pay for additional upgrades by speaking to the Architect.

◆ Shops make the largest contribution to Monteriggioni's value once open, but are commensurately expensive.

◆ Having all five shops open for business adds an immediate bonus of 5,000*f* to Monteriggioni's value. Completing all upgrades confers an additional increase of 15,000*f*. Income from shops constitutes the lion's share of the maximum Chest Income.

◆ As a side benefit, shopping at vendors based in Monteriggioni enables Ezio to take advantage of discounts. These can be increased with successive building upgrades.

SHOP INVESTMENTS

NAME	LEVEL 1	LEVEL 2	LEVEL 3	TOTAL
Art Merchant	1,000*f*	5,000*f*	8,000*f*	14,000*f*
Bank	1,500*f*	5,000*f*	9,000*f*	15,500*f*
Blacksmith	-	7,000*f*	12,000*f*	19,000*f*
Doctor	-	3,000*f*	5,000*f*	8,000*f*
Tailor	1,000*f*	2,500*f*	5,000*f*	8,500*f*
Grand Total				**65,000*f***

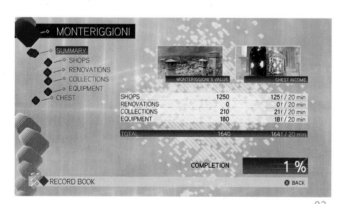

02

03

04

44

05

2. RENOVATIONS

As with Shops, all Renovations are performed by speaking to the Architect.

◆ Renovations are one-shot investments: once you pay the Architect, the building work is complete. There are no further upgrades.

◆ Completing all Renovations leads to a completion bonus of 10,000*f* to Monteriggioni's value.

◆ Some Renovations open routes to otherwise inaccessible Treasure Chests in – and, with the Mines, underneath (Fig. 5) – the town.

RENOVATION INVESTMENTS

NAME	COSTS
Brothel	3,000*f*
Mines	4,000*f*
Church	4,000*f*
Military Barracks	3,000*f*
Thieves Guild	3,000*f*
Well	4,000*f*
GRAND TOTAL	**21,000*f***

3. COLLECTIONS

The Collections category covers an assortment of miscellaneous items that Ezio can acquire during the course of the story.

◆ **Models & Portraits:** Automatically awarded after specific Memories are complete.

◆ **Codex Pages:** There are 30 in total: 10 given at specific milestones, four picked up during a Memory in Sequence 03, and a further 16 distributed around the towns and cities that Ezio visits. These are technically optional until Sequence 14, when they must be collected in order to finish the game. You cannot find all Codex pages until the start of Sequence 11. Codex pages must be placed on the Codex Wall at Villa Auditore to be counted in the ledger.

◆ **Feathers:** Found throughout the game world, they actually contribute very little to Monteriggioni's value until you have all 100 – and, even then, the nominal income increase will only be of interest to hardcore completists. The Feather collection cannot be completed until Sequence 11 at the very earliest. Those you have collected must be placed in the box in Maria's room to be taken into account in Claudia's ledger.

◆ **Seals:** All six are collected during special expeditions in Assassin Tombs, with the last one made available during Sequence 09. See "Introduction: Secret Locations" on page 52 for more details on these missions.

◆ **Paintings:** These can be bought from Art Merchants in each town Ezio visits, with a unique selection of works available in each locale. It's possible to acquire all of these by early in Sequence 07.

In total, the Collections contribute a relatively small amount to Monteriggioni's value, with a high percentage of the maximum florin total available through final completion bonuses alone. For this reason, you should regard Collections as a project to undertake much later in the game.

4. EQUIPMENT

Every weapon and piece of armor collected by Ezio adds to Monteriggioni's value.

◆ You can buy 22 weapons in total, with a reasonable completion bonus for having all of them. However, a few later armaments are incredibly expensive, and one can only be acquired after you collect 50 Feathers.

◆ There are five armor classes, which you can technically complete by Sequence 09. A full set of Missaglias armor costs in excess of 75,000*f*, though – which is one of the reasons why you should start spending on Shops and Renovations at a relatively early stage.

◆ In total, a full Equipment collection contributes a fairly high sum to Monteriggioni's maximum value, but is still much less important than Shops or Renovations.

UPGRADE STRATEGY

Though Monteriggioni's initial contribution to Ezio's fighting fund is inconsequential, investing in the town's infrastructure will soon increase the totals received every 20 minutes. Indeed, doing so is necessary in order to easily afford weapons, armor and many other purchasable items that are unlocked as you complete forthcoming Sequences. In other words, if you neglect Monteriggioni now, you'll lose out later.

1: Your first step is to go out and collect all eight Statuettes hidden around the village. This should take no more than 15 minutes if you use the guide printed overleaf, and will furnish Ezio with an additional 8,000*f* to spend. This is a great head-start.

2: Speak to the Architect and open the Art Merchant, Bank and Tailor. This will only cost 3,500*f*, but will immediately increase your Chest Income to over 900*f* per 20 minutes, and the Maximum Chest Capacity to not far from 4,000*f*. Before you invest any more, we suggest that you go spend florins on the full set of Leather Armor. Sequence 04 features much more combat, so the extra protection is arguably more important right now.

3: The next step is to complete all buildings in the Renovations category. This should be your baseline objective by the end of Sequence 04 if you're keen to have the Villa generating greater revenue for later expenses. The cost is not inconsiderable at 21,000*f*, but will boost your Chest Income to over 4,000*f* per 20 minutes, and the Maximum Chest Capacity to just over 16,000*f*.

4: Now focus your attention on the Shop upgrades, returning to Monteriggioni to collect funds and spend them with the Architect whenever Chest Income accumulates in sufficient quantities. You could also work on Secondary Memories to pick up extra funds. Completing most of those available up to and including Sequence 06 will easily furnish you with the necessary capital to upgrade the stores to the maximum Level 3. This will increase your Chest Income to over 10,000*f* per 20 minutes, and the Maximum Chest Capacity total to approximately 42,000*f*.

5: Finally, work on completing armor, weapon and paintings, stopping by at Villa Auditore whenever the chest is almost full to fund another spending spree. Certain sections of the Equipment and Collections categories will require more effort than others, but you'll find more information on these later in the guide.

HOW TO PLAY

WALKTHROUGH

REFERENCE & ANALYSIS

EXTRAS

USER INSTRUCTIONS

MAP: FLORENCE

PRESENT 01

SEQUENCE 01

SEQUENCE 02

MAP: TUSCANY

SEQUENCE 03

SEQUENCE 04

SEQUENCE 05

MAP: ROMAGNA

SEQUENCE 06

PRESENT 02

MAP: VENICE

SEQUENCE 07

SEQUENCE 08

SEQUENCE 09

SEQUENCE 10

SEQUENCE 11

SEQUENCE 14

PRESENT 03

There are eight statuettes of Roman gods hidden on walls throughout Monteriggioni. Once these have been collected, Ezio can place pairs of them on four pedestals situated to the west, northwest, northeast and east of the path leading around Villa Auditore to obtain a welcome reward of 8,000*f*.

VENUS: West face of the building just northwest of the wall where you collect the Mars statue.

MARS: On a wall directly southwest of the Villa Auditore entrance.

APOLLO: Next to a large window above an arch with an alleyway beneath.

DIANA: On the north face of the building directly in front of the town entrance.

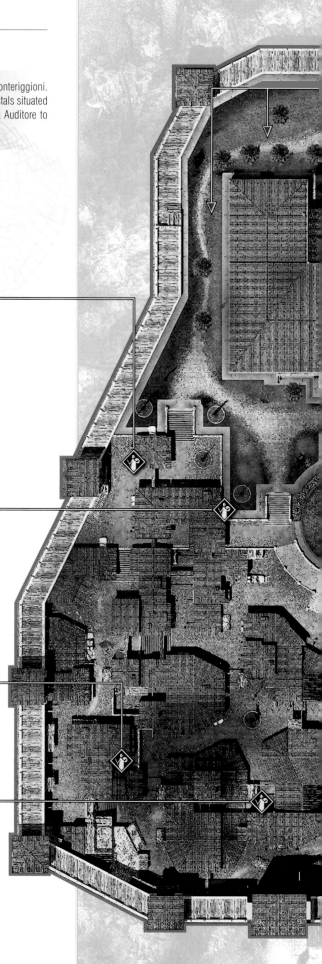

Pedestals.

NEPTUNE: On a wall directly southeast from the Villa entrance, just past a tree.

PLUTO: Behind a tree north of the church entrance.

JUPITER: On the rear wall of the church.

MINERVA: Just above a sloped roof on the southeast side of the building.

HOW TO PLAY

WALKTHROUGH

REFERENCE & ANALYSIS

EXTRAS

USER INSTRUCTIONS

MAP: FLORENCE

PRESENT 01

SEQUENCE 01

SEQUENCE 02

MAP: TUSCANY

SEQUENCE 03

SEQUENCE 04

SEQUENCE 05

MAP: ROMAGNA

SEQUENCE 06

PRESENT 02

MAP: VENICE

SEQUENCE 07

SEQUENCE 08

SEQUENCE 09

SEQUENCE 10

SEQUENCE 11

SEQUENCE 14

PRESENT 03

SEQUENCE | 04

MEMORY 01

PRACTICE WHAT YOU PREACH: A short yet instructive Memory, this unlocks new assassination techniques. Practice each one in turn (and as often as you like), being sure to try both the high and low profile variants of Assassinate from Ledge and Assassinate from Hiding (Fig. 1). When ready, return to Leonardo to complete the final objective and receive the Double Hidden Blades.

01

MEMORY 02

FOX HUNT: The Mercato Vecchio contains a common street pest: the Harasser. These infuriating individuals can recognize Ezio and will draw unwanted attention with their songs and shouts. For the same reason, you should also avoid individuals bearing crates. They will steer towards you but won't collide with you if you stand still.

Once you locate your target with Eagle Vision, move in close to trigger a cutscene. During the chase that follows (Fig. 2), the biggest challenge is to avoid colliding with guards (and, to a lesser extent, common citizenry). Once you draw close, tap the Empty Hand Button to tackle your quarry. Do not, under any circumstances, use your weapons – this will cause immediate desynchronization.

02

MEMORY 03

SEE YOU THERE: A free running exercise en route to Santa Maria Novella. The Memory ends once your companion leaves, but there is still the question of how to deal with the guards blocking the route to your next objective. Courtesans or Mercenaries (Fig. 3) both have their merits if your funds allow it, though a short free running session over the wall with the arches or an honest brawl will be just as effective in securing access to the catacombs.

03

USER
INSTRUCTIONS

MAP: FLORENCE

PRESENT 01

SEQUENCE 01

SEQUENCE 02

MAP: TUSCANY

SEQUENCE 03

SEQUENCE 04

SEQUENCE 05

MAP: ROMAGNA

SEQUENCE 06

PRESENT 02

MAP: VENICE

SEQUENCE 07

SEQUENCE 08

SEQUENCE 09

SEQUENCE 10

SEQUENCE 11

SEQUENCE 14

PRESENT 03

ASSASSINATION TECHNIQUES

The first Memory of Sequence 04 provides you with new ways to assassinate foes.

◆ Assassinate from Ledge (Fig. 4) is great for archers, or guards patrolling rooftop destinations. If your target is alone, bear in mind that the high profile variant (where Ezio jumps up to perform the kill) may draw less attention than throwing him to the streets below. Then again, if you need a distraction, hurling a dead sentry to the ground should have the desired effect.

04

◆ Having Air Assassinations in your repertoire means that you can stalk certain targets on high ground, leaping down to kill as you catch them if in hot pursuit, or once situated in a suitably secluded locale if they are oblivious to Ezio's presence. Though thoroughly useful (not to mention spectacular) in many instances, this attack is especially handy when you need to kill a corrupt Official to reduce Notoriety.

◆ With forward planning, Assassinate from Hiding kills are extremely satisfying. The low profile type is naturally hard to execute, but is an abrupt remedy whenever there is a danger that a guard may discover Ezio as he lies concealed in a pile of straw or leaves. The high profile variation is just a cool way to kickstart a brawl in style.

◆ The Double Hidden Blades enable Ezio to assassinate two targets at once if they are stood in close proximity. This feat can be performed either at ground level or via an Air Assassination. Note that even though the timing window is much tighter than with other weapons, successful Counter Kills performed with the Double Hidden Blades are instantly lethal.

HARASSERS

Harassers are a special class of citizen who exist solely to irritate, impede your progress, and sorely test your ability to refrain from slaying innocents. Whenever Ezio moves within approximately 15 meters of their starting position, these distinctive dandies will run over and stand in front of him to hinder forward motion, causing a commotion with their songs, shouts and capering. This will lead other citizens and – worse – nearby enemies to pay attention.

The best way to deal with a Harasser is to avoid him entirely, bypassing his position or Blending with a moving group. The luxury of being able to plan in advance is not always yours to enjoy, though, especially while attempting to travel to a destination or waypoint at pace. Once detected, you have four options. Drawing a weapon will make the Harasser flee, but causes a commotion that may lead enemies to attack. Throwing florins will cause the nuisance to scurry away in search of coins. Pushing into a Harasser will prompt him to drop his lute. The most effective solution, though, is to restrain the digit moving purposefully towards the Weapon Hand Button, and simply make a run for it.

ENEMY MORALE

Though the most instinctive course of action in large-scale fights is to deal with weaker enemies first, targeting and killing the strongest opponents first can actually be beneficial – if you have the skill to pull it off. All opponents (with the exception of assassination targets) have a hidden "morale" attribute. Surviving assailants have their total reduced whenever Ezio dispatches one of their peers, with bonuses applied for certain techniques (see below). However, enemies can receive morale boosts whenever Ezio is hurt, enters critical status, or attempts to flee.

We analyze the system in its entirety later in the guide (see page 135), but the following guidelines should help you to take advantage of it during the battles ahead.

◆ Once his morale reaches zero an opponent will flee, never to return.

◆ As a general rule, the tougher an opponent, the higher their total morale.

◆ The deaths of senior or stronger adversaries cause the greatest morale penalties. Kill a lowly militiaman, and his superiors will barely blink; execute an opponent of high rank, and nearby militiamen will surely waver, if not bolt at the first opportunity (Fig. 5).

◆ For the time being, you can inflict additional morale penalties for Counter Kills and weapon-based finishing moves whenever Ezio grabs an enemy.

05

▌MEMORY 04 ▬▬▬▬

NOVELLA'S SECRET: This mission is covered in greater depth across the page, but those seeking to beat it with minimal assistance should simply bear in mind that studying your environment carefully is the key to completing the early stages. Later on, free running and combat skills are more important.

▌MEMORY 05 ▬▬▬▬

WOLVES IN SHEEP'S CLOTHING: Wound Francesco to drive him away (it's not possible to kill him here), then defend Lorenzo de' Medici from a large wave of assailants (Fig. 6). Once these are defeated, escort him through the chaos in the streets until you reach his residence. You will be attacked by other enemies as you travel: judicious use of Counter Kills is the trick to keeping each battle suitably short. As all this combat may take a toll on Ezio's health, armor and supplies, be sure to restock, repair and heal before starting the next Memory. Throwing Knives could be especially useful.

06

▌MEMORY 06 ▬▬▬▬

FAREWELL FRANCESCO: Head up to the rooftops and travel to the waypoint where de Pazzi seemingly awaits your arrival. Climb the back end of the Palazzo della Signoria and study the positions of Francesco's men (Fig. 7). His archers are your foremost priority. If you can discretely kill these first (ideally with the low-profile Assassinate from Ledge move), the combat that follows will be far less fraught with danger.

Your target flees once you reach the upper level, so give chase immediately – losing him will send you back to the previous checkpoint. Francesco is an accomplished free runner. Concentrate on keeping up with him at first, only taking risks to close the gap when you are confident that the consequences for any mistakes will be small. Once you draw sufficiently near, ready the Hidden Blade and wait for the right moment to strike.

07

HOW TO PLAY

WALKTHROUGH

REFERENCE &
ANALYSIS

EXTRAS

1: Use the lever to open the first gate, then climb up and take the left-hand exit. Free run over the exposed poles and beams (Fig. 8) to reach a second lever, then head through the central passage. Again, use the beams to free run to a broken platform where a third and final lever can be found to open the gate at the waypoint marker. Perform a Leap of Faith from the ledge into the pile of straw below to quickly return to the bottom level. Note that should you accidentally fall to the lower level (and survive) before activating the second lever, you can climb a ladder to reach a path that leads back to the starting point.

Secret: Walk to the edge of the initial broken staircase and look down to see a short piece of wood protruding from the wall. Drop down and use the Grasp function to quickly catch it as Ezio falls past. Leap across to the nearby broken floor section to find a chest.

08

USER
INSTRUCTIONS

MAP: FLORENCE

PRESENT 01

SEQUENCE 01

SEQUENCE 02

2: Free run over the broken wall sections (to your left as you enter the room) to reach the upper level. There are Templar guards on either side. Use the Assassinate from Ledge move to kill the first on your left, then sneak up on the second. Free run over the poles extending from the wall above the locked gate; for the final jump, aim for the hanging rope to swing around to safety (Fig. 9). Activate the glowing switch mechanism.

Secret: Drop through the broken floor to find a secret chest.

09

MAP: TUSCANY

SEQUENCE 03

3: Still on the upper level, leap over to protruding stones on the east wall (Fig. 10), then climb to the wooden platform and jump to the adjacent balcony. Hop over to the sarcophagus raised by the mechanism, then turn left and use the pole to reach a second balcony. Here, operate the device to open the gate. Jump to the pole left of it after the cutscene, then perform a Leap of Faith from the ledge to return to the lower level.

10

SEQUENCE 04

SEQUENCE 05

MAP: ROMAGNA

SEQUENCE 06

4: Templars enter the room and begin investigating, but you can ignore these and make a break for the individual just through the gate. Approaching him triggers a frantic chase through ruined corridors. You can't "fail" during this sequence, so feel free to take risks. The athletic Agile Templar will do everything in his power to curtail Ezio's pursuit (Fig. 11), but every blocked route has an alternative path next to it.

11

PRESENT 02

MAP: VENICE

SEQUENCE 07

SEQUENCE 08

SEQUENCE 09

5: When you reach a long set of stairs leading to a tunnel with a raised path on the left, you have a choice. If you choose to follow him on the low ground, you won't catch him before he reaches the door. The Templar then warns four of his associates, leading to a fight. If you take the high ground, though, it's possible to perform a spectacular jumping execution at the end (Fig. 12), thus preventing him from raising the alert and avoiding the battle entirely.

Move to the waypoint to find a switch. After the cutscene, head down and open the sarcophagus. Don't forget to open the nearby Treasure Chests before you exit to the outside world.

12

SEQUENCE 10

SEQUENCE 11

SEQUENCE 14

PRESENT 03

ENEMY ARCHETYPE: AGILE

The Agile is a special class of enemy that excels at free running. Indeed, their straight-line sprinting speed is superior to that of Ezio, and it is this that makes them most dangerous. They can be readily identified by their slender build.

◆ When Ezio is fleeing, Agile opponents will follow close behind and attempt to impede his progress, barging him from behind to throw him off-balance. Weaving precisely through crowds or performing daring feats of free running may enable you to lose an Agile, but the best strategy is often to dispatch them before fleeing, or after drawing them away from their slower peers.

◆ In combat, Agiles dodge more frequently than other enemy types and may follow evasive maneuvers with a counter, but are very weak. They also have fairly low morale ratings (though higher than generic militia), which will cause them to flee from the scene if Ezio slaughters their allies efficiently.

◆ Though they have boundless energy while chasing, Agiles will grow tired if forced to dodge repeatedly. After evading a few attacks, a typical Agile will enter a "fatigued" state for approximately ten seconds before their stamina is replenished. During this period, they can be killed with almost casual ease.

SEQUENCE 04: SECONDARY MEMORIES

FREE MISSIONS

SAN MARCO SCUTTLE (RACE)	
Location:	Behind Santa Croce in the southeast corner of Florence.
Special Conditions:	Run through all gates within the allotted time limit.
Advice:	Ignore any guards that give chase, and focus on learning the route on your initial attempts. The most difficult part of the course comes just after gate 12, where there is a jump to a rooftop that is just outside Ezio's range. The solution is to angle your run to climb the wooden crane (Fig. 1), then leap from there. There are a lot of gates to pass through, but you actually have enough time to make a few (small) mistakes.

01

EQUIPMENT UPGRADES & CODEX PAGES

Equipment: Sequence 05 marks the debut of two new swords: the Florentine Falchion (notable for its high Deflect rating) and the Captain's Sword (which offers a better Speed statistic). You can now also buy the full set of Helmschmied armor, though don't rush to make a purchase if your current Leather garb is still offering sufficient protection – it's a significant investment that might be better spent on upgrading Monteriggioni.

Codex Pages: If you have been neglecting these so far, take the time to storm Banks in Florence and Tuscany to obtain the seven Philosophical Codex pages available at this time (five and two in the respective locales), then take them to Leonardo for translation.

INTRODUCTION: SECRET LOCATIONS

The completion of Novella's Secret during Sequence 04 unlocks additional excursions to Secret Locations: six **Assassin Tombs** and three **Templar Lairs**.

◆ There are five main optional Assassin Tombs to play, these being unlocked gradually during the course of the game. Each one contains a special Seal as its final reward (in addition to florins), which will eventually enable you to unlock the Armor of Altaïr. We'll let you know as soon as they become available.

◆ There is a bonus Assassin Tomb available for those who sign up for the Uplay service. This has no seal, but makes a contribution to both the overall story and Ezio's purse.

◆ Owners of the Black Edition have three exclusive Templar Lairs. These work in the same way as Assassin Tombs, but offer florins as a final reward – plus, naturally, the satisfaction of beating them.

◆ All Tombs and Lairs contain two hidden Treasure Chests. These provide extra florins, but it's not mandatory that you find them all.

◆ Tombs and Lairs tend to feature more demanding climbing tasks than Ezio's exploits above ground. One advanced move in particular is required to complete some of these optional adventures, or at least to reach hidden Treasure Chests. It consists of a vertical wall run followed immediately by a wall jump at the peak of Ezio's ascent. In practice, this means you run up a featureless surface before leaping in the necessary direction (Fig. 2).

02

Entrance: On the north side of Santa Maria del Fiore – the switch is clearly visible from the street.

1: Climb the wall to the left of the main doors (located not far west of your starting position), then move onto the platform to the right. Free run to the second of the two decorative arches on the north wall. Now jump onto the beams and make your way to a first chandelier. From here, use the other chandeliers and wooden beams to reach a platform on the south wall (Fig. 3). Landing here will create a first shortcut back to the upper level.

2: Run along the beam and climb to the top platform, then turn and jump to the beam near the window; now swing, free run and jump along the face of the south wall to reach a chandelier. Now head to the beam in the north via the chandeliers and wooden platform (Fig. 4). From the beam, jump to the stone platform then climb to its upper level. Again, free run and swing your way to a chandelier to the east. Turn right and make your way over the obvious free run elements to reach a platform on the south wall. Move to the end of the beam, then use the poles to the east to arrive at a platform below. This will activate a second ladder shortcut.

3: Jump to the circular structure, then jump over to the small balcony below the organ pipes. Face north, then use the beams and chandelier to reach an identical balcony on the opposite side of the room; from there, jump to the other side of the circular structure. Move around to the west. Climb onto the nearby platform via the wooden planks and beam (Fig. 5), then jump to another platform further north.

4: Walk over the beams and leap over to a platform on the north wall. Climb to the balcony above it, then use the wooden beams to get to a suspended platform. Jump to the stone ledge, then swing via the pole to a wooden platform below; from there, use the chandelier to reach a platform further south. Use the wooden ledges to traverse to the left (Fig. 6), then climb up to the walkway above. Use one of the two beams to reach a larger wooden beam to the west; move onto the protruding section to leap over to the nearby balcony.

Hidden Treasure #1 (optional): On the south side of the balcony, move out onto the beam and face south. Use the pole and beam directly ahead to arrive at a platform below, then climb up to the ledges and to the top of the window above. Now spring back to reach the chandelier, then jump to the barrier to the southeast of your position (Fig. 7). After opening the Treasure Chest, climb the surface to the right of it to reach a wooden beam; climb up, then move to the center. Jump and swing on the pole to get to a suspended platform.

5: Jump over to a suspended wooden platform (if you collected Hidden Treasure #1, you're already there), then hop over to the next balcony. Free run up to the ladder, then climb to the top. Free run all the way around the outer edge of the dome until you reach an area of climbable brickwork revealed by camera view.

Hidden Treasure #2 (optional): At the end of the dome path (just before you reach the brickwork mentioned in Step 5), drop over the edge of the barrier and climb down the scaffold below (Fig. 8). Drop to the platform, open the Treasure Chest, then climb on top of the nearby screen. Jump to the hand-holds in the bricked-up window to reach the scaffold and return to the upper level.

6: Climb up to the wooden beams, then leap over to a platform in the center of the dome. At the top of the ladder, open the sarcophagus to receive the Seal of Iltani, then exit via the flashing window.

HOW TO PLAY

WALKTHROUGH

REFERENCE & ANALYSIS

EXTRAS

USER INSTRUCTIONS

MAP: FLORENCE

PRESENT 01

SEQUENCE 01

SEQUENCE 02

MAP: TUSCANY

SEQUENCE 03

SEQUENCE 04

SEQUENCE 05

MAP: ROMAGNA

SEQUENCE 06

PRESENT 02

MAP: VENICE

SEQUENCE 07

SEQUENCE 08

SEQUENCE 09

SEQUENCE 10

SEQUENCE 11

SEQUENCE 14

PRESENT 03

Entrance: On the west side of the Palazzo Medici, situated in the north of Florence's San Marco district.

1 – Courtyard: Head into the waypoint marker and kill the soldiers who attack Ezio. Look for a platform on the west wall of the courtyard, then use it to free run up to a lighting fixture. Climb up, then jump across to another directly ahead, then jump onto the beams. Free run over the flat tops of the posts to get to the east wall, then turn right and face south. (Fig. 9). Use the lighting fixtures to reach the beams further ahead. Turn right again and jump to the top of the post, then turn left and hop onto the beams. Swing on the poles to the south to reach a wooden beam; climb up when the camera angle changes, then drop through the hole to arrive at the Palazzo interior.

09

2 – First Floor: Jump down to kill the guards, then pull the lever. Climb to the top of the cupboards to the right of the fireplace, then free run over to the west wall. Wall run to the top of the nearest painting, then traverse all the way to the right. Now turn and free run to the passage that the lever opened in the east wall (Fig. 10), then climb the ladder to reach the second floor.

10

Hidden Treasure #1 (optional): Turn to face east when you first arrive on the second floor and move onto the ledge in front of the painting, Wall run vertically, then spring back to grab the decorative beam (Fig. 11). From there, leap to the upper ledge and pull the lever. This will open two cupboards, each containing a Treasure Chest.

11

3 – Second Floor: Approach the door to trigger a cutscene. Once it ends, you can hide behind the door and wait for two guards to walk into the room, then wait for them to walk away for an easy Double Assassination opportunity. However the battle begins, kill all hostiles in the area. Climb through the window on the north wall of the corridor, then make your way to the open window on the opposite side of the courtyard (Fig. 12). Slay the guards inside, then climb onto the movable steps in the northwest corner of the room. Free run to the east and scale the bookcases to reach the balcony above.

12

4 – Third Floor, Part 1: Climb to the top of the cupboard, turn and jump to a beam, then use the chandeliers to reach the opposite balcony. Kill the guards on the other side, then exit to the inner walls via the open window. Free run to the east wall, then turn right and head for the open window to the south (Fig. 13).

Hidden Treasure #2 (optional): Instead of entering the corridor, turn right and free run to another window to the west. Climb up to the platform to open the chest, then retrace your steps.

13

5 – Third Floor, Part 2: Sneak along the corridor and try to kill at least one of the two Brutes before you are detected, then fight his enraged cohorts. Return to the east end of the corridor and climb the bookcase. Move through the hole, then jump to the ornate framing above the door to your right (Fig. 14). Traverse to the left until you reach the top of a cupboard. Jump onto the top of the bed, then leap into the alcove. Pull the lever, then drop down and return to the corridor. Climb the bookcase again, but this time jump over to the chandelier. Use the two lighting fixtures to get to a second chandelier further along the corridor, then jump into the secret passage. Follow the linear path to reach Lorenzo's treasure room. Loot the large chest, then interact with the glowing door to exit.

14

Entrance: Look for the glowing door west of the Training Ground in Monteriggioni (Fig. 15).

Note: There are glowing stone plates located throughout the Auditore Family Crypt that relate the story of one of Ezio's ancestors. Press the Head Button to read each one you encounter. As they are pretty much impossible to miss, we don't specify their positions in the walkthrough.

1: Run down the steps, then climb through the opening in the northeast corner of the room. Wall run on the east wall, then jump left to grab the ledge. Continue forward until you reach a lever. This raises a barrier far north of your position, but only for a limited time. Activate the mechanism, then jump onto the beam. Hit the ground running and, without breaking stride, turn left and leap to the pole; from there, swing to the wooden walkway below. Run through the opening and hop onto the column; jump onto the wooden platform (Fig. 16) and hop to another column to your right. Face north and free run up to the gate, then dash through before it falls. Turn the corner and drop down to reach another lever.

Hidden Treasure #1 (optional): Walk past the lever and jump into the water. Swim beneath the gate in the northwest corner of the flooded area, then climb the north wall (Fig. 17). Jump left to land on a wooden beam. Face west, then wall run and jump left to a small (and unobtrusive) hand-hold. From there, scale the south wall to reach the Treasure Chest.

2: Before you go any further, climb the steps at the north edge of the area and note the position of the closed gate. This should help to prevent any confusion later. Return to the lever and activate it to raise a barrier to the east, then swim beneath it before it closes. Here comes the tricky part. Activate the next lever, then turn and leap from the balustrade to the beam. Climb up, turn right, then wall run and leap to the right to reach a wooden platform. Jump to the beam to the south, then jump again to reach a stone wall. Run forward and wall run, then jump right to reach another wooden beam; climb up and hop over to the wall, then to the stone platform. Run onto the small wooden beam and jump into the water below (Fig. 18). Jumping from this precise position will enable Ezio to clear the submerged barrier. Finally, rush over to the gate you examined earlier and run through before it slams shut.

3: Drop into the corridor, then head north to reach the next lever. Activate it, then hop over to the wooden platform. Turn right and free run up to the broken staircase (Fig. 19), then run over the wooden beam and swing down via the two poles. At the end of the tunnel, hop onto the stone platform directly ahead, aiming to land on the left-hand side of it. Now wall run and leap left before the gate closes.

Hidden Treasure #2 (optional): Climb the boxes to the west of the final lever, then wall run and jump right to grab a ledge. Climb up to find the Treasure Chest.

4: There is one last timed run to reach the final room. Pull the lever, then free run to the east until you get to a broken wall (Fig. 20). Here, jump to the wall section to your right, then continue east until you come to a wooden platform. Stand on top of the boxes and wall run, then spring back to reach a beam, then jump over to the broken walkway. Now turn right, jump to the platform and sprint through the entrance. After reading the final plate and looting the Treasure Chests in the burial chamber, use the hatch to exit.

15

16

17

18

19

20

HOW TO PLAY

WALKTHROUGH

REFERENCE & ANALYSIS

EXTRAS

USER INSTRUCTIONS

MAP: FLORENCE

PRESENT 01

SEQUENCE 01

SEQUENCE 02

MAP: TUSCANY

SEQUENCE 03

SEQUENCE 04

SEQUENCE 05

MAP: ROMAGNA

SEQUENCE 06

PRESENT 02

MAP: VENICE

SEQUENCE 07

SEQUENCE 08

SEQUENCE 09

SEQUENCE 10

SEQUENCE 11

SEQUENCE 14

PRESENT 03

SEQUENCE | 05

▌MEMORIES 01 & 02 ▌

FOUR TO THE FLOOR: A very simple task: meet de Medici on the Ponte Vecchio and view a cutscene. Once it ends, head over to the waypoint to meet Leonardo.

A BLADE WITH BITE: Another short and uncomplicated objective. When you reach his workshop, Da Vinci prepares a new gadget for Ezio – the Poison Blade. If you have any optional engagements that you'd like to work on in Florence, do so now as you'll be leaving the city for the rest of this Sequence. Once ready, either travel to Monteriggioni on foot or on horseback or, better still, try out a hugely convenient Fast Travel Station (Fig. 1).

01

▌MEMORY 03 ▌

EVASIVE MANEUVERS: On your return to Monteriggioni, speak with Mario to begin this short yet instructive Memory. Pay special attention to the Dodge and Disarm tutorials (Fig. 2), as these abilities will grow in significance as Ezio faces ever more varied and well-armed adversaries.

Note: Memories 04 to 07 are all made available after the completion of Memory 03. We cover the progression followed by the DNA menu, though there's no reason why you can't chose a different order if you prefer. All four events occur in and around San Gimignano. You can find a map of this region on page 37.

▌MEMORY 04 ▌

TOWN CRIER: The Memory Start position is just outside Santa Maria Assunta in San Gimignano; we suggest that you pick up Throwing Knives on your way there if your stocks are low. Figuring out the best way to reach Antonio Maffei is a puzzle of sorts, but we've prepared a reliable solution.

1: Begin by climbing a ladder behind a hay cart northeast of your starting position (Fig. 3). Eliminate the nearby rooftop archer, then climb the short tower directly south of the one where Maffei is holding forth.

2: When you are almost at the top, stop and observe the two sentries. One stands in the center, turning to face a new direction at regular intervals. His companion, though, walks around the outside of the roof – making him an easy target for a stealthy Assassinate from Ledge move as he passes your position. Naturally, you should do this while his companion is looking elsewhere. Once you've sent him plummeting, bide your time and kill the second archer.

3: A rope bridge links this tower and your destination, so drop down to it and head over to Maffei's tower. At the top, your target is guarded by a few soldiers. When you reach the wooden platform, ensure that there is no one above before climbing up. At this point, the manner in which you deliver the *coup de grace* is yours to choose – though, it must be said, it's a *long* way down…

02

03

USER INSTRUCTIONS

MAP: FLORENCE

PRESENT 01

SEQUENCE 01

SEQUENCE 02

MAP: TUSCANY

SEQUENCE 03

SEQUENCE 04

SEQUENCE 05

MAP: ROMAGNA

SEQUENCE 06

PRESENT 02

MAP: VENICE

SEQUENCE 07

SEQUENCE 08

SEQUENCE 09

SEQUENCE 10

SEQUENCE 11

SEQUENCE 14

PRESENT 03

04

down his employer, which is almost comical when it works. If an opportunity arises to stealthily administer Poison to your actual objective, though, it may be that you can arrange to be far away before he expires and the alarm is raised. If Ezio's quarry is located at a height where a fall could be fatal, you could wager on which will kill them first: the poison, or the unyielding surface that awaits below…

◆ A poisoning could also be used to cause a commotion that will enable Ezio to sneak by undetected.

◆ Poison Blade refills can be purchased from any Doctor for a nominal fee.

PICKPOCKETS

If you have come to regard Harassers as a greater scourge than any Templar you have encountered, you'll just *love* Pickpockets. It could be that Ezio's purposeful gait identifies him as a man of means, or that the jingling of coins collected from Monteriggioni's coffers rings out like a clarion call to such folk; we cannot say for sure. What is certain, though, is that failing to notice these scoundrels in a timely fashion will dent Ezio's finances.

05

◆ Pickpockets are represented on the Mini-Map with a distinct icon: a red purse with an exclamation mark in the center. The best way to avoid them is to pay them a wide berth, though establishing eye contact is enough to make them give up the idea of stealing from you. They seem disinclined to follow targets onto rooftops, so that's always a good way to avoid their attention.

◆ If they can get close enough, Pickpockets will bump into Ezio, automatically relieving him of a variable sum of florins, before attempting to escape. Like Borgia Couriers, they are adept at climbing and free running, though not so skilled as to leave Ezio trailing in their wake (Fig. 5). To retrieve stolen money, get close enough to perform a tackle or an assassination move. The former should cause the terrified coin-snatcher to relinquish his ill-gotten gains, plus the contents of his own purse as compensation. If you opt for violence, you can loot the florins from his corpse.

◆ If you lose sight of a Pickpocket during a chase, you have mere moments to get them back in view before they (and Ezio's florins) vanish for good. Once the icon disappears from the Mini-Map, the pursuit is over.

POISON BLADE

Though introduced with relatively little fanfare, you should not regard the Poison Blade as anything less than a valuable addition to Ezio's arsenal. When used on a viable target, it will cause him to stagger or sway almost drunkenly at first. After this initial stage, the afflicted individual will endure a psychotic episode where he draws a weapon (if he has one) and begins to swing it wildly – even hitting his companions as he labors to fight off assailants that only he can perceive (Fig. 4). The final indignity, barring a merciful intervention, is collapse and death.

It should go without saying that this most fiendish toy has some interesting applications.

◆ After selecting this blade from the radial menu, the usual "Assassinate" option is replaced by "Poison" when you stand sufficiently close to a target. If you stab your chosen victim discretely, ensuring that all potential witnesses are looking elsewhere, citizens and soldiers alike will be oblivious to Ezio's involvement. Note that you cannot fight or perform Air Assassinations or Assassinations from Ledges with the Poison Blade. If you try any of these moves, the Double Hidden Blades will be automatically used instead.

◆ If a target is walking when stabbed, he will continue to stumble forward for a time, keeping step with his allies (if applicable); stationary victims are less inclined to move from their position.

◆ On a tactical level, the Poison Blade facilitates novel assassination opportunities. Stabbing a bodyguard might cause him to inadvertently cut

06

07

▌MEMORY 05 ▌

BEHIND CLOSED DOORS: The Memory Start position is located far outside the walls of San Gimignano, so you may prefer to complete the nearby Memory 06 beforehand. This is an extremely combat-oriented mission, so stock up on Throwing Knives and Medicine and repair Ezio's armor before you head for the waypoint just southeast of Villa Salviati.

Once you start the Memory, head north to the buildings on the east side of the villa. All soldiers in the region have been briefed to expect you, so waste no time: order your Mercenaries to attack each group you encounter, then try to stalk the periphery of each melee, performing easy one-hit kills on opponents facing away from you. When you reach the houses, make the archers your priority. The tallest building here is high enough to enable Ezio to leap straight over to the villa walls (Fig. 6). With Throwing Knives at the ready, turn left and follow this high path until you reach the main gate, dispatching sentries with as little ceremony as possible.

Take a deep breath, then jump down and open the gate – the mechanism is clearly visible beside it. Once your allies engage the many soldiers here, your target is easy to identify: he is, after all, the only combatant wearing nightclothes. If you engage and dispatch him quickly, your sole remaining objective is to escape.

▌MEMORY 06 ▌

COME OUT AND PLAY: Bernardo Baroncelli is the most cautious assassination target you have faced so far. The streets leading to his location are blocked by guards, so you need to find and climb a building on the western edge of the highlighted zone. The specific one you need has a ladder leading to its roof (Fig. 7).

Move over to the Leap of Faith position on the east face of the building. Observe the scene below, then activate Eagle Vision to identify Baroncelli. Ensure that he is facing away and there are no guards moving underneath, then dive into the cart full of hay just below. Watch your target closely as he walks around the area, regarding groups and potential hiding spots with great suspicion. Wait until he is facing away from you, then jump out and Blend with the nearby crowd. Finally, pick a group that lies directly on his "patrol" route and lie in wait. Activate Target Lock as he approaches, then strike with the Hidden Blade once he moves in range. For a more exotic finish, you could opt for the Poison Blade instead – on either Baroncelli or his bodyguards. If you remain concealed throughout, you may be able to Blend straight into another group once the deed is done, escaping detection entirely.

Should Baroncelli spot Ezio, he will flee immediately, with surrounding guards rushing to his aid. Don't get sidetracked by fighting – aim to catch your quarry and perform a quick kill before making your escape.

Though you may have already faced a few, the number of enemies carrying armaments of the "Heavy" or "Long" varieties increases in Sequence 05. These two-handed weapons occupy a distinct class of their own, and are distinguished from standard one-handed weapons (the type you are most familiar with at this point) by several features.

08

The most important thing to keep in mind is that Ezio cannot reliably perform Counter Kills on an opponent wielding a Heavy or Long weapon type unless he is carrying one himself, or fighting with the Double Hidden Blades. Indeed, attempting to do so with a one-handed weapon (such as a sword or dagger) will usually enable the aggressor in question to break through his guard and score a direct hit.

Blocking still works perfectly well, of course (with the exception of "special" techniques – more on that in a moment), as do the one-shot Deflect Counters, but Counter Kills are most definitely out. With this powerful riposte being the most efficient way to kill large numbers of standard guards, this is clearly a problem. There are two solutions. One is to refine your fighting skills with one-handed weapons, learning how to identify Long or Heavy weapons in brawls and using Counter Kills carefully. The second is to start fighting with fists or the Double Hidden Blades whenever you face groups with mixed weapon types, making regular use of the Disarm move if you opt for pugilism. As a fringe benefit, successful Disarms on a two-handed weapon carrier will grant you a "free" guaranteed kill on your next Counter Kill.

09

Heavy and Long weapons each have a special "power-up" technique that both enemies and Ezio (after he's learned them from the Training Ground) can use. You'll soon learn to identify the tell-tale signs that an assault of either type is imminent. They can be averted without consequence if you hit the assailant in question before the charge period is complete. If not, you'll need to dodge with great accuracy to avoid big damage.

◆ Fighters carrying Long weapons (spears and halberds) can execute the Sweep attack (Fig. 8), which knocks Ezio from his feet.

◆ Combatants holding Heavy weapons (including the two-handed sword and axes) can perform a Smash attack (Fig. 9). This breaks through all defenses (with the exception of an accurately timed Disarm attempt) to inflict large damage. Once fully charged, this move can also smash a weapon from a target's grasp – and this applies to Ezio, too.

ENEMY ARCHETYPE: BRUTES

These imposing soldiers possess great strength and endurance. Utterly fearless, they will always move to the front of any battle and engage Ezio at close range.

◆ Brutes favor two-handed Heavy weapons. This means that you should be cautious before committing to Counter Kills in groups where a Brute is present – unless, of course, you favor the Double Hidden Blades for combat, or have acquired a suitable two-handed weapon of your own.

◆ Their combo assaults are very powerful. More so than any other generic enemy, effective dodging and strafing is vital, especially when such evasive maneuvers set up quick ripostes as a Brute follows through on an inaccurate attack. You also need to be wary of their special techniques, particularly the devastating Smash Attack.

◆ Due to their huge bulk and heavy armor, Brutes are poor athletes. Their running speed is slower than most assailants you face, and their climbing skills are negligible. This means that you can conceivably scale a building, lure a Brute's associates to your position, then drop back down to fight him once they have been dispatched.

◆ Brutes have the highest hidden morale level of all standard enemies. No matter how many of their comrades you slaughter, they will never run from battle. However, they are also highly regarded by their peers – and this is something that you can exploit, as killing a Brute can cause weaker enemies to abandon the battle immediately.

HOW TO PLAY

WALKTHROUGH

REFERENCE & ANALYSIS

EXTRAS

USER INSTRUCTIONS

MAP: FLORENCE

PRESENT 01

SEQUENCE 01

SEQUENCE 02

MAP: TUSCANY

SEQUENCE 03

SEQUENCE 04

SEQUENCE 05

MAP: ROMAGNA

SEQUENCE 06

PRESENT 02

MAP: VENICE

SEQUENCE 07

SEQUENCE 08

SEQUENCE 09

SEQUENCE 10

SEQUENCE 11

SEQUENCE 14

PRESENT 03

■ MEMORY 07 ■

THE COWL DOES NOT MAKE THE MONK: Stefano da Bagnone is seeking refuge inside the Monte Oliveto Maggiore, located southeast of San Gimignano. Though it may seem that you can stroll straight in, activating Eagle Vision will reveal that certain groups of monks are actually disguised guards. Those patrolling outside will be suspicious of Ezio as he passes, but are easy to avoid. Those inside the building, however, are more attentive, and will attack on sight if they see Ezio enter. Complicating matters somewhat, the area marked in red on your Mini-Map is a "forbidden zone". This encompasses two possible entrances.

Given the need to identify Bagnone with Eagle Vision before you make the kill, a discrete approach definitely works best. One tactic is to slip through the entrance on the north face of the building (Fig. 10) and immediately Blend with a crowd (good timing and judgment are essential here); you can then make use of the numerous hiding spots available to move into position and strike as Bagnone walks by. Another tactic is to sneak onto the rooftop and perform an Air Assassination once your target strolls out into the center of the cloister. Either way, the Smoke Bombs given to Ezio at the start of the mission will facilitate the quick escape required once the deed is done. If you leave via the exit on the north face of the building, one dropped just outside should suffice.

10

■ MEMORY 08 ■

WITH FRIENDS LIKE THESE: Before you start this Memory, take the time to reduce Ezio's Notoriety level to zero and replenish your stock of Throwing Knives.

Identify Jacopo de' Pazzi with Eagle Vision, then trail him out of the town. He will become suspicious if Ezio approaches him too closely, or causes any kind of commotion – even colliding with a civilian may lead him to backtrack and investigate. If you lose a direct line of sight with your target, you have 25 seconds to lay eyes on him again, or Desynchronization will follow. His destination is a secret meeting in the Antico Teatro Romano ruins not far outside the town.

The best approach is to take to the rooftops, though you will need to swiftly slay a few archers with well-aimed Throwing Knives. Follow him out of the square, and scale the first suitable wall once you note the direction in which he is travelling. When Jacopo reaches the main gate, note that there are guards blocking the exit. Wait on a roof until your target strolls through, then use the wooden scaffold to the west of the gate to climb onto the town's outer wall. When he walks past your position, free run on the beams and poles extending from the nearby tower to reach the next wall section (Fig. 11).

When Jacopo reaches the steps leading into the ruins, wait until he and his guards walk down the steps into the ruined amphitheater, then use the Leap of Faith to return to ground level. Do not attempt to follow them down. Approach the waypoint marker that appears from the south (look out for a stone "bridge" over a passage below) and stroll over to the glowing circle to trigger a cutscene.

Make use of the powerful Disarm ability in the fight that ensues (see Combat Tips for guidance), then approach the mortally wounded Jacopo to end his suffering. The Memory ends with a pitched brawl against enemies carrying weapon types that you may not have encountered so far. See "Primer: Weapon Classes" on page 59 for advice specific to these new armaments.

11

USER
INSTRUCTIONS

MAP: FLORENCE

PRESENT 01

SEQUENCE 01

SEQUENCE 02

MAP: TUSCANY

SEQUENCE 03

SEQUENCE 04

SEQUENCE 05

MAP: ROMAGNA

SEQUENCE 06

PRESENT 02

MAP: VENICE

SEQUENCE 07

SEQUENCE 08

SEQUENCE 09

SEQUENCE 10

SEQUENCE 11

SEQUENCE 14

PRESENT 03

12

13

ADVANCED COMBAT TIPS

Ezio's armory and repertoire of skills continue to grow, but his enemies are also evolving. Unless you are bullying poorly trained militiamen in a deserted backstreet or country road, the days of pummeling the Weapon Hand Button in combat are over. Use the following advice to adapt your fighting style accordingly.

◆ More adept enemies will now begin to perform counters against Ezio's basic attacks. Learn to react quickly to deflect or dodge these.

◆ If enemies are fighting defensively, attempt to isolate one from the group and unleash a withering combo. Try for measured button presses every time a strike connects – don't just hammer wildly. A good rhythm will be more effective, and also make it easier to immediately stop and block incoming attacks.

◆ With a little practice and careful observation, you'll notice that enemies carrying Long or Heavy weapons rather telegraph the Sweep and Smash moves.

◆ Enemies with their backs to Ezio can be slain instantly (Fig. 12). This is difficult to engineer when he fights alone, but makes Mercenaries worth every last florin if you have the opportunity to hire them for big combat encounters.

◆ Use the Deflect Counter (stop blocking when sparks appear during an enemy attack and immediately tap the Weapon Hand Button) to wear down large groups of skilled adversaries if more aggressive tactics are failing.

◆ The Disarm move makes unarmed fighting a viable tactical option. Indeed, it's probably the safest way to deal with groups of mixed opponents where some carry Long or Heavy weapons. The drawback, of course, is that punches are rather weak. Once opponents carrying Heavy or Long armaments have been forcibly removed from the fray, though, it's safe to go back to a favored weapon.

◆ As with Counter Kills, the Disarm move will only drain a small amount of health if an enemy successfully repels Ezio.

◆ A Disarm attempt during the last blow of an opponent's combo will always be successful against generic enemies.

◆ Weapons acquired through a productive Disarm are uniquely powerful, especially two-handed varieties. Counter Kills will frequently finish enemies instantly, no matter their overall health, with Ezio often leaving the stolen weapon in the body of his victim. These can sometimes be retrieved, but only by quickly disengaging Target Lock. Taking the risks into account, weapons concealed beneath or firmly embedded in corpses are best left where they are.

◆ Brutes and Seekers aside, you can be sure that your Counter Kills and Disarms will be successful on any enemy that looks tired.

SMOKE BOMBS

For those who find extended farewells tiresome, Smoke Bombs can facilitate a near-instantaneous *arrivederci*.

◆ Enemies caught in the immediate radius of a Smoke Bomb will lose sight of Ezio, and will remain frozen in place for at least a few seconds (Fig. 13). This could make Smoke Bombs a handy distraction if other methods are unlikely to work.

◆ With enemies close behind, don't be too quick to throw Smoke Bombs at the first opportunity – instead, bide your time and lead pursuers into an optimal position, such as a narrow alley, gate or door. They could also be employed to mask a transition from street to rooftop, or a quick dive into a hiding spot.

◆ Smoke Bombs can be purchased from Blacksmiths.

SEQUENCE 05: SECONDARY MEMORIES

EQUIPMENT UPGRADES

Those who favor scintillating swordplay can now invest in the Scimitar: a blade as sharp as the intake of breath that most players will involuntarily experience once they notice the 11,300*f* price tag. Alternatively, you could allow Ezio's purse to be bludgeoned by the acquisition of the Flanged Mace for 10,500*f*. The appearance of Metal Vambraces marks the start of a new armor set to collect; the remaining parts become available at the start of Sequence 07.

If you have a penchant for unarmed combat, the Metal Cestus is a genuine bargain at 2,000*f*. This increases the damage inflicted by Ezio's punches. It is a permanent upgrade, and need not be equipped once purchased.

INTRODUCTION: ASSASSINATION CONTRACTS

Assassination Contracts are optional Memories that can be initiated from pigeon coops located on rooftops (Fig. 1). They are marked on both the Mini-Map and the main area map as a crosshair icon. Which coop you visit isn't actually that important: all contracts within a region are played in a strictly linear order, with the completion of one contract unlocking the next in line (though we do mention when using a particular start point will cut down on travelling time). If you fail a contract, you will usually restart at the nearest pigeon coop.

01

A total of 15 Assassination Contracts are unlocked in Sequence 05 (eight in Florence, seven in Tuscany), and you can complete these whenever you wish. However, we strongly advise that you speak to Lorenzo at the start of Sequence 06 before you begin. Once Ezio has accepted his generous gift of the Medici Cape, you can fulfill the terms of each contract without worrying about cumulative Notoriety penalties.

ASSASSINATION CONTRACTS (FLORENCE)

There are three pigeon coops in Florence: one in the southeast of the Santa Maria Novella district, a second in San Giovanni, and a third not far from the city gate in the San Marco district.

DAY AT THE MARKET	
Brief:	Kill a merchant at a marketplace in the San Marco district.
Special Conditions:	The target will run if he recognizes Ezio; contract is failed if he escapes.
Advice:	Travel to the waypoint marker, then stroll around the area with Eagle Vision active to identify your target. A good place to look is by a Tailor and Art Merchant on the east side of the green circle on your Mini-Map. You can either wait until he is facing away from Ezio and walk over for a quiet kill, or just run over and finish it – either ending is fine.

FALLEN ARCHERS	
Brief:	Kill three archers.
Special Conditions:	Targets will attack if they detect Ezio.
Advice:	The three archers are arranged in a line in the south of the San Marco and San Giovanni districts. The target on the right is alone beside the river, and can be dispatched with an Air Assassination; the central target is on a rooftop, which makes him ripe for the Assassinate from Ledge technique from the south face of the building; the target on the left walks back and forth between the river and a cart full of leaves, with the latter being the prime location to strike. There is no penalty for engaging them directly in combat, but the low-key approach we suggest here removes the need to fight additional guard patrols or rooftop archers.

POLITICAL SUICIDE	
Brief:	Kill a target north of San Lorenzo in the Santa Maria Novella district.
Special Conditions:	Desynchronization occurs if the target detects Ezio.
Advice:	The target is located beneath an archway, with two groups of four bodyguards blocking the path on either side. Hire the Courtesans standing just north of San Lorenzo, then escort them close enough to lure away one group of guards. Use Eagle Vision to identify which of the two noblemen is your quarry, but don't make your move yet. Instead, wait for a group of civilians to walk towards the arch, then Blend with them. When you draw level with the target, finish him with a quick Hidden Blade kill. Make your escape instantly – your Blended status will end the moment the body is detected.

CAVEAT EMPTOR	
Brief:	Kill the Salvucci family member found in a marketplace in the Santa Maria Novella district.
Special Conditions:	Desynchronization if the target detects Ezio.
Advice:	Look for a Blacksmith and an Art Merchant in the highlighted area. Identify the target with Eagle Vision (he is conversing with his bodyguard), then watch him approach the Blacksmith as you draw near. Hide among citizens by the Art Merchant to avoid the Harasser in the center, then wait for a crowd to pass between the bodyguard and your target. Blending in again, walk over and stab him with the Poison Blade before retreating to a safe distance.

HOW TO PLAY

WALKTHROUGH

REFERENCE & ANALYSIS

EXTRAS

USER INSTRUCTIONS

MAP: FLORENCE

PRESENT 01

SEQUENCE 01

SEQUENCE 02

MAP: TUSCANY

SEQUENCE 03

SEQUENCE 04

SEQUENCE 05

MAP: ROMAGNA

SEQUENCE 06

PRESENT 02

MAP: VENICE

SEQUENCE 07

SEQUENCE 08

SEQUENCE 09

SEQUENCE 10

SEQUENCE 11

SEQUENCE 14

PRESENT 03

MEETING ADJOURNED

Brief:	Follow a corrupt official to a meeting, then kill all marked targets.
Special Conditions:	The official must not detect Ezio before he reaches the conspirators; all targets must be killed before they can escape.
Advice:	There are Harassers stationed by the corrupt official's location, so be sure to Blend to avoid them as you approach. The journey is uncomplicated, with the standard 25-second period of grace in effect whenever Ezio loses sight of his target. Once you arrive at the destination and the conspirators are revealed, hire the nearby Courtesans and order them to distract the guards. Climb onto the wall and use the Flying Knives special technique to fell numerous targets immediately, then throw a Smoke Bomb at the sole exit to prevent anyone from moving through once you mop up any survivors. If you haven't acquired the Flying Knives ability, use multiple Smoke Bombs and perform Hidden Blade assassinations instead.

NEEDLE IN A HAYSTACK

Brief:	Find and kill a conspirator near Santa Maria Novella.
Special Conditions:	The target must not detect Ezio.
Advice:	The target is located in one of several courtyards that may or may not be guarded; the exact location is chosen randomly for each attempt. A search at street level will be both time-consuming and dangerous, so stock up on Throwing Knives and head to the rooftops. Methodically travel to each courtyard in turn and examine the occupants with Eagle Vision. That's the hard part. Once you have identified the conspirator, finish him with the Air Assassination technique.

PEACEKEEPER

Brief:	Kill 10 Brutes within a time limit.
Special Conditions:	60-second time limit once the first guard is killed.
Advice:	The Brutes are on a bridge in the far south of the San Marco district. Hire a group of Mercenaries on your way there (you can find one just west of the bridge), then start the battle by ordering them to attack. The clock will only start counting down from the moment of the first death. Unless you are already a master at performing Counter Kills with the Double Hidden Blades, don't attempt to fight the Brutes directly. Instead, try to get behind them and perform quick assassinations while they are distracted. Smoke Bombs can be useful here – throw one, and you'll enjoy a brief period where you can slay disoriented Brutes before they recover.

LEADER OF THE PACK

Brief:	Tail a guard to his garrison and assassinate his leader.
Special Conditions:	Avoid detection while tailing the guard.
Advice:	This contract ends with a particularly vicious battle, so ensure that Ezio's health and armor are in top condition before you start. Harassers are the only complication during the first part of the journey, but you should be reasonably adept at dealing with these pests by now. When the target and his companions walk through a guarded entrance, you have a choice. The first is to hire the nearby Courtesans and use their talents to secure passage to the alleyway, then fight your way through the guards until you can engage and execute their commander. The second is to climb to the roof of the building and observe the assembled troops before the time expires, then perform an Air Assassination. Either way, it's definitely a good idea to use a Smoke Bomb to mask your escape once the target is dead.

FREE MISSIONS

SPEAR OF INFIDELITY (BEAT UP)

Location:	Speak to a woman in an alleyway not far north of San Gimignano's south gate.
Advice:	The target is a Seeker, and he's stationed on the southeast section of the city wall. As with all Beat Up missions you must not kill him, so engage the cad with fists alone. This Seeker will flee if you succeed in a Disarm attempt and makes regular use of the Sweep technique, so it's best to knock him over with flurries of fast combos. Step back when he yields, and the Memory will soon end.

SPEEDY DELIVERY (COURIER)

Location:	Outside a Bank on the main street that leads from San Gimignano's south gate to the center of town.
Special Conditions:	You must complete "Wedding Bells Are Ringing" (see page 42) before you can start this Memory. There is a time limit of 2:30 with three separate destinations.
Advice:	Sprint to the south gate and grab a horse; you don't have a hope of reaching all three drop-off points without one. Dismount to speak to each recipient, then quickly get back on the horse and set off for the next destination. A journey with no hitches should leave you with approximately 25 seconds to spare, so rest assured that minor mistakes won't be punished harshly.

ASSASSINATION CONTRACTS (TUSCANY)

There are two pigeon coops in San Gimignano – one near the south entrance, the other in the northeast of the town. As was the case in Florence, there is actually no real difference between these: you still play the Memories in the order related here, with the completion of each contract unlocking the next in line.

REAP WHAT YOU SOW

Brief:	Find a Pazzi benefactor on a farm east of San Gimignano and kill him.
Special Conditions:	Target is located within a Restricted Area, with guards poised to attack if they spot Ezio.
Advice:	There is no reason why you can't burst into the Restricted Area and slay the target (and, for that matter, his guards). However, a more satisfying scenario is to approach the farm from the hill to the west. Run down to the tower and watch the patrol for a moment; when the coast is clear, calmly walk over and hide in the leaf-filled cart. The subsequent assassination will be noticed by his bodyguard, but you can easily outrun anyone who gives chase – especially if you have a horse waiting nearby.

DON'T GET YOUR HANDS DIRTY

Brief:	Kill four conspirators in San Gimignano.
Special Conditions:	Lorenzo suggests that Ezio assassinate the targets without using weapons, but this is not mandatory.
Advice:	Start this contract from the pigeon coop in the south of San Gimignano, then work your way north. If you would like to follow Lorenzo's guidance (and it really is just that – there's no penalty for Hidden Blade kills), consult the following tips.

- ◆ Target #1 can be found in the marketplace where you assassinated Bernado Baroncelli earlier. Throw him into the wooden cage.
- ◆ Target #2 is on top of a tower. Climb up and throw him from the south edge of the roof; in any other direction, there's a slim chance he may survive the fall.
- ◆ Target #3 is on top of a much taller tower. You can throw him in any direction you please.
- ◆ Finally, Target #4 is located on a rooftop. Hurl him over the edge to end the Memory.

SUPPLY IN DEMAND

Brief:	Locate a guild leader by tailing one of his employees, then kill him.
Special Conditions:	The hireling must remain unaware of Ezio's presence.
Advice:	Maintain a safe distance, dealing with or bypassing Harassers quietly, and the journey is unexceptional in every way. When you reach the guild leader, just run straight over to perform the assassination with a bare minimum of ceremony. His unarmed companions will attack Ezio, but how you deal with their misplaced loyalty is very much at your own discretion.

FLEE MARKET

Brief:	Kill a pair of conspirators in a marketplace close to Santa Maria Assunta.
Special Conditions:	Targets are inside a Restricted Area; nearby guards will attack Ezio on sight.
Advice:	Travel to the north side of Santa Maria Assunta, then climb to the upper roof area. You will see a courtyard to the south – this is where your two targets are located. Kill the closest archer (but without allowing his body to slide or fall from the rooftop), then creep over to the Leap of Faith position above a cart full of leaves. Track the movement of your targets until their backs are turned, then jump down into the hiding spot. Both targets will stop by this position. Stealth isn't an option from this point onward, so leap out for a High Profile Assassination, then cut down the second conspirator before he can run far. The final objective is to escape, which shouldn't be too difficult if you head for the south end of the town.

VERTICAL SLICE

Brief:	Kill five Borgia henchmen.
Special Conditions:	Desynchronization will be immediate if Ezio is detected – stealth kills are mandatory.
Advice:	The best way to approach this contract is to move to a position west of the Borgia soldiers, then work your way through them in the sequence outlined below.

- ◆ Target #1 is patrolling near the west edge of the town. Hide behind the wall to the right of a well, then emerge and assassinate him from behind when he walks to the north.
- ◆ Approach the nearby steps and Blend with crowds to make your way to Target #2. There is a pile of hay on his patrol route, but any stealth kill will do just fine as long as he doesn't see Ezio.
- ◆ Target #3 is the man furthest south. Climb onto the nearby rooftop and approach the wall beneath him when he faces away, then jump up and hang from a position just below the fence to avoid detection. When he moves close, use the Assassinate from Ledge technique.
- ◆ Target #4 is the man furthest north. Once again you should approach him carefully, observe his patrol route, then strike either when his back is turned, or by waiting patiently on a ledge until he stands above Ezio.
- ◆ You are now free to tackle Target #5 on top of the tower. Jump to its east face from the adjacent building to begin climbing. Be very cautious when you reach the top: accidentally moving onto the roof when the target is facing Ezio will force you to replay the contract from the start, which will be enormously frustrating. Wait patiently for the guard to move to your position, then use the Assassinate from Ledge technique to safely conclude the Memory.

NO CAMPING

Brief:	Kill the leaders of three groups of soldiers in the countryside surrounding San Gimignano.
Special Conditions:	A time limit of five minutes.
Advice:	Start this mission from the southern pigeon coop – this way, you can quickly sprint to the south gate and pick up a horse. With each group, the leader is your only concern: you simply do not have time to fight all of their soldiers as well. Ride your horse to each waypoint, then identify the commander with Eagle Vision. Run in for a quick Hidden Blade kill (a flurry of Throwing Knives will also work), then get back on your horse and travel to the next target. If you're quick and direct, you should be able to finish this contract with a couple of minutes to spare.

SHOWTIME

Brief:	Assassinate a target taking a stroll through the Antico Teatro Romano ruins southwest of San Gimignano.
Special Conditions:	The ruins are designated as a Restricted Area for the duration of the contract, so guards will be swift to attack Ezio if they spot him; if the target sees Ezio, you must catch him before he escapes.
Advice:	Initiate this contract at the southern pigeon coop to cut down on travel time. The east side of the ruins is heavily guarded, with your target taking a stroll in the "corridor" that runs from north to south around the outer edge of the complex. Head to the north end of this walkway and assassinate the guard at the end, then the guard patrolling above. Stand in an unobtrusive position where you can wait and watch for your quarry to approach with his bodyguards. Once you have identified him, use the Air Assassination technique to complete the contract. Escape before the guards can gather in numbers to attack.

Entrance: In an alleyway behind the Palazzo Comunale in San Gimignano

1: Climb up to the ledge that runs around the inside of the well, then make your way to the gate; throw the lever to open it. Head up the stairs. The wine cellar is patrolled by a small collection of guards, so it's prudent to silence them before you continue. Climb on top of a wooden rack holding eight barrels, then jump over to the platform in the southwest corner of the room (Fig. 2). Leap over to the ledge to the right, then traverse laterally to reach a walkway. At the end of this, jump over to a ledge on your left. Move to the right, around a corner, and climb onto the platform.

02

Hidden Treasure #1 (optional): It may be wise to kill the guard on the balcony as outlined in Step #2 before you begin. Head up the stairs in the southeast corner of the room and climb into an opening there. Use the rings on the wall (Fig. 3) to reach a small room to the north. Open the chest, then pull the lever to open the gate. Jump to the pole and swing to the beam. Rejoin the walkthrough at Step 3.

2: This route is only necessary if you choose to leave Hidden Treasure #1. Run up the stairs, then jump to a beam. Climb up to the balcony and assassinate the guard there. Hop over to the chandelier, then leap to the ropes just to the north. Move left to reach a platform, then leap over to the beam.

03

3: Climb over the barrier and walk forward to trigger a cutscene. Remain concealed and watch the movements of the three guards if you intend to perform stealth kills, or just burst into the library and fight them if you are not averse to the idea of a quick brawl. When you are ready, climb on top of a bookcase in the southeast corner of the room (Fig. 4). Free run to the wooden beams to the west, then jump over to a wall ring. Climb up to the balcony and assassinate the guards. Use the chandeliers as a route to the north wall, then jump over to a window and climb to the platform above. Now free run (via the poles and ropes) to the next balcony and kill the guard.

Hidden Treasure #2 (optional): Climb the door (and rings above it) on the east side of the balcony, then spring backwards to reach the rafters. Follow the obvious route to the stone platform and open the chest. Turn around and run over the rafters to the south to return to the balcony.

04

4: Walk through the open door on the west side of the balcony to reach the tower area. Run up the ramp, then use the hanging beams to continue your ascent. When you get to the second beam on the south wall, turn around and hop over to the balcony; this short-cut will enable you to assassinate the guard without first alerting him (Fig. 5). Climb the ladder, then free run around the outer walls of the tower until you reach a collection of wall rings. Jump over to these. When the camera view changes, watch the movements of the guard to judge the best moment to climb up and strike.

05

5: Climb up and grab the lintel above the window, then use the wall ring to reach a wooden beam. Jump over to the wall rings, then climb into the rafters. Hop over the beams to a group of three rings in the northwest corner (Fig. 6). Climb to the wooden ledges, then traverse to the right to get to a higher beam. The wall rings to your right enable access to the final room. Collect the Seal of Wei Yu from the sarcophagus, then exit via the ceiling hatch.

06

HOW TO PLAY

WALKTHROUGH

REFERENCE & ANALYSIS

EXTRAS

USER INSTRUCTIONS

MAP: FLORENCE

PRESENT 01

SEQUENCE 01

SEQUENCE 02

MAP: TUSCANY

SEQUENCE 03

SEQUENCE 04

SEQUENCE 05

MAP: ROMAGNA

SEQUENCE 06

PRESENT 02

MAP: VENICE

SEQUENCE 07

SEQUENCE 08

SEQUENCE 09

SEQUENCE 10

SEQUENCE 11

SEQUENCE 14

PRESENT 03

Apennine Mountains & Florence

Forlì

Rocca di Ravaldino

Abbazia di san Mercuriale

USER
INSTRUCTIONS

MAP: FLORENCE

PRESENT 01

SEQUENCE 01

SEQUENCE 02

MAP: TUSCANY

SEQUENCE 03

SEQUENCE 04

SEQUENCE 05

MAP: ROMAGNA

SEQUENCE 06

PRESENT 02

MAP: VENICE

SEQUENCE 07

SEQUENCE 08

SEQUENCE 09

SEQUENCE 10

SEQUENCE 11

SEQUENCE 14

PRESENT 03

Palazzo Comunale

Avamposto Veneziano

Venice

Please note that collectible items do not appear on this map to avoid potential spoilers. You can find them on dedicated maps in the Secrets section of the Extras chapter.

SEQUENCE 06

MEMORY 01

ROAD TRIP: Medici's gratitude (and, perhaps more importantly, his rewards) mark a fitting end to Ezio's time in Florence. Once you have spoken to him, this is a good time to begin completing Secondary Memories that remain, particularly the (relatively) new Assassination variety. Though you can return to Florence and its surrounding towns later, spending a little time in pursuit of florins (and upgrading Monterigionni) will be of great benefit in the long term.

When you are ready, head to Leonardo's workshop to receive further instructions.

MEMORY 02

ROMAGNA HOLIDAY: Follow the Memory Start marker to reach the Apennine Mountains zone, where Ezio is reunited with Leonardo and a brief yet unusual gameplay sequence begins. The horse-drawn carriage is sturdier than most, but collisions will inflict gradual damage reflected by a gauge in the top left-hand corner of the screen. Use the Movement Stick to steer, but don't bank too sharply – should the carriage overturn, you'll be returned to an earlier checkpoint.

Naturally, there's more to this set-piece event than negotiating obstacles. Assailants will jump from horses to grab either side of the carriage, progressing from there to the roof, before finally attacking Ezio. Those on the sides can be dislodged by brushing against roadside scenery, though this is a fairly high-risk strategy. To deal with enemies who reach the roof, sharp banking mixed with quick left-right motions can cause them to lose their balance and fall (Fig. 1). Driving beneath low branches has a more immediately satisfying result. Should an attacker reach Ezio, tap the Empty Hand Button rapidly to thwart his assault.

In the second stage of the escape, Ezio's opponents use Greek fire to set sections of road ablaze. If you can evade the flames while attending to combatants on the carriage, you should reach the third and final part of this mission, where Ezio jumps out to challenge his pursuers directly. Make the Brute your priority, and his death should weaken the resolve of his surviving allies.

01

MEMORY 03

TUTTI A BORDO: Feel free to take in the sights and sounds of rustic Forlì and its surrounding wetlands before you head to the dock to meet Leonardo. There is a brief (and, of course, appropriate) gondola tutorial to complete before Ezio sets sail for Venice (Fig. 2), but the onscreen prompts will furnish you with all the guidance you need.

02

HOW TO PLAY

WALKTHROUGH

REFERENCE & ANALYSIS

EXTRAS

USER INSTRUCTIONS

MAP: FLORENCE

PRESENT 01

SEQUENCE 01

SEQUENCE 02

MAP: TUSCANY

SEQUENCE 03

SEQUENCE 04

SEQUENCE 05

MAP: ROMAGNA

SEQUENCE 06

PRESENT 02

MAP: VENICE

SEQUENCE 07

SEQUENCE 08

SEQUENCE 09

SEQUENCE 10

SEQUENCE 11

SEQUENCE 14

PRESENT 03

MEDICI CAPE

Lorenzo gives Ezio the princely gift of a Medici Cape at the start of Sequence 06. Wearing this special apparel marks him as a friend of the ruling regime in Florence and Tuscany, and has the rather profound effect of freezing the Notoriety gauge at zero. Though patrolling Medici guards will still draw swords and attack in reaction to illegal acts such as murder, assault and trespass, all lesser transgressions will inspire nothing more severe than a rebuke – and there are no cumulative consequences for any action. This makes the process of finding collectibles and completing Secondary Memories in the affected areas far less time-consuming.

TRICKS & TRIVIA

◆ The Apennine Mountains map does not contain any Feathers, Glyphs or Codex Pages, though you can find several Treasure Chests and ride through on a horse to admire the scenery if you're so inclined.

◆ Fast Travel Stations enable you to move swiftly to destinations you have previously visited. The fees are nominal, and the length of the journey is limited solely to load time. This makes it a convenient way to frequently go to Monteriggioni in order to upgrade buildings or pick up funds for purchases.

◆ Covered gondolas in the Romagna region (and, later, Venice) can be looted to obtain florins. The sums are smaller than those found in Treasure Chests, but not so trivial that you can casually walk on by at this stage of the game.

◆ If you perform a Hidden Blade or Poison Blade assassination while Blended in a group, try to leave the scene quickly, or move to another, more distant collection of civilians if continued stealth is necessary. Dead bodies (or other sources of similar alarm) cause nearby collections of pedestrians to temporarily disperse, thus removing the Blend effect.

03

ENEMY ARCHETYPE: SEEKERS

Seekers (Fig. 3) are the third and final of the three unique enemy archetypes to make an appearance. They can be identified by the spears that they carry – their weapon of choice and, as you'll soon discover, a tool of their trade that isn't only used for combat.

◆ Seekers are vigilant and inquisitive. While other guards will often stroll past a hiding spot, oblivious to Ezio's presence, these experienced investigators will regularly examine places where he might conceivably seek refuge.

◆ They will stop to look at every hiding spot with the exception of benches if Ezio is currently Incognito. If he is discovered, the Seeker will roust him from his place of concealment and scold him. If they find him when he is Notorious or still technically in active combat (blue ring surrounding the Mini-Map), a fight will ensue.

◆ In combat, Seekers maintain a greater distance from Ezio to take advantage of the long reach offered by their weapons. They have a propensity for launching attacks whenever Ezio attempts a special technique such as a Smash with a stolen two-handed axe. They are rather susceptible to the Disarm move.

◆ Seekers use Sweep attacks, which will knock Ezio from his feet for sizable damage if they connect.

◆ A good strategy when you fight a Brute and Seeker at the same time is to Disarm the latter and use his weapon for a guaranteed Counter Kill on the former.

SEQUENCE 06: SECONDARY MEMORIES

 ASSASSINATION CONTRACTS

There are two pigeon coops in Romagna – one in the center of Forlì, and another in the countryside to the north. As in Florence and Tuscany, each contract beyond the first is unlocked once the previous commission has been completed.

THIN THE RANKS	
Brief:	Assassinate six guards inside Forlì.
Advice:	This first contract in Romagna is easy – the only real work is travelling to each waypoint. The targets are all found in pairs: two in the north of Forlì, two in the south, with the last two found patrolling the west town wall. Simply reaching the final damned duo is something of a puzzle at first, but you can easily jump across to the wall via a building next to the first wall tower north of the Rocca di Ravaldino.

BEGINNINGS OF A CONSPIRACY	
Brief:	Kill three targets.
Special Conditions:	Ezio must avoid detection by the targets or their allies – stealth kills are a must here.
Advice:	All three victims are located inside the walls of Forlì, so use the pigeon coop in the center of town when you accept the contract.

- The closest target is an Elite patrolling with three subordinates beneath your starting position. If he is walking at the rear of the formation, simply fall into stride behind him and stab him with the Poison Blade while no one is looking. If he is to the side or front of the formation, you may need to arrange a distraction. Hire the nearby Mercenaries and order them to attack, then discretely poison the target once the battle begins.
- The target in the north of the town is a civilian, and the only one of the three targets to become suspicious on sight of Ezio. He and his bodyguard will start moving as you approach. Hire the Courtesans on the street and order them to distract the guard, then sneak behind the target to administer Poison.
- The final target is solitary, so you are free to perform a Hidden Blade kill when he faces the water.

ARCH ENEMIES	
Brief:	Eliminate the 10 Borgia archers.
Special Conditions:	Kill all targets within the allotted time limit.
Advice:	Throwing Knives are a must for this contract; you should also start it from the pigeon coop in the center of town. Take a quick look at the area map once the Memory is underway, and you'll see that the archers form a line that snakes towards the south gate. In essence, this is a race where the ten Borgia archers act as checkpoints. Focus on the allotted targets, ignoring any local guards who give chase, and this challenge will pose no problems.

WET WORK	
Brief:	Swim or row to a ship anchored just off the coast, then make your way on board and kill the captain.
Advice:	You can reduce travel time by starting this Memory at the pigeon coop north of Forlì. Grab a gondola from the dock northwest of the ship, then row to the east of the waypoint marker, taking care to stay clear of the other boats and red Restricted Area. Now jump out and, after checking that there are no guards looking out in your direction, swim to the rear section of the vessel. Move to the right-hand side to begin climbing, then traverse back to the aft section. From the ledge, dispatch the two guards that pass your current position with the Assassinate from Ledge technique. Once they have been eliminated, you are free to climb up when the captain stands by the wheel. Assassinate him, then jump off the boat before anyone notices.

HOW TO PLAY

WALKTHROUGH

REFERENCE &
ANALYSIS

EXTRAS

USER
INSTRUCTIONS

MAP: FLORENCE

PRESENT 01

SEQUENCE 01

SEQUENCE 02

MAP: TUSCANY

SEQUENCE 03

SEQUENCE 04

SEQUENCE 05

MAP: ROMAGNA

SEQUENCE 06

PRESENT 02

MAP: VENICE

SEQUENCE 07

SEQUENCE 08

SEQUENCE 09

SEQUENCE 10

SEQUENCE 11

SEQUENCE 14

PRESENT 03

01

02

DEAD ON ARRIVAL	
Brief:	Kill the agent.
Special Conditions:	Ezio must not lose the target.
Advice:	The Agile can be found on a rooftop in the northwest of Forlì. Once he espies Ezio, he will do what he does best: run. This initiates a chase that features ambushes designed to stall Ezio's pursuit. However, if you approach his building from street level, then climb up on the west face, it is possible to jump up and assassinate him before he can take more than a single stride (Fig. 1).

GO TOWARDS THE LIGHT	
Brief:	Kill the commander guarding the lighthouse.
Advice:	The target is on top of the lighthouse in the far northeast of Romagna, with the structure (and immediate surroundings) designated as a Restricted Area for the duration of the mission. Make your way to the water in the very northeast of the map, then cautiously swim south to reach the jetty by the arch. Climb up the wall, then wait and watch from the ledge. If you time it carefully, it's possible to kill the Brute then the archer before either can react. Climb to the next level of the lighthouse and dispatch the archers there; finally, make your way to the top and slay the target in whichever manner you deem appropriate.

MARK AND EXECUTE	
Brief:	Locate a woman marked for execution, then kill the target who is with her.
Special Conditions:	Ezio must not be detected.
Advice:	The woman is held captive in a courtyard behind a large building in the northeast of the map. All entrances at ground level are heavily guarded, so hire the Mercenaries to the east and order them to attack the guards stationed at the south entrance. Now carefully walk through the melee and identify the target. Wait until he faces away (Fig. 2), then stroll behind the target and guard to perform a Double Assassination. If this mission proves too problematic (the target is easily alerted), you can return to it later once Ezio acquires a new weapon during Sequence 09.

EQUIPMENT UPGRADES & CODEX PAGES

Equipment: The Medium Knife Belt is a must for your trip to Venice – there are rooftop archers *everywhere* in the City of Bridges. If you are still running around in outmoded Leather attire, this would be an optimum time to upgrade to the newly available set of Metal armor if your budget allows for it, or the more affordable Helmschmied ensemble if not.

Codex Pages: There are three Philosophical Codex pages in Forlì. If you already possess the seven from Florence and Tuscany, collecting these will enable you to obtain another square on Ezio's Health Meter once Leonardo is settled in Venice.

FREE MISSIONS

WANTON HUBBY (BEAT UP)	
Location:	A short walk from Forlì's north gate.
Advice:	The husband is outside a house east of a bridge within the highlighted area. Unlike other Beat Up targets so far, he has friends who will attack Ezio once the fight begins. Disable these first, then punch the cheat until he submits.

PROMISCUITY KNOCKS (BEAT UP)	
Location:	In the northeast of Forlì, not far from the gate.
Special Conditions:	Wanton Hubby must be completed first.
Advice:	Your target is near the Rocca di Ravaldino in the southwest corner of Forlì, but this is a public area with several guards in the immediate vicinity. As the act of assaulting a citizen will draw their attention (and, subsequently, their swords), you'll need to create a distraction. Hire a group of Mercenaries and order them to attack the main patrol; this should pull all unwanted potential aggressors into a fight. Now approach the husband and administer the necessary beating. Be careful not to knock him into the water – this counts as killing him, and will force you to replay the Memory from the start.

THE MESSENGER'S BURDEN (COURIER)	
Location:	Near a Bank west of Abbazia di San Mercuriale in the center of Forlì.
Special Conditions:	Deliver the message within the allotted time limit.
Advice:	Run east from the starting position, then take the second street to the left. Climb the wall to the right of a group of Courtesans to reach a rooftop, where you will find a rope "bridge" providing easy access to Forlì's east wall (Fig. 3). Jump from the Leap of Faith position directly ahead, and the recipient is just a short sprint to the south. How you deal with the final twist is entirely up to you – there are no penalties or additional rewards either way.

03

ROMAGNA HUSTLE (RACE)	
Location:	Behind a house directly north of Forlì.
Special Conditions:	Finish the course before the clock reaches zero.
Advice:	Use the following tips and tricks, and you'll find this to be one of the easier Races.
	◆ As ever, ignore guards and archers – even if they attempt to attack Ezio, you'll soon lose them.
	◆ There are a few instances here where you can save a lot of time by simply leaping from a rooftop for a necessary return to ground level. Heal while running, and this trick will enable you to cut many seconds from your time.
	◆ When you leap over the wall on the west side of Forlì, mount the nearby horse to make your way back to the start. Jump off and finish the final two gates on foot.

HORSEPLAY (RACE)	
Location:	Not far from the Fast Travel Station south of Forlì.
Special Conditions:	You must have completed Romagna Hustle to start the Memory; complete the course within the allotted time limit.
Advice:	The trick to negotiating the course quickly is to regulate your pace by releasing the Legs Button whenever you need to move the horse between obstacles or over bridges. Though it's a trifle callous, there's also no reason to slow down for pedestrians. That's really all there is to it.

ASSASSIN TOMB: RAVALDINO'S SECRET

Entrance: On the outer wall of the Rocca di Ravaldino in Forlì.

1: Dive into the water and swim to the platform to the north. Hop over to the upper area, then climb the wall to reach a ledge. Spring back onto the stone platform. Now make your way to the lever to the south via the wooden beams. Activate it to raise the portcullis, then quickly jump down and sprint through before it drops.

Hidden Treasure #1 (optional): After running beneath the portcullis, turn left and wall run up to the wooden ledge (Fig. 4). Spring back to grab the beam, then climb up and free run to the nearby Treasure Chest.

2: Drop down until you reach the water, then dive under the metal gate. Climb onto the brickwork, then turn left and free run to the bottom of the well. Wall run up to the first ledge, then spring back to reach another; repeat the process until you trigger a cutscene at the top. Assassinate the guard, then dispatch all of his companions. Make your way to the southwest corner of the area and climb on top of a scaffold (Fig. 5), then jump to the east and enter the room — watch out for another guard here if he didn't enter the fray earlier. Wall run up to the top of a decorative shield, then spring back to reach a ledge.

Hidden Treasure #2 (optional): Pull the lever, then free run to the north. At the end of this first "corridor", turn left and jump onto the low wall. Wall run up to a ledge underneath the pole, then spring back to reach another ledge on the column. Traverse around it until Ezio takes hold of the pole, then swing to the ledge to the west (Fig. 6). Move left and jump to a beam, then climb on top of it. Jump to the shield on the wall, then leap sideways to the pole and swing to the Treasure Chest. Pull the lever to open a shortcut back to the start of Step 3.

3: Pull the lever to lower the gate, then free run through before it raises. On the other side, operate a second lever to lower another gate, then free run to the south wall. Turn left and jump over to the beams, then move to the top of the wall. Grab the small (and easily missed) ledge just above (Fig. 7), then traverse to the left and drop onto a beam. Run down the stairs and climb through the opening at the bottom.

4: Deal with all guards in the vicinity, then head to the northeast corner of the lower area. Climb to the top of the fence (Fig. 8), then free run in a clockwise route to get to a balcony. Use the shields to reach and climb through a hole in the wall. The final trial is to activate the lever, then follow a reasonably complicated path to run through a gate before it slams shut. You may find it helpful to practice at least once before you begin. Once you are ready, pull the lever and jump to the right-hand wall section at the start of the tunnel. Jump to the left, onto the broken arch, then run north and jump to a beam. Wall run to the ledge on your left, then spring back to reach a platform. Jump to the beam then, last but not least, swing on the pole and hit the ground running to pass through the gate before it closes. Collect the Seal of Qulan Gal from the sarcophagus, then exit via the trapdoor.

04

05

06

07

08

HOW TO PLAY

WALKTHROUGH

REFERENCE & ANALYSIS

EXTRAS

USER INSTRUCTIONS

MAP: FLORENCE

PRESENT 01

SEQUENCE 01

SEQUENCE 02

MAP: TUSCANY

SEQUENCE 03

SEQUENCE 04

SEQUENCE 05

MAP: ROMAGNA

SEQUENCE 06

PRESENT 02

MAP: VENICE

SEQUENCE 07

SEQUENCE 08

SEQUENCE 09

SEQUENCE 10

SEQUENCE 11

SEQUENCE 14

PRESENT 03

Madonna dell' Orto

Cannaregio District

San Giobbe

Leonardo's Workshop

Romagna (Forlì)

Gilda dei Ladri di Venezia

San Polo District

Santa Maria Gloriosa del Frari

San Giacomo di Rialto

Romagna (Forlì)

Santa Maria dei Camini

Dorsoduro District

Santo Stefano

Squero di San Trovaso

Romagna (Forlì)

Santa Maria della Visitazione

San Marco District

Scuola Grande di San Marco

Santi Giovanni e Paolo

Arsenale di Venezia

Ponte di Rialto

Torre dell' Orologio

Castello District

Campanile di San Marco

Palazzo Ducale di Venezia

Basilica di San Marco

San Zaccaria

Romagna (Forli)

San Pietro di Castello

USER
INSTRUCTIONS

MAP: FLORENCE

PRESENT 01

SEQUENCE 01

SEQUENCE 02

MAP: TUSCANY

SEQUENCE 03

SEQUENCE 04

SEQUENCE 05

MAP: ROMAGNA

SEQUENCE 06

PRESENT 02

MAP: VENICE

SEQUENCE 07

SEQUENCE 08

SEQUENCE 09

SEQUENCE 10

SEQUENCE 11

SEQUENCE 14

PRESENT 03

Please note that collectible items do not appear on this map to avoid potential spoilers. You can find them on dedicated maps in the Secrets section of the Extras chapter.

PRESENT   02

▌WAREHOUSE ▌

Desmond's athleticism is now equivalent to that of Ezio, so meet Lucy in the warehouse to put his newfound prowess to the test. The task she sets is to operate a series of small sensors. These are all located in the area that Lucy unlocks: two on the lower level, with the final pair on the walkways above (Fig. 1).

▌ACRE ▌

Chase the individual who initially stands underneath the raised portcullis, but runs as you approach. If you lose your way, your destination is the largest tower inside the walled area (Fig. 2). Climb to the top to reach a cutscene. Though the urge to explore may be great, moving outside the white "boundaries" or a fatal fall will force you to resume from the beginning – there are no checkpoints.

SEQUENCE   07

▌MEMORIES 01 & 02 ▌

BENVENUTO: This is but a stroll through the streets of Venice, taking in evocative sights and sounds as you follow your two companions. Feel free to explore and unlock a few viewpoints before you start.

THAT'S GONNA LEAVE A MARK: Heal, repair armor and replenish your stocks of finite items before you begin – a full set of Throwing Knives, in particular, will make a massive difference. After the opening cutscene ends, your job is to escort the wounded Rosa as she attempts to escape. This does not begin auspiciously, as you are thrown directly into a fight with nearby guards. Rosa's Health Meter is displayed in the upper left-hand corner of the screen. Attract your opponents by attacking them, even if the risk exposes Ezio to damage. While he will have opportunities to heal during this action-heavy Memory, his newfound ward will not.

Rosa has a surprisingly high level of mobility at first, so endeavor to keep up with her once the first set of guards have been dispatched. You will encounter numerous small skirmishes with Borgia forces as you progress through the streets, so a secondary benefit of staying close is that it may enable you to perform quick Hidden Blade kills on stronger enemies. After a number of encounters, Rosa will collapse. For the next section of the Memory, your job is to carry her. There are further attacks, but this time certain individuals will come to your aid. It's best to drop Rosa and help out, then continue towards the waypoint.

For the final stage, Rosa is on board a gondola. Run alongside the boat as it moves along the canal, slaying all archers on its path (Fig. 3). Throwing Knives facilitate the perfunctory brand of kill required, though some are in a suitable position for Hidden Blade finishes. It's a good idea to move ahead and work in advance (the route isn't complicated), though don't stray too far. Don't put your controller aside when you reach your destination – the scenes that follow require your interaction, which can lead to different outcomes.

01

02

03

USER
INSTRUCTIONS

MAP: FLORENCE

PRESENT 01

SEQUENCE 01

SEQUENCE 02

MAP: TUSCANY

SEQUENCE 03

SEQUENCE 04

SEQUENCE 05

MAP: ROMAGNA

SEQUENCE 06

PRESENT 02

MAP: VENICE

SEQUENCE 07

SEQUENCE 08

SEQUENCE 09

SEQUENCE 10

SEQUENCE 11

SEQUENCE 14

PRESENT 03

04

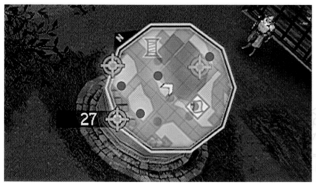

05

06

WELCOME TO VENICE

◆ As with Florence before it, only a portion of Venice can be visited at first, with new areas unlocked as you complete future Sequences. Attempting to travel through the distinct boundaries will, as ever, result in Desynchronization.

◆ As befits a larger city (and a thriving hub of European commerce), Venice features an increased militia presence. The local patrols are trained to a higher standard, carry better and more varied weapons, and frequently count at least one Agile among their number (Fig. 4). This means that you'll often need to be a little more creative when making an escape, though a well-placed Smoke Bomb will always give you a head start. Brutes and Seekers are also more common here.

◆ Rooftop sentries are present in greater numbers. This means that you must regularly consult your Mini-Map and plan your routes carefully when you leave street level (Fig. 5). If you have no moral objection to leaving a trail of bloodstained tiles in your wake, a regularly restocked supply of Throwing Knives will always be of benefit. The archers of Venice are made of sterner stuff than their peers in Florence or Tuscany, though, and will only fall after two knife hits. If ammunition is low, an alternative is simply to hurl them into the canals far below.

◆ Though travel on rooftops is more complicated than you might hope, use of gondolas (or, at a push, swimming) turns certain canals into handy expressways.

◆ Before you set off to explore and reach viewpoints, note that the Santa Maria Gloriosa dei Frari tower in San Polo cannot be scaled before Ezio acquires a new ability. A later Memory actually involves climbing this building, so there's no real need to worry about it for now.

◆ Look out for locations marked in red on your Mini-Map (Fig. 6): these are "Restricted Areas". Entering one of these will cause any guard that espies Ezio to attack without prior warning or rebuke.

MEMORIES 03 & 04

BUILDING BLOCKS: Enter the Thieves Hideout (Gilda dei Ladri di Venezia) office to meet Antonio for a brief cutscene. Once it ends, there are three Memories (04, 05 and 07) that you can approach in any order you please, with two of these unlocking a new Memory (06 and 08) on completion. As with our Sequence 05 walkthrough, we follow the order of progression that appears in the DNA menu.

BREAKOUT: Meet Ugo on a rooftop to the east of Santa Maria Gloriosa dei Frari to begin this Memory. There are three locations where you will find cages containing groups of four Thieves (Fig. 7). These are guarded at street level by several soldiers who will attack Ezio if he enters the designated Restricted Areas, marked in red on your Mini-Map. Once you free a group of captives, you must escort them back to Ugo, who awaits your return at the Memory Start location. It's only mandatory that one Thief survives (the number required is marked onscreen), but it's still prudent to keep them out of trouble and not to outdistance them.

07

MEMORY 05

CLOTHES MAKE THE MAN: Meet Ugo on the dock east of the Thieves Hideout to begin this Memory. The first objective is to secure the services of Thieves and use them to lure away the guards surrounding three Treasure Chests (Fig. 8). The two containers closest to the starting position are a cakewalk: just stroll over once the guards give chase and retrieve the contents. The final chest, located close to a bridge, requires a little more in the way of planning. In addition to the guards stationed around it, there is also a street patrol and a Harasser. Time your approach carefully to send the Thieves in at the right moment.

The second objective is to steal a gondola from a Restricted Area. Approach it from the rooftops, picking up another group of Thieves on the way and, once again, order them to create a diversion. The journey back to the final waypoint marker should be short and uneventful.

08

MEMORY 06

CLEANING HOUSE: Speak to Antonio inside the Thieves Hideout. The approximate locations of the three traitors are marked by green circles on the Mini-Map. Once inside this zone, carefully avoid the attentions of any nearby guards and use Eagle Vision to identify each culprit (Fig. 9).

One is found on a ship surrounded by other vessels, with a perimeter of keen-eyed archers making a direct approach difficult. A second stands alone on a rooftop. The third can be found strolling near a marketplace, with several opportunities for an Air Assassination. All three targets will attack and raise the alarm if they spot Ezio. See the page to your right for advice on a stealth-oriented approach.

09

CLEANING HOUSE: STEALTH STRATEGY

North Target (Coast Area)

The target is on a ship surrounded by other vessels, each one guarded by archers. Start from the dock at the southwest edge of the circle then make your way to the nearest boat, swimming underwater for the last part of the approach to remain undetected. Kill the two guards on board then move to the closer of the two large ships, again employing the Submerge ability to stay out of sight. Climb to the top of the near side of the aft section and, hidden from view, use Eagle Vision to pick out the target. Quietly dispose of the nearby guard with the Assassinate from Ledge technique, then do the same with the traitor when he saunters by. Drop back into the water and return to dry land.

South Target (Rooftop)

This traitor is unguarded, and can be found on a rooftop. He will attack if he sees Ezio, though falls easily to a single Throwing Knife from behind.

East Target (Marketplace)

The final traitor can be found wandering around the market east of the Palazzo Della Seta, and he's accompanied by a bodyguard. Don't approach his hangout at street level – the Harasser in this area will surely blow Ezio's cover. Instead, make your way to a dock on the east edge of the marketplace via the rooftops or canals. Identify your victim, then hide in the cart full of hay and wait for him to approach. Once he turns his back to Ezio, climb out and strike (Fig. 11); we recommend the Poison Blade for a subtle finish.

USER
INSTRUCTIONS

MAP: FLORENCE

PRESENT 01

SEQUENCE 01

SEQUENCE 02

MAP: TUSCANY

SEQUENCE 03

SEQUENCE 04

SEQUENCE 05

MAP: ROMAGNA

SEQUENCE 06

PRESENT 02

MAP: VENICE

SEQUENCE 07

SEQUENCE 08

SEQUENCE 09

SEQUENCE 10

SEQUENCE 11

SEQUENCE 14

PRESENT 03

11

HIRING THIEVES

The final "group hire", Thieves are a great compromise as they can fight like Mercenaries and distract like Courtesans, though they're slightly less efficient at both.

◆ Acquire a Target Lock on a guard with a group of Thieves in tow and press the Head Button to use their special ability: Lure. They will go over to infuriate the specified individuals, before running off; any guards in the immediate vicinity will then give chase.

◆ The Lure command is a one-shot ability: you lose the group once you use it. You should also note that guards will eventually return to their original posts, so go about your business quickly.

◆ Unlike Courtesans and Mercenaries, Thieves can climb and perform free running moves. That said, they don't possess Ezio's incredible level of agility and are noticeably slower. If you take a complicated route at great speed, they will soon fall behind (or, in at least a few unfortunate instances, to their deaths on the streets below).

◆ Thieves will leap to Ezio's aid if he is attacked (or enters combat voluntarily), though their effectiveness is lower than Mercenaries.

◆ Once they are hired, you cannot Blend with groups of Thieves.

BREAKOUT: USEFUL TIPS

◆ Returning each group of prisoners via the rooftops is definitely the best strategy (they're all accomplished at climbing and free running), so take the time to eliminate all archers on your way to each cage. Try to pick a relatively straightforward route to avoid unintentional casualties, and don't move too far ahead.

10

◆ It is possible to use distraction techniques to draw the soldiers at each street-level entrance away (Fig. 10), but remaining undetected requires lots of patient reconnoitering of the area and extremely delicate timing once you put any plan into action. Even if you're favoring stealth over combat whenever possible, it's probably sensible to resign yourself to bloodshed in this Memory.

◆ Make your way to the rooftop directly above each cage, then observe the scene below. In two instances you should wait for certain soldiers to leave the area before you make your way down – listen out for dialogue.

◆ There is a single guard outside each cage, with others stationed by nearby entrances – but not all of these will attack if you're quick and quiet. Start with a deadly Hidden Blade kill, then dispatch any adversaries who attack. You can only open a cage while Ezio is in the Anonymous state.

12

MEMORY 07 & 08

MONKEY SEE, MONKEY DO: Speak to Rosa outside the Thieves Hideout to play a short Climb Leap tutorial.

BY LEAPS AND BOUNDS: Having acquired a valuable new technique you can finally scale the tower at Santa Maria Gloriosa dei Frari, so meet Rosa there to begin this Memory. There is a time limit to reach the viewpoint, but it's actually rather generous. The most obvious route is to scale the east face, by the starting position, but you may find it easier and faster to run to the southwest corner of the building and climb from there (Fig. 12). Synchronize before you dive back down, then speak to Rosa to stop the clock.

13

MEMORY 09

EVERYTHING MUST GO: After killing the five archers on the surrounding rooftops (an uncomplicated task that requires no real strategy barring the obvious suggestion that Throwing Knives will help), return to Antonio. Hire a group of Thieves stationed nearby, then make the short journey to the Palazzo Della Seta's western entrance. You'll find it guarded by four soldiers. Instruct your helpers to lure them away, or Double Air Assassinate the Brutes. Run over to the northwest corner (beside the canal) to begin scaling the wall, employing Climb Leap as required until you reach a balcony.

Once the cinematic interlude ends, the challenge is to assassinate Emilio before he departs on a boat stationed at the north face of the Palazzo. While he waits for his minions to load select possessions on board, he will stroll around the inner walls, loudly bemoaning his lot in what little of his life remains. You can climb down and fight your way to your target if you like, but the north face of the building presents an opportunity for a more creative finish. Climb in through the open window on the right, then look over the safety barrier to the left. See the beam below? Drop onto it, and you can wait silently for Barbarigo to move into position for departure, then end the Memory with a stylish Air Assassination (Fig. 13).

USER INSTRUCTIONS

MAP: FLORENCE

PRESENT 01

SEQUENCE 01

SEQUENCE 02

MAP: TUSCANY

SEQUENCE 03

SEQUENCE 04

SEQUENCE 05

MAP: ROMAGNA

SEQUENCE 06

PRESENT 02

MAP: VENICE

SEQUENCE 07

SEQUENCE 08

SEQUENCE 09

SEQUENCE 10

SEQUENCE 11

SEQUENCE 14

PRESENT 03

15

16

17

USING CLIMB LEAP

The Climb Leap ability is the final addition to Ezio's athletic repertoire.

◆ With Ezio in position on a suitable ledge, hold the Movement Stick up and press the High Profile Button and the Legs Button to Climb Leap, then press the Empty Hand Button to grab any hand-hold in range before he falls back down (Fig. 14).

◆ If your timing of the Grasp move is inaccurate, or the hand-hold is out of range, Ezio will always automatically grab onto the ledge where he started.

◆ Certain buildings or towers encountered from this point forward can only be scaled by employing Climb Leap in specific positions, but it's an ability that will prove useful in other instances. If you are adept at picking routes while climbing walls, you will notice that this new skill can occasionally be used to take short-cuts.

◆ If Ezio is targeted by an archer, Climb Leap can be employed to quickly evade incoming arrows.

14

GUARD RANKS

In addition to the three special enemy archetypes (Agile, Brute and Seeker), all members of the "generic" soldiery you encounter hold one of three ranks: Militia, Elite or Leader. The seniority of these individuals has an effect on their combat prowess and hidden morale level. Militia are easy prey to well-timed Counter Kill or Disarm moves, and will soon bolt when Ezio cuts down their cohorts. Leaders are more inclined to fight to the death, will often repel instant kills until sufficiently wounded, and may employ counter-attacks against Ezio's combos. Elites lie somewhere between both in terms of their combat proficiency and resolve. Note that Militia respond to thrown money by racing over to pick up coins themselves. This means that any patrol with such members in its formation will stop to wait for them to finish picking up coins and rejoin.

To easily identify a guard's rank, look at his helmet. No matter the uniform, Militia wear caps (Fig. 15), Elites favor open-faced helmets (Fig. 16), while Leaders have headgear with additional facial protection (Fig. 17).

SEQUENCE 07: SECONDARY MEMORIES

ASSASSINATION CONTRACTS

The San Polo pigeon coop is located on a rooftop close to the ship to Romagna (where Ezio disembarks on his arrival in Venice), southwest of the Ponte di Rialto.

THICKER THAN WATER	
Brief:	Follow a gondola to reach the target.
Special Conditions:	Immediate Desyncronization if you are detected by a guard.
Advice:	Grab a gondola en route to the waypoint marker, then follow another gondola through the Venetian canals. When it eventually emerges into the open sea, it will head over to a boat. Your target is on board. For a quiet kill, steer the gondola to the far side of the vessel – avoiding the Restricted Area – then jump out and swim underwater to reach a position just behind the marked man. Wait until his guards are facing away, then strike from the water.

ZERO TOLERANCE	
Brief:	Eliminate a target who is chasing a woman.
Special Conditions:	The woman must not identify Ezio or witness the deed.
Advice:	When you reach the marked area, head to the herald standing beside the Blacksmith inside the green circle. Face south, activate Eagle Vision, and wait. You'll see the woman first, with your target in hot pursuit. Watch the Mini-Map for a minute to familiarize yourself with the route they take. When they enter an alleyway to the left of your position (heading east), quickly run south, past the Blacksmith, and take the first right. Climb into the cart filled with hay or the adjacent well. After scanning the area to ensure that there are no guard patrols passing by, use the Assassinate from Hiding Spot technique to end your quarry's amorous pursuit (Fig. 18).

EQUIPMENT UPGRADES

As Sequence 08 begins, Assassins working on a tight budget should first invest their florins in the mighty Schiavona. It's not cheap at 25,000 *f*, but this is categorically the best sword you can own right now. Other new additions are the Notched Cinquedea, a powerful dagger priced at 9,300 *f*, and the Missaglias Greaves – the first piece of the second most durable armor class.

18

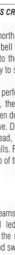

19

20

21

22

Entrance: On the north face of the Santa Maria Gloriosa dei Frari bell tower in the San Polo district – climb onto the adjacent roof, and the glowing door is easy to spot.

1: From the beam, perform a Leap of Faith into the hay pile below, then climb the ladder and walk through the open doorway to enter the church nave. Drop down and run straight ahead, then turn left into the choir stalls. Free run over the northern side to reach the top of the arch (Fig. 19).

2: Jump onto the beams to the south, then climb up the nearby wall ledges; from there, spring backwards to reach the next set of beams. Jump on the chandelier and swing on the horizontal bar, then continue forward until you reach the east wall of the church, just above the main entrance. Free run past the paintings until you reach the north wall, then use three emblems to climb higher; from the topmost of these (Fig. 20), spring backwards to reach a beam. Run over this to reach a wooden platform (and a first checkpoint).

3: Swing on the first lighting fixture to reach a beam; leap to the chandelier and, from there, to the platform opposite. Swing on the beam to the west to reach a triangular wall fitting, then drop to the platform below. This will trigger a cutscene where Ezio is thoughtfully rewarded with a short-cut to use in the event of a fall. Walk to the end of the plank bridge and leap over to the brickwork above a stained-glass window (Fig. 21). Climb up and to the left to reach a metal pole; swing from this to reach a wooden platform. Walk over the plank bridge and use the pile of bricks to reach a beam. Walk to the right of the pillar, and hop over to another beam a short distance to the south.

Hidden Treasure #1 (optional): Instead of walking across to the south side, turn and face the pillar to the north. Climb via the emblems to the top of the pillar, move around to the right, then spring backwards to land on a beam. Hop onto the chandelier and then jump to the emblems opposite. Climb up to find the Treasure Chest. Retrace your steps to reach the platform at the end of Step 3.

4: Run over to the pillar to the south and use the emblems to climb it. At the top, use the scaffold to traverse around to the right and reach a metal pole. Swing to the next pole and, from there, the platform below. Jump to the ladder and descend to the bottom, then walk down the wooden ramp; once Ezio is safely on the next platform, this will fall to create another short-cut. Leap over to the beam and climb to the ledge above; now spring to the opposite ledge. Move right onto the beam, then haul Ezio up and jump to the light fixture (Fig. 22). Now swing to the wooden platform directly ahead. Hop onto a beam and, once again, use the reachable ledge to spring back to another behind Ezio, traverse to the right to reach a beam, then jump to a wooden platform at a lower elevation.

Hidden Treasure #2 (optional): Hop onto the stone ledge to the west and, from there, the wooden platform on the other side. Jump onto the stained-glass windows and climb to the top. Perform a backwards jump onto the pole and swing to the beam. Jump down to the stone platform and enter the small alcove where the Treasure Chest is hidden. Hop over to the wooden beam to the east and drop onto the platform below to continue.

5: Jump to the wooden fixture to the north, then climb via the emblems to reach a ledge above. Use the horizontal bars (Fig. 23) to swing to a platform close to the far north wall. Perform a Leap of Faith into the hay pile and open the door to the basement. Open the strong box to obtain the Templar's treasure, loot other chests in the room, then approach the glowing wall section to find the exit.

23

HOW TO PLAY

WALKTHROUGH

REFERENCE & ANALYSIS

EXTRAS

USER INSTRUCTIONS

MAP: FLORENCE

PRESENT 01

SEQUENCE 01

SEQUENCE 02

MAP: TUSCANY

SEQUENCE 03

SEQUENCE 04

SEQUENCE 05

MAP: ROMAGNA

SEQUENCE 06

PRESENT 02

MAP: VENICE

SEQUENCE 07

SEQUENCE 08

SEQUENCE 09

SEQUENCE 10

SEQUENCE 11

SEQUENCE 14

PRESENT 03

SEQUENCE 08

01

02

MEMORY 01

BIRDS OF A FEATHER: Feel free to explore the new San Marco district, then travel to the waypoint marker beside Santo Stefano – though we strongly advise that you reduce your Notoriety level before you begin.

Follow the two Templar conspirators from a safe distance, Blending with groups to avoid detection. Be watchful for Harassers, and swiftly take refuge in crowds whenever you spot one. You will soon reach a bridge guarded by soldiers where your targets will cross (Fig. 1). Either hire the nearby Courtesans to distract them, or cross via the next bridge along.

After the cutscene, follow the group and hire the first Courtesans you encounter. These will both enable you to pass waiting Harassers, and distract guards blocking the path that the Templars take. The final leg of the journey (up until you reach the Ponte Rialto) is uncomplicated, though be careful to avoid (or gently push) citizens carrying boxes – collisions will cause breakages, which could draw attention to Ezio.

MEMORY 02

IF AT FIRST YOU DON'T SUCCEED: Once again, you should ensure that Ezio's Notoriety is low or non-existent before you begin this Memory. Walk with Antonio to reconnoiter the imposing Palazzo Ducale. The journey to the first waypoint is no more than a leisurely stroll.

You have four locations to scout. The first is a short distance away, beside the Campanile di San Marco. The second is on top of a tower to the southeast. If you have yet to visit this location, be sure to synchronize with the viewpoint before you jump back down (note that the pile of hay is on the left).

Now head to the marker at the northeast corner of the Palazzo. Antonio will comment on the easy route to the top of the basilica, where the final waypoint awaits. Ensure there are no guards nearby – you could create a suitable distraction with Courtesans hired from the nearby piazza if necessary (Fig. 2), or use the Throw Coins move to lure soldiers into the alleyway – then climb up with Antonio following close behind. The Memory ends when you enter the final waypoint.

HOW TO PLAY

WALKTHROUGH

REFERENCE &
ANALYSIS

EXTRAS

USER
INSTRUCTIONS

MAP: FLORENCE

PRESENT 01

SEQUENCE 01

SEQUENCE 02

MAP: TUSCANY

SEQUENCE 03

SEQUENCE 04

SEQUENCE 05

MAP: ROMAGNA

SEQUENCE 06

PRESENT 02

MAP: VENICE

SEQUENCE 07

SEQUENCE 08

SEQUENCE 09

SEQUENCE 10

SEQUENCE 11

SEQUENCE 14

PRESENT 03

TRICKS & TRIVIA

◆ Some adversaries may now use a special "grab and restrain" attack on Ezio. Should this happen, tap the Empty Hand Button and shake the Movement Stick repeatedly to wrestle free before another guard can land a blow.

◆ Struggling to find a free gondola? Try stealing one. If Ezio climbs onto an occupied gondola, its operator will take fright and dive into the water.

◆ If you can acquire a Target Lock on a victim above, and Ezio can climb the surface below them, the Assassinate from Ledge technique also works while he is treading water (Fig. 3).

◆ Did you know that Ezio can attack opponents while climbing ladders? Press the High Profile Button and Weapon Hand Button to punch upwards while ascending a ladder; he will kick if moving downwards. The latter could be gainfully employed to discourage a particularly tenacious Agile.

◆ Here's something to try on a return visit to Romagna or Tuscany: Ezio can leap straight onto the back of a waiting horse from a low rooftop, or any surface at a similar height.

◆ You may have noticed citizens carrying brooms, rakes and hoes, but probably haven't guessed that Ezio can pick these up and use them as improvised weapons. There's no need to harm the worker in question to obtain them – a little jostling will suffice. All three count as two-handed weapons, which makes them highly useful if you're intending to pick a fight with groups of guards that include Brutes or Seekers (Fig. 4).

◆ If there is a shop nearby, you can take advantage of a handy trick to temporarily lose a pursuing Harasser. Just enter the shop menu, then leave immediately.

03

04

The Harasser will slowly walk back to his starting position before running to engage Ezio a second time. This may give you sufficient time to Blend with a crowd.

◆ Throwing an archer from a rooftop is a great way to create a distraction on a street below. Though a trifle macabre, you could also kill one in advance, then carry and hurl his corpse over the edge, if you're aiming for a very precise spot. Naturally, it pays to ensure that there isn't a balcony just below before you try either trick…

05

06

MEMORIES 03 & 04

NOTHING VENTURED, NOTHING GAINED: This is actually a disguised tutorial, designed to familiarize you with Leonardo's remarkable invention before a later set-piece. The cutscene that follows segues straight into the next Memory.

WELL BEGUN IS HALF DONE: For players who don't shy away from physical confrontations, completing this Memory is a simple matter of incapacitating all marked targets. Those who prefer a more studied approach can employ the following stealth kill tips.

◆ **Area #1:** The first targets are two Brutes standing on a bridge just east of the start point. Other soldiers patrolling this area will rush to their aid if you engage them directly. Wait until no one of consequence is watching, then stab one with a Poison Blade from behind, before switching to the Hidden Blade to instantly slay his companion (Fig. 5). If you're quick, you can leave the scene before anyone notices.

◆ **Area #2:** Your victims are a pair of Brutes on the deck of the ship, with another four guards patrolling nearby (though the latter are not actually targets). It's a Restricted Area, as the red zone on the Mini-Map warns you, so don't just stroll up the gangplank. If you climb onto the rear section of the boat from the water, you can use the Assassinate from Ledge technique as the two Brutes walk past your position.

◆ **Area #3:** Two Brutes occupy separate positions on a covered walkway to the west of the Palazzo. Both stand in small Restricted Areas, with other guards poised to get involved if Ezio trespasses. Jump into the canal and submerge to avoid detection until you reach a position just beneath one of the targets, then use the Assassinate from Ledge technique. Rinse and repeat for the second Brute.

◆ **Area #4:** Eliminate a group of sentries stationed on rooftops north of the piazza.

MEMORY 05

INFREQUENT FLIER: You can find a diagram that illustrates the optimum route to the Palazzo Ducale on the page to your right. As a general rule, don't worry too much about dodging arrows. Instead, focus on swooping just above the fires, as the rapid uplift they provide is a more efficient form of evasive maneuver than any amount of zigging or zagging.

Once you reach the roof, you must avoid detection as you follow the roof to a waypoint in the northeast corner of the Palazzo. Desynchronization will be pitilessly swift if a sentry spots Ezio. Use the chimneys as cover (Fig. 6), watching each archer closely before striding out for a quiet Hidden Blade kill when they turn their backs. Climb down the ladder when you reach it and, from there, leap over to the glowing marker.

Grimaldi will loudly condemn Ezio as the true killer of the Doge, so ready yourself for a fight. If you're sufficiently fleet-footed, you can evade the guards and kill your target straight away. Your only remaining objective is then to put distance between Ezio and the scene of the crime. Once you lose your pursuers, the Sequence draws to a close.

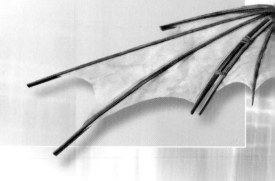

ACHIEVEMENT/TROPHY ALERT!

To all those attempting to amass the full 1,000 Gamerscore or Platinum Trophy for Assassin's Creed II: *pay close attention*. The Infrequent Flyer Memory is the only opportunity to obtain the Fly Swatter accomplishment. To avoid the (for hardcore completists, rather crushing) disappointment of missing out during your first playthrough, be sure to Target Lock and make contact with a guard before you crash land on the roof of the Palazzo Ducale (Fig. 7). If necessary, deliberately crash before touchdown to try again.

07

INFREQUENT FLIER: ROUTE MAP

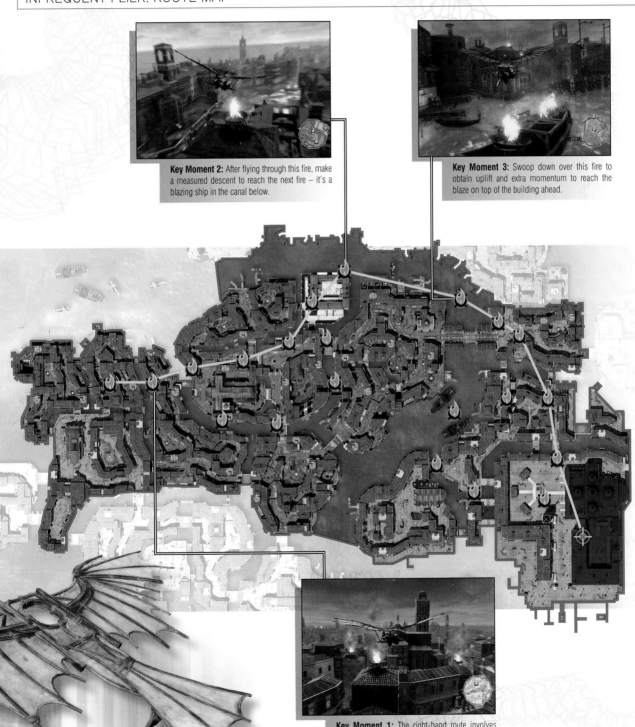

Key Moment 2: After flying through this fire, make a measured descent to reach the next fire – it's a blazing ship in the canal below.

Key Moment 3: Swoop down over this fire to obtain uplift and extra momentum to reach the blaze on top of the building ahead.

Key Moment 1: The right-hand route involves low-level flight through a narrow passage, so head for the flames to your left instead.

HOW TO PLAY

WALKTHROUGH

REFERENCE & ANALYSIS

EXTRAS

USER INSTRUCTIONS

MAP: FLORENCE

PRESENT 01

SEQUENCE 01

SEQUENCE 02

MAP: TUSCANY

SEQUENCE 03

SEQUENCE 04

SEQUENCE 05

MAP: ROMAGNA

SEQUENCE 06

PRESENT 02

MAP: VENICE

SEQUENCE 07

SEQUENCE 08

SEQUENCE 09

SEQUENCE 10

SEQUENCE 11

SEQUENCE 14

PRESENT 03

SEQUENCE 08: SECONDARY MEMORIES

ASSASSINATION CONTRACTS

The pigeon coop in San Marco is on a rooftop in the southwest corner of the district. You must have completed the Zero Tolerance contract (see page 82) before you can attempt these Memories.

see page 82

BLADE IN THE CROWD	
Brief:	Find and kill three targets without alerting them to your presence.
Special Conditions:	Time limit of three minutes; immediate Desyncronization if Ezio is detected.
Advice:	You'll need to use Eagle Vision to identify each individual, and approach them from behind to perform the necessary Hidden Blade finish (Fig. 8). Try to note the positions of potential Blend opportunities as you move, and be quick to use them to avoid detection if a target is facing Ezio when you locate him. The Poison Blade could be a fine solution if any one of the three is walking close to a patrol or stationary guards.

HONORABLE THIEF	
Brief:	Follow an informant to the target's location.
Special Conditions:	Keep up with the Thief; ensure that he is not killed.
Advice:	Throwing Knives and the Large Knife Belt (unlocked at the start of Sequence 09) are beneficial here. The route taken by the Thief isn't too taxing, but you'll need to stay hot on his heels to be ready to kill each archer. The target has bodyguards when you reach him, but it's a fairly undemanding brawl as long as you stay well clear of the outer edge of the rooftop.

08

EQUIPMENT UPGRADES

The Large Knife Belt should be regarded as a mandatory purchase – with rooftop archers everywhere, it's worth every last florin of the 6,000*f* retail price. Sequence 09 also introduces the Missaglias Vambraces and Missaglias Chest Guard for 12,000*f* and 27,900*f* respectively. If the Villa coffers are currently empty, there's no need to rush to buy these – there's relatively little in the way of challenging combat until the last mission of the coming Sequence.

Entrance: You'll find a ladder on top of the Basilica di San Marco, with the secret entrance just below (Fig. 9).

Introduction: From your starting position, head straight to the waypoint marker and use the switch to set up four free running and climbing trials – one each for the north, east, south and west areas of the church. These "physical puzzles" challenge you to discover and follow a very specific route to reach a lever within a short timeframe. Take too long, and the lever will retract. We advise that you practice each course at least once before you attempt it against the clock.

Once all four trials have been completed, drop down into the secret area to collect your prize: the Seal of Amunet.

09

1 – Transept Puzzle (North): Stand on the north switch plate, then hop over the fence and climb the pulpit to your right. Jump over to the stone pillar and, from there, to the platform on the left. Use the poles to the north to reach the lintel over the doorway, then jump to the ledge on the right. Move along until you reach an arch, then use the decorative fittings to climb up to the balustrade above (Fig. 10). Run alongside the north wall and free run over the boxes; wall run up to the hanging rings. Move to the top, then spring backwards to land on the beam. Finally, jump onto the lever before it retracts.

10

2 – Apse Puzzle (East): Stand on the east switch plate, then sprint forward to reach two tables covered in white cloth at the back end of the apse; use these to reach an alcove. From here, jump onto the platform to the left, then turn left again and make your way onto the platform at the center of the area. Climb onto the balcony to the north, then head left and left again. Free run over the improvised "bridge" (Fig. 11) to reach a ledge on the far side. Traverse to the left, past the pillars, and climb up onto the balcony. Scale the organ pipes to reach the flat surface on top and, from there, leap to the lever.

11

3 – Transept Puzzle (South): Stand on the south switch plate, then climb the pulpit to the left. Free run to the south (via a pole and suspended platform) until you reach a thin dividing wall. Turn right and run along the wall until you pass under an arch; hop over to the platform directly ahead. Turn right and use the wooden beams to reach a ledge on the left-hand side of the arch, then climb up and over the balustrade to reach the upper walkway. Leap over to the first of two hanging cruciform decorations (Fig. 12), then drop and traverse to its easternmost arm; climb back up and hop over to the next one and do the same again to reach the walkway. Turn right and free run over the beams to arrive at the south wall, then climb to the center of the window and spring back to grab the lever.

12

4 – Nave Puzzle (West): Stand on the west switch, then free run over the left-hand column of benches and climb onto a decorative screen. Move under the archway and use the two platforms to reach a ledge to the west. Traverse around until you see a beam beneath Ezio, then drop onto it. Use the beams that extend from the west wall to progress north (Fig. 13); at the far side, climb via the ring to reach the upper level. Run around the corner to reach the huge window, and climb the cross at the center. When Ezio reaches the top, spring backwards and then swing via the two poles to reach the lever.

Hidden Treasure #1 (optional): Follow the Nave Puzzle instructions until you reach the upper walkway, then walk east until your path is blocked. Turn to examine the far side of the archway (Fig. 14). See the dark fixtures on the wall? That's your route up. Drop over the adjacent balcony and traverse to reach the first of these hand-holds, then use Climb Leap to get to the top. Now spring backward to reach a wooden beam. Run up the north wall to another sequence of hand-holds, then move east until Ezio is above a wooden beam. Drop down and hop over to the nearby platform to find the chest.

14

Hidden Treasure #2 (optional): Follow the route taken to Hidden Treasure #1 until you reach the first wooden beam, then leap over to the white platform. Drop down to the other (east) side of the obstruction, and follow the walkway until it curves to the left. Facing north, you now need to leap from the balustrade to the wooden beams far below (Fig. 15). From the beams, jump onto the ledge on the right-hand side of the arch to the north, then traverse to the left until you come to the chest.

15

HOW TO PLAY

WALKTHROUGH

REFERENCE & ANALYSIS

EXTRAS

USER INSTRUCTIONS

MAP: FLORENCE

PRESENT 01

SEQUENCE 01

SEQUENCE 02

MAP: TUSCANY

SEQUENCE 03

SEQUENCE 04

SEQUENCE 05

MAP: ROMAGNA

SEQUENCE 06

PRESENT 02

MAP: VENICE

SEQUENCE 07

SEQUENCE 08

SEQUENCE 09

SEQUENCE 10

SEQUENCE 11

SEQUENCE 14

PRESENT 03

SEQUENCE 09

▌MEMORY 01

KNOWLEDGE IS POWER: Visit Leonardo's Workshop to obtain the Carnevale Mask and, of far greater import, the Pistol. Head to the waypoint marker and practice by shooting the three target dummies (Fig. 1), then return to Da Vinci. Replenish your Pistol ammunition at a Blacksmith on the way to the next Memory Start.

▌MEMORIES 02 & 03

DAMSELS IN DISTRESS: The murderer will flee from Ezio, but don't be too eager to catch up with him – there's a twist to this Memory that will soon become abundantly apparent. After a short distance your quarry will stop, holding a Courtesan at knifepoint. If you approach him, he will stab her and run; were you to repeatedly make the same mistake, he would leave a trail of corpses on the street before Desynchronization occurred. The solution, naturally, is to use the Pistol. When he stops to issue threats, blade poised, acquire a Target Lock and wait for a clear shot (Fig. 2). Once you have one, fire to exact immediate retribution. A single direct hit will end the Memory immediately.

NUN THE WISER: Walk with Teodora and Antonio to the Squero di San Trovaso. Once the journey is complete, you can complete the first three Carnevale competitions in any order you like. As before, our walkthrough follows the order used in the DNA menu.

01

02

▌MEMORY 04

AND THEY'RE OFF: You can find this Memory Start located next to Santa Maria Della Visitazione. It's a checkpoint race with a two-minute timer. As with other races, a measured and careful approach is better than pure speed. Wasting several seconds through caution (though not outright timidity) will not cause you to fail, but falling in certain positions certainly will.

The course isn't particularly complicated, but there are two points that may lead to a little confusion. Firstly, the path after gate number seven might not be immediately apparent, but it's easy when you know how: you're supposed to swing around the corner of the building via the hanging basket (Fig. 3). If you have approximately one minute left when you reach the rooftops, you're making excellent time, though as little as 40 seconds is sufficient to reach the finish line. After gate twelve, dive down into the canal. It's then a straight sprint through crowds to reach the final gate.

03

USER
INSTRUCTIONS

MAP: FLORENCE

PRESENT 01

SEQUENCE 01

SEQUENCE 02

MAP: TUSCANY

SEQUENCE 03

SEQUENCE 04

SEQUENCE 05

MAP: ROMAGNA

SEQUENCE 06

PRESENT 02

MAP: VENICE

SEQUENCE 07

SEQUENCE 08

SEQUENCE 09

SEQUENCE 10

SEQUENCE 11

SEQUENCE 14

PRESENT 03

CARNEVALE MASK

The Carnevale Mask (Fig. 4) is worn up until the final Memory of Sequence 09, and enables Ezio to maintain the necessary Incognito status until that point. It works in much the same way as the Medici Cape. Guards will still attack if they witness him perform an illegal act (such as murder or assault), but there is no Notoriety increase after either killing or escaping them.

04

USING THE PISTOL

◆ With the Pistol equipped, acquire a Target Lock, then press and hold the Weapon Hand Button to aim. Once an uninterrupted line forms, release the button to shoot and kill your target instantly.

◆ Ezio cannot move while aiming the Pistol, but will automatically twist to track the movements of a target.

◆ After every shot, reloading takes three seconds. Ezio cannot fire again until this time has elapsed, though he can perform all other actions (such as blocking or changing weapons).

◆ Releasing the Weapon Hand Button before the direct line between Pistol and target appears greatly reduces the likelihood of a hit – and especially so at long range.

◆ Guards will not react to Ezio aiming the Pistol if he is Incognito. You could use this fact to target a potentially troublesome Leader or Brute before combat begins.

◆ Firing the Pistol is a reprehensible action, and will always cause nearby guards to attack Ezio. It will also scare civilians in the vicinity (Fig. 5).

◆ Using the Pistol successfully in open combat can be difficult, as Ezio is completely defenseless while aiming. Blind-firing at point-blank range can work, but you'll need to choose your moment carefully. One perk of using the Pistol is that guards find it utterly terrifying. The very act of aiming it during a battle will Intimidate all present, causing them to suffer gradual morale reductions, with an additional penalty levied after each successful kill. Even so, it's not the most efficient way to fight. We would suggest using it to initiate combat, if just for the morale-sapping effect, then switching to another tactic.

◆ Note that the Disarm technique is available while the Pistol is equipped. You can use this to make a fluid transition into more conventional combat.

◆ Replenish your stock of ammunition (up to a maximum of six bullets) by purchasing it from a Blacksmith.

05

▌MEMORIES 05 & 06 ▌

CTF: The Memory Start location is near Santa Maria dei Carmini. Ezio must beat an Agile in a game of Capture the Flag, with victory awarded to the first to score three wins. If Ezio reaches the flag first, he must evade his rival and return to his rooftop "base" (his start position). If his opponent gets to it first, sprint through the streets and over rooftops to perform a Shove or Tackle and retrieve it before the Agile can score. Refer to the tips on the page to your right if you experience any difficulties.

RIBBON ROUND-UP: This Memory starts at the Squero di San Trovaso, so it's most likely the first game you will participate in after Antonio and Teodora leave. The objective is extremely simple: walk up to each group of women marked on the Mini-Map, and then hold the Legs Button to steal their bundle of ribbons (Fig. 6). Work your way around the square first, then head for the marker to the east. Now follow the trail of waypoints to retrieve the rest of the ribbons with ease.

▌MEMORY 07 ▌

CHEATERS NEVER PROSPER: Heal and repair armor before you head to the Squero di San Trovaso to begin this Memory. There are three fights against generic soldiers; after these, Dante Moro enters the ring. The only rule for these four bouts is that you don't kill your opponents, though stamping on prone bodies is permissible. Stick to counters, and you can clear each one with an air of indifference.

When Silvio's armed henchmen enter the ring, the prior restriction on fatalities is relaxed. Practiced Assassins can now equip the Double Hidden Blades and opt for Counter Kills, though use of Disarm is fine if you prefer (Fig. 7). The Memory ends when the final Agile falls.

▌MEMORY 08 ▌

HAVING A BLAST: Travel to the waypoint marker and locate Dante Moro, but don't get too close: if he recognizes Ezio, the Memory ends. He's initially located in a small garden in the north of the highlighted area. When he walks out, send groups of Courtesans to follow him. With a large entourage surrounding your mark, Blend and perform the necessary theft (Fig. 8). Objective accomplished, follow the waypoints to reach the party.

When Dante arrives to expose Ezio's deception, your priority is to avoid the guards. Move from group to group and hire some Courtesans to maximize your chances of remaining unnoticed. The Seeker is the principle danger here as he will move between Blend opportunities, dispersing each little crowd as he encounters them.

Once the timer expires, the final task is to assassinate Marco Barbarigo, if possible by timing a Pistol shot in order to have its distinctive report masked by the exploding fireworks. When he falls, make a swift exit from the party (via the water if circumstances dictate), then return to La Rosa Della Virtù to complete the Sequence.

CTF: STEP BY STEP

1: After leaving your starting "base position", be sure to jump over the wooden fences (Fig. 9) during the initial sprint along the tiles – scaling the higher rooftop that blocks your path will waste precious time.

2: From this position, run towards the waypoint, and leap straight off the edge of the building to land on a stone platform not far below (Fig. 10). From here, leap directly to the flag. Ezio will sustain a significant amount of damage, but this is easily healed between rounds.

3: Turn and climb the ladder to return to the rooftops (Fig. 11). If your opponent is rushing towards your position, making a quick circular run to throw him off track may be a good idea.

4: When Ezio is two points up, his competitor will begin to reach the flag much more quickly. At this point, don't even bother to compete for the first capture. Instead, run over the ropes beside your base (to the left of Ezio from the start). Now turn right and cross a second set of ropes to a third rooftop (Fig. 12). See the rooftop hutch far to the west, beyond the viewpoint tower? This is your opponent's base. Track his movements from above. Once he begins his climb, get into position and wait. The moment he sets foot on the rooftop, plant Ezio's shoulder into his body to retrieve the flag, then make good your escape.

09

10

11

12

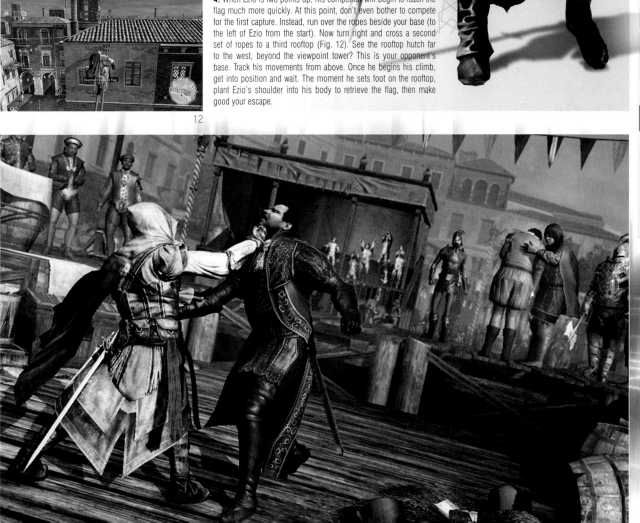

HOW TO PLAY

WALKTHROUGH

REFERENCE & ANALYSIS

EXTRAS

USER INSTRUCTIONS

MAP: FLORENCE

PRESENT 01

SEQUENCE 01

SEQUENCE 02

MAP: TUSCANY

SEQUENCE 03

SEQUENCE 04

SEQUENCE 05

MAP: ROMAGNA

SEQUENCE 06

PRESENT 02

MAP: VENICE

SEQUENCE 07

SEQUENCE 08

SEQUENCE 09

SEQUENCE 10

SEQUENCE 11

SEQUENCE 14

PRESENT 03

SEQUENCE 09: SECONDARY MEMORIES

ASSASSINATION CONTRACTS

The pigeon coop for this district is located on a rooftop west of the Squero di San Trovaso. You must have completed each Venice-specific contract up to and including Honorable Thief (see page 88) to access these.

NO LAUGHING MATTER

Brief:	Identify and kill specific individuals disguised as harlequins among the Carnevale crowds.
Special Conditions:	None, but the targets will flee if they see Ezio.
Advice:	The target in the northwest is alone, and is the easiest of the three to kill. The other two are initially located in separate private gatherings surrounded by guards. Approach from the canals in both instances, then give chase should they flee before you can perform an assassination. Actually, allowing them to see Ezio may be the best approach – that way, you can tail them to a suitably secluded area to perform the necessary finish.

CRASH A PARTY

Brief:	Follow a guest to a party, then kill the host.
Special Conditions:	Maintain distance from target while following; timer appears if eye contact is broken; party is in a Restricted Area.
Advice:	The first part of the contract is simple enough: just don't cause a commotion or get too close to the guest. When she turns into an alleyway blocked by guards, quickly scale the building. Eliminate rooftop archers as required, then reestablish eye contact before the timer expires. The party is a Restricted Area, with patrols (including a Seeker) poised to detect Ezio if he lingers in the open. The target is standing beside one of the painters at the west edge of the enclosure; climb down the outer wall there for easy access. Blend with the nearby crowd until the patrols face elsewhere, then emerge to strike.

FALSE LEGACY

Brief:	Eliminate a single target (and, as a fringe benefit, free kidnapped artists to decorate the Medici family crypt).
Special Conditions:	None.
Advice:	The target is a Brute, ostensibly secure behind a screen of guards with patrols covering the nearby area. The obvious strategy is to fight your way through, but a more prudent alternative is to hire a group of Mercenaries and order them to attack. Once the melee unfolds, stroll calmly into the center of it and cut the Brute down with the Double Hidden Blades. The proximity of water makes the subsequent escape a formality.

EQUIPMENT UPGRADES

As Sequence 10 begins, Tailors will now sell the Large Poison Vial, capable of carrying the maximum 15 doses, and you can also complete your Missaglias armor collection with a set of Pauldrons – if you have 21,300*f* to spare, that is. If you haven't bought the Sword of Altaïr yet, consider doing so now. With a base price of an astonishing 50,000*f*, the blade is the undisputed leader in its weapon class. It can only be purchased from the Blacksmith in Monteriggioni.

HOW TO PLAY

WALKTHROUGH

REFERENCE & ANALYSIS

EXTRAS

USER INSTRUCTIONS

MAP: FLORENCE

PRESENT 01

SEQUENCE 01

SEQUENCE 02

MAP: TUSCANY

SEQUENCE 03

SEQUENCE 04

SEQUENCE 05

MAP: ROMAGNA

SEQUENCE 06

PRESENT 02

MAP: VENICE

SEQUENCE 07

SEQUENCE 08

SEQUENCE 09

SEQUENCE 10

SEQUENCE 11

SEQUENCE 14

PRESENT 03

13

Entrance: On the west face of the tower at Santa Maria Della Visitazione.

Opening Chase: Head along the tunnel and perform a Leap of Faith from the beam. Assassinate the Brute, then give chase as the Agile flees. Pay special attention when you reach the final corridor (Fig. 13). If you can free run from a sheet-covered step to a wooden platform suspended over the lower path, there is an opportunity to perform a perfect Air Assassination at the end. You can then stroll through the open gate and past the oblivious guards in the adjacent room. If you don't catch the Agile in time, you will instead need to climb through a gap to the right of the closed gate, and then fight him and a group of his cohorts.

However this section ends, open the door and head down the stairs to reach a large chamber.

14

Hidden Treasure #1 (optional): You can find this Treasure Chest just outside the gate that the Agile closes if he survives. Look for a set of boards on the west wall (Fig. 14). Jump onto these, then Climb Leap to the rings above. Spring backwards onto the beam. Wall run vertically and, at the peak of Ezio's ascent, leap to the right to grab a pole. Swing over to the ledge, then climb into the alcove to claim your reward.

Hidden Treasure #2 (optional): Once you enter the underground chamber, turn left. Notice the ledges on the east wall? Swim over and climb these. On the small platform area, perform a wall run up the surface to Ezio's left, then jump over to the ledges to the right. From there, spring back again to reach the topmost ledge on the left-hand side. Climb up to find the chest. Use the nearby pole for a rapid return to the lower level.

Timed Run: There are four pressure-sensitive bars in this cavern (though these are retracted at present). Ezio must land on each one of these to open a door to the burial chamber. By pulling the lever you activate a mechanism that both extends each bar and rotates three pillars. The pillars move poles into position, creating a complete course that takes you around the chamber in a clockwise route (Fig. 15). The catch, of course, is that the pillars return to their original positions once a timer expires, making it impossible to complete the run unless you're already in position to jump to the final bar.

Before moving to step-by-step guidance, the best advice we can offer is to take it steady. Stopping occasionally to measure tricky leaps or to regain your composure will not prevent you from reaching the final lever in time; falls due to over-confidence or poor judgment most definitely will. You should also note that you will need to perform a wall run followed immediately by a wall jump (where you run up a featureless surface before leaping in the necessary direction) on several occasions here.

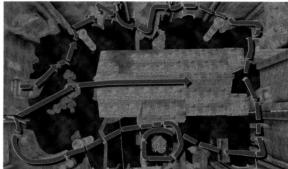

15

16

1: Free run up to the pole on the tower (Fig. 16) and swing to the stone platform. Move to the right-hand side of the platform, then wall run and jump right to reach the first bar.

17

2: Once the cutscene ends, swing to the steps. Wall run up the shield (Fig. 17) and jump left. Free run and swing over the poles in quick succession to reach the southeast corner of the chamber. Wall run and jump right to reach the second bar.

18

3: Swing to the ledge below and sprint to the ruined railing (Fig. 18). Free run over the wall sections in the southwest corner to reach the third bar.

4: This is the most difficult stretch. Don't allow the acceleration of the mechanism to panic you. Swing from the bar to a broken column, then free run to a platform further north. Follow it around to reach a surface with (rather eye-catching) streaming water; approach it and wall run, then jump left to reach a higher level. Jump over the gap to another platform (past the back of the statue), then turn to face north (Fig. 19) and gather your wits for the finale: a free running sequence over two bars, a broken column and a pole to reach the raised area in the northwest corner. Jump to the final bar to unlock the way forward.

Enter the burial chamber to retrieve the Seal of Leonius. If you have collected the other four "optional" seals (in addition to the one obtained in Sequence 04), you can now return to Villa Auditore to unlock Altaïr's ancient yet powerful armor in the Assassin Sanctuary.

19

SEQUENCE | 10

▌MEMORIES 01 & 02 ▌

AN UNPLEASANT TURN OF EVENTS: Speak to Antonio to view a cutscene.

CAGED FIGHTER: Talk to the wounded Mercenary to begin the Memory. Your objective is to free Bartolomeo D'Alviano from his prison (Fig. 1) and return him to his residence just west of San Zaccaria. If you're not happy to bludgeon your way to success, we've prepared a more subtle step-by-step walkthrough on the page to your right.

▌MEMORY 03 ▌

LEAVE NO MAN BEHIND: Forget stealth: this mission is all about smiting, and plenty of it. From the east side of San Zaccaria, cross the nearby bridge and climb the roof of the prison on the south side to set up a Double Air Assassination (Fig. 2). With the guards dead, open the cage door. Four of the Mercenaries inside will choose to fight with Ezio, which proves useful at the more heavily guarded second prison. Attack quickly on arrival, stalking the periphery of the fight to secure easy kills against opponents distracted by your companions, then open the cage. With your expanded army in tow, head to the third prison for a concluding brawl.

01

02

USER INSTRUCTIONS

MAP: FLORENCE

PRESENT 01

SEQUENCE 01

SEQUENCE 02

MAP: TUSCANY

SEQUENCE 03

SEQUENCE 04

SEQUENCE 05

MAP: ROMAGNA

SEQUENCE 06

PRESENT 02

MAP: VENICE

SEQUENCE 07

SEQUENCE 08

SEQUENCE 09

SEQUENCE 10

SEQUENCE 11

SEQUENCE 14

PRESENT 03

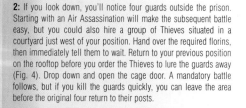

CAGED FIGHTER: STEP BY STEP

1: Head north until you approach the southern edge of the Restricted Area surrounding the waypoint marker, then climb onto the nearby rooftops for the next leg of the journey. Follow the line of rooftops adjacent to the Arsenale wall, eliminating sentries on the way, to reach a final group of buildings to the north. You'll definitely hear Bartolomeo D'Alviano long before you lay eyes on him. Look for two archers standing on a wooden platform (Fig. 3); D'Alviano is imprisoned directly below. Wait until a third sentry further north faces away, then take out the pair of archers with a Double Assassination, before dispatching the third with Throwing Knives.

03

2: If you look down, you'll notice four guards outside the prison. Starting with an Air Assassination will make the subsequent battle easy, but you could also hire a group of Thieves situated in a courtyard just west of your position. Hand over the required florins, then immediately tell them to wait. Return to your previous position on the rooftop before you order the Thieves to lure the guards away (Fig. 4). Drop down and open the cage door. A mandatory battle follows, but if you kill the guards quickly, you can leave the area before the original four return to their posts.

04

3: Head to the next waypoint which, once again, lies at the center of another Restricted Area. Any guards you encounter will immediately attack Bartolomeo, so try to pay them wide berth. Your destination is just inside an alleyway in the northeast region of the circle (Fig. 5). If you hire another group of Thieves, you could use them to distract the soldiers stationed outside the nearby Bank. There is another mandatory battle at the final waypoint. Once the captain and his lieutenant fall, open the gate to conclude the Memory.

05

▌MEMORY 04 ▐

ASSUME THE POSITION: Your objective here is to escort Mercenaries to strategic locations marked by Bartolomeo and kill the guards stationed there (Fig. 6). There are two catches: any soldiers that you pass on your way there will automatically attack, and the number of Mercenaries accompanying Ezio is reduced after you secure each of the two initial waypoints. Use the Mini-Map to pick routes that enable you to avoid unnecessary combat if you prefer.

06

▌MEMORY 05 ▐

TWO BIRDS, ONE BLADE: Head to the top of the designated viewpoint (you'll need to use Climb Leap on a few occasions to scale it), then run to the subsequent waypoint to provide aid to Bartolomeo. That accomplished, run to the next marker to fight Dante. Unless you have a pressing need to defend yourself, ignore the other combatants – *signore* Moro is your sole objective here. He will run once his health is depleted.

After the cutscene, an onscreen timer will reveal a deadline for the successful assassination of both Dante and his master, Silvio. Head to the rooftops and follow them from above. This entirely removes the need to fight at street level, though you will need to deal with a few archers. When you near the ship, look for a gray building close by (Fig. 7). Climb the loading crane on top of it and jump to reach the nearby beam, then perform a Double Air Assassination to execute Silvio and Dante in a single spectacular finish. Alternatively, you could also swim to your destination and stealthily make your way to your targets if you're so inclined.

07

NOTORIETY: LIVE WITH IT

As Sequence 10 focuses almost exclusively on combat, it makes sense to temporarily stop the usual practice of reducing Ezio's Notoriety level between or even during Memories. The distances that you must walk between later Memory Start positions are rather trivial, so it's no trial to Blend on the rare occasions that you need to dodge a patrol (Fig. 8).

08

TRAINING: DOUBLE HIDDEN BLADES

The final section of the "Two Birds, One Blade" Memory offers a perfect opportunity to practice the peerlessly devastating art of fighting with Double Hidden Blades alone (Fig. 9). If you give chase to Silvio and Dante at street level, waves of guards will run to support them. As the only consequence for failure is a short journey back to the previous checkpoint, there's no reason why you can't attempt to defeat all of them.

USER INSTRUCTIONS

MAP: FLORENCE

PRESENT 01

SEQUENCE 01

SEQUENCE 02

MAP: TUSCANY

SEQUENCE 03

SEQUENCE 04

SEQUENCE 05

MAP: ROMAGNA

SEQUENCE 06

PRESENT 02

MAP: VENICE

SEQUENCE 07

SEQUENCE 08

SEQUENCE 09

SEQUENCE 10

SEQUENCE 11

SEQUENCE 14

PRESENT 03

09

The most efficient way to fight with Double Hidden Blades is to eschew direct aggression in favor of instant-death ripostes (Fig. 10). The timing window is definitely smaller than for Counter Kills with other weapons, or Disarm attempts, but it's possible to hone your skills to the point where practically every enemy attack is their last. The trick is to time the Counter Kill later than usual. This will initially lead to partial failures where Ezio blocks instead (too early, and enemies will land their blow successfully), but you can gradually work on refining your response each time. Whenever adversaries appear reluctant to lash out, a quick Taunt is always a satisfying remedy.

Once you reach the point where you can conquer all challengers (main assassination targets aside) with plenty of time to spare and no significant damage to Ezio's Health Meter, feel free to complete the Memory.

10

SEQUENCE 11

▌MEMORY 01

ALL THINGS COME TO HE WHO WAITS: Walk with Leonardo until he departs at the start of the Sequence, then travel to the Castello district to reach the Memory Start marker. A full belt of Throwing Knives will be of great service, so be sure to stop at a Blacksmith at some point during the journey.

As with previous Memories of this variety, there are four golden rules: maintain a safe distance from your target, don't fall too far behind, keep him in sight whenever possible, and don't cause a scene. You should stick to the rooftops at first, then move down to continue stalking at street level when you reach a church (Fig. 1). If you require further guidance for the pursuit, consult the complete walkthrough on the page to your right.

▌MEMORY 02

PLAY ALONG: Press the Empty Hand Button to pick up the box when prompted, then follow the Templar henchman through the city streets. Regulate your pace to match stride with him and the two guards who fall into formation behind Ezio. With due irony it appears that every merchant in Venice has scheduled a delivery for this point in time, so be sure to weave deftly past all individuals carrying crates (Fig. 2). When you reach the waypoint, watch carefully for interactive prompts during the cutscene to slay the three guards.

The fight against Borgia has three stages. In the first, it's a one-on-one confrontation. Disarm and Counter Kill attempts will only be partially successful (a minor health drain rather than the desired effect), so equip your most powerful weapon and either use Deflect Counters to whittle down his Health Meter, or dodge each assault and follow up with a strike of your own. The Templar will perform his own counters against combos, though this isn't really an issue if you have a full pouch of Medicine.

With Ezio's nemesis bruised but not beaten, several guards will enter the fray. These can be dispatched in any way you please. Ignore the Templar for now: the additional combatants are your sole concern. Purists will switch to Hidden Blade counters for quick finishes, though be sure to only block any attacks that Borgia performs. For the concluding stage where you are joined by allies, you should only kill the guards that engage Ezio directly, then focus your attention on Rodrigo alone.

After the closing cutscene, Ezio is automatically transported to a new location – to avoid spoilers, we'll just say that it isn't Venice. However, you are free to return here immediately to complete Secondary Memories if you wish.

01

02

STEP BY STEP:
ALL THINGS COME TO HE WHO WAITS

If you crave a stern test of your wits and free running prowess, try following the courier to his destination without once returning to street level. This is a genuinely challenging accomplishment, though it is of course entirely optional – there is no reward other than personal satisfaction. For those who prefer an easy life, we've prepared a direct route through this enjoyable Memory.

As the positions of archers may change between sessions, we can only suggest that you kill any that lie in Ezio's path, and simply ignore those that do not directly engage him. Equip the Throwing Knives in advance once the action resumes, then head south along the walkway. Turn right onto a wooden platform, then leap over to the rooftop below. You can re-establish contact with the courier here. Head north until you reach a wooden beam that extends from the last house in a row, then leap to the platform suspended by ropes and, from there, to the left-hand rooftop. Continue north, trailing your target's movements. When you reach the east face of the Santi Giovanni e Paolo church in the northeast corner of the Castello district, jump down to street level. The courier will now cross a canal via a mooring post, then sprint along a path to reach a courtyard. If you successfully trail him there, you'll receive a welcome checkpoint.

Hire Thieves to distract the guards, then follow the courier into alleyways. After he crosses a canal, wait until he moves around a corner before dispatching the solitary guard with a quiet Double Hidden Blades kill. On the next street, the courier will begin to run. Shadow his movements from a safe distance, being careful not to create a disturbance of any kind. He will eventually cut into an alley on the right-hand side of the street and cross another canal. The route briefly becomes a little too circuitous for any description to be useful here, but it's not difficult to follow his movements. What is certain, though, is that the number of potential hazards is suddenly increased – particularly in terms of citizens carrying boxes, and Harassers running to assail Ezio. Weave through these until you see the target free running above the street. There's actually no need to follow him up there – just walk beneath at a discrete distance and wait for him to return to ground level.

The courier will eventually walk through a guarded entrance, triggering a brief cutscene and another checkpoint. Your next challenge is to reach and kill him within 90 seconds, avoiding detection entirely. Run to the south to find two ladders leading to the rooftops. Climb these, then make your way to a wooden platform just above the target's position to set up a perfect Air Assassination opportunity (Fig. 3).

03

VENETIAN CAPE

Once you complete Play Along, Ezio is awarded the Venetian Cape (Fig. 4). This has the same basic effect as the Medici Cape, but works in Venice and Romagna instead. It makes the process of finding Feathers, Glyphs and Codex Pages far less time-consuming, as there is no need to address cumulative Notoriety penalties accrued through assorted confrontations.

To change capes, visit the Outfits page in the Inventory menu.

04

USER INSTRUCTIONS

MAP: FLORENCE

PRESENT 01

SEQUENCE 01

SEQUENCE 02

MAP: TUSCANY

SEQUENCE 03

SEQUENCE 04

SEQUENCE 05

MAP: ROMAGNA

SEQUENCE 06

PRESENT 02

MAP: VENICE

SEQUENCE 07

SEQUENCE 08

SEQUENCE 09

SEQUENCE 10

SEQUENCE 11

SEQUENCE 14

PRESENT 03

SEQUENCES 10 & 11: SECONDARY MEMORIES

ASSASSINATION CONTRACTS

The final pigeon coop is located in the Castello district, due east of the Basilica di San Marco. You must have completed each Venice-specific contract up to and including False Legacy (see page 94) to obtain this last contract.

HUNTING THE HUNTER	
Brief:	Kill a target to obtain the location of a bounty hunter trailing Ezio, then eliminate him.
Special Conditions:	The body of the first target must be looted to continue.
Advice:	The initial target is an Agile, and you'll find him standing beside the west wall of San Pietro di Castello. Approach the church from the east side, climb to the roof, and you could easily slay him with Throwing Knives before he has the opportunity to run (Fig. 5). Naturally, it pays to ensure that there are no patrols in the vicinity before you do this. Now loot the body to reveal a new waypoint. Approach the center of the marked area from the south; a cursory examination will reveal that your target is actually a crude dummy. Ready yourself for the inevitable ambush before you approach it, then defeat all combatants to complete the final assassination contract.

FREE MISSIONS

VENETIAN RUSH (RACE)	
Location:	Near the front entrance of the Basilica di San Marco
Advice:	This is an enjoyable challenge, with a perfectly manageable three minute time allocation. If you don't complete it the first time, your greater familiarity with the course should make the second run a certainty. There are only a few areas that may be problematic. Firstly, one of the initial gates at street level forces you to briefly cut through the Restricted Area surrounding the palazzo. Don't worry about this: just sprint straight through and ignore the guards. Finally, the latter section of the Race features two instances where you free run over beams above water. Falling here will lose you more time than you can spare, so favor caution over speed for both.

PHILANDERER ON THE ROOF (BEAT UP)	
Location:	Cannaregio district
Advice:	Travel to the waypoint marker and make your way up to the rooftop. As with all other Beat Up Memories, it's vital that you don't kill the target. Launching combos is risky (you might accidentally knock him over the edge), so stick to counters. After five or six of these, the scoundrel will yield.

THE PERFECT MARRIAGE (COURIER)	
Location:	Cannaregio district
Special Conditions:	You must loot the Thief's body, so don't do anything that might cause him to fall into water.
Advice:	Ezio is asked to retrieve a letter by killing the man who stole it. Naturally, he's of the Agile archetype. There is a five minute time limit, but you can remove the need for a chase by approaching the target from behind (Fig. 6). From his position on the rooftops, he faces east; sneak up from the west for a fuss-free Hidden Blade kill. Should he spot Ezio, switch to Throwing Knives to cut the pursuit short. Loot the body and return to the final waypoint.

05

06

TEMPLAR LAIR: SHIPWRECKED

NOTE: ASSASSIN'S CREED II BLACK EDITION ONLY

HOW TO PLAY

WALKTHROUGH

REFERENCE & ANALYSIS

EXTRAS

USER INSTRUCTIONS

MAP: FLORENCE

PRESENT 01

SEQUENCE 01

SEQUENCE 02

MAP: TUSCANY

SEQUENCE 03

SEQUENCE 04

SEQUENCE 05

MAP: ROMAGNA

SEQUENCE 06

PRESENT 02

MAP: VENICE

SEQUENCE 07

SEQUENCE 08

SEQUENCE 09

SEQUENCE 10

SEQUENCE 11

SEQUENCE 14

PRESENT 03

Entrance: In the Castello district – look for a glowing door at the base of a tower in the Arsenale di Venezia when you reach the waypoint marker.

First Shipyard, Part 1: Jump into the water and dive to pass underneath the gate. Climb the wall and use the Assassinate from Ledge technique to kill the guard standing above.

Hidden Treasure #1 (optional): After assassinating the first guard, jump into the water below and swim to a gate a short distance to the north (Fig. 7). Submerge and swim beneath it, then do the same with the three gates in the tunnel leading east. Climb onto the platform, then jump over to the ledge. Traverse to the right, then leap over to a beam further along. Climb up to find the chest, then pull the lever to open the cage.

07

Hidden Treasure #2 (optional): After opening the first Treasure Chest, drop down to the lower level and enter the hole in the east wall (Fig. 8). Use the two poles to reach a ledge, then jump over to another ledge to your right. Traverse all the way to the left, then spring back to reach the platform where the chest is located. Return to the main shipyard area and make your way up to the guards by the north wall.

08

First Shipyard, Part 2: If you choose to skip the Treasure Chests, climb to the top of the metal cage to the north, then assassinate the guards below. Scale the north wall via the boxes and traverse right, then jump to the platform in the northeast corner. Run south and use the wooden bar to reach the boat section in the center. Hop over the incomplete timbers to reach the other side (Fig. 9), then leap to the platform. Jump over to the boat section to the east, Climb leap to the upper ledge, then leap to the platform on your left. Free run over to the balcony and kill the guards stationed there.

09

First Shipyard, Part 3: Leap from the west edge of the balcony to reach a stone ledge below, then traverse to the left until the camera angle changes to show a pole behind Ezio's position (Fig. 10). Spring back to reach it, then swing to the balcony. Kill the Brute once the cutscene ends, then sprint in pursuit of the fleeing Agile.

10

Agile Chase, Part 1: Turn left when you reach the south wall, then leap over to a platform on the left. Ezio can make the jump to the platform further north if you position him on the longer of the two broken bridge supports, but you can easily climb up to it if you accidentally drop to the level below. Run into the boat section and climb the scaffold to the upper level (Fig. 11), then hop over the timbers to reach the balcony. Turn right and follow the Agile into the second shipyard.

11

Agile Chase, Part 2: Swing over the poles and free run over beams to return to the lower level, then run around to the other side of the ship and hop over the wooden supports. Enter the part-built vessel via the ramp, then turn right and run through the lower level until you reach a ladder. At the top, run north to reach another ladder, then turn and follow the guard to the south wall, before running all the way back to the north. Free run over the top of the ship, then jump over to the balcony on the north wall. Now chase the Agile into the tunnel. After the first turn to the right, the next corridor has a section of broken brickwork (Fig. 12) that leads to a hole in the left-hand wall that Ezio can swing through to reach a rusty chandelier. Once there, jump and swing over to a lower chandelier and perform an Air Assassination as your victim runs underneath. Taking this short-cut will enable you to catch the Agile before he can alert other guards near the treasure room entrance. If you don't catch him in time, you'll need to fight them to continue. After looting the Templar stash, use the highlighted exit to return to Venice.

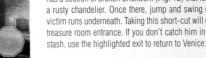

12

COLLECTING CODEX PAGES

There are 30 Codex pieces in total and you can only start the first Memory of Sequence 14 if you have collected all of them. Ezio automatically obtains 14 of these during Memories before this point in time, so you actually only need to look for 16 Philosophical Codex pages. These are hidden in guarded Banks and marked on area maps and the Mini-Map with a distinctive icon. We'll let the game itself reveal why this is necessary: suffice to say, if you haven't acquired them by this point, you'll need to do so now.

13

Use Fast Travel Stations to reach each location quickly, and wear the Medici and Venetian Capes where applicable to avoid Notoriety penalties as you kill the guards outside each Bank (Fig. 13). Once they have been dispatched, stroll through the open door to retrieve your prize from the chest inside (Fig. 14).

14

You should also note that, from the start of Sequence 14, Leonardo moves to the Villa in Monteriggioni. Once you have the necessary pages, visit him in Claudia's office to have him decode them.

PHILOSOPHICAL CODEX PAGES: LOCATIONS

REGION	DISTRICT/AREA	CODEX PAGES
Florence	San Giovanni	1
	San Marco	2
	Santa Maria Novella	2
Tuscany	San Gimignano	2
Romagna	Forlì	3
Venice	San Polo	2
	San Marco	1
	Dorsoduro	1
	Castello	1
	Cannaregio	1

RECAP: OPTIONAL PURSUITS

After the first memory of Sequence 14, Assassin's Creed II ends its final chapter in a new locale – and you cannot return to previous regions once you commit to the journey. Though it is possible to find collectibles, complete Secondary Memories and just have fun in the sandbox after the closing credits, we thought this an appropriate time to remind readers of secondary pursuits and activities that they may actually wish to complete before then.

Monteriggioni Upgrades
If you have neglected the Villa management side-quest, this would be a good time to complete all building upgrades and restore the village to its former glory. If you do this now, you'll gradually accrue the necessary funds to complete weapon, armor and art collections while you explore other diversions. See page 43 onward for a complete overview of the Villa management system.

Villa Art Gallery
It serves no real purpose other than an incremental step towards 100% completion, but there's something undeniably satisfying about strolling around the Villa's gallery room once all 30 masterpieces have been acquired.

USER INSTRUCTIONS

MAP: FLORENCE

PRESENT 01

SEQUENCE 01

SEQUENCE 02

MAP: TUSCANY

SEQUENCE 03

SEQUENCE 04

SEQUENCE 05

MAP: ROMAGNA

SEQUENCE 06

PRESENT 02

MAP: VENICE

SEQUENCE 07

SEQUENCE 08

SEQUENCE 09

SEQUENCE 10

SEQUENCE 11

SEQUENCE 14

PRESENT 03

Armor and Weapon Collections

You will need the Villa to generate florins at close to the maximum rate to afford all weapons and armor in a reasonable timeframe, particularly the full Missaglias set and the remarkably expensive Sword of Altaïr (sold exclusively by the Monteriggioni Blacksmith). There is one special weapon (the Condotierro War Hammer) that can only be purchased once 50 Feathers have been stored in a chest in Maria's room. We would suggest that completionists wait until after the final credits to perform the necessary scavenger hunt, then use the annotated maps in the Extras chapter to find them with (relative) ease.

Free Missions

If you have neglected them so far, give these side-missions a try. There are four types in total: Races, Beat Up events, Courier assignments and Assassination contracts. Most are short, and can be completed in no more than a few minutes; some of them offer experiences or challenges that you won't have seen during main story missions. If you have left Monteriggioni to languish in squalor until now, the florins obtained for completing Secondary Memories located in Venice will make a valuable contribution to your restoration fund.

Secret Locations

Completing the five Assassin Tomb Secondary Memories (in addition to Novella's Secret in Sequence 05) is the only way to unlock the Armor of Altaïr, which remains locked in the Sanctuary beneath the Villa until you collect Seals for each one. Even if you have little interest in the ultimate reward, these optional adventures are highly enjoyable in their own right. Players who own the Black Edition of Assassin's Creed II can also raid three Templar Lairs for fun and florins, and there is a bonus Assassin Tomb available beneath the Villa for those who sign up online to the Uplay service. The accompanying table provides page references to walkthroughs for all nine of these distinct and entertaining side-quests.

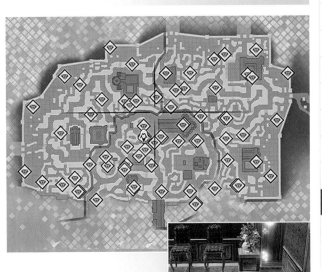

Treasure Chests

This huge endeavor is one for compulsive collectors alone. As you should know by now, Treasure Maps purchased from Art Merchants reveal the location of all Treasure Chests on designated area or district maps. There are 330 individual troves hidden throughout the game world, so this is truly no trivial undertaking. What's more, there is no ultimate reward for opening every one. Most players will consider this a futile undertaking, but we admit to feeling a sense of solidarity with those who will regard it as an irresistible compulsion…

NAME	TYPE	PAGE
Il Duomo's Secret	Assassin Tomb	53
Torre Grossa's Secret	Assassin Tomb	65
Ravaldino's Secret	Assassin Tomb	73
San Marco's Secret	Assassin Tomb	89
Visitazione's Secret	Assassin Tomb	95
Home Invasion	Templar Lair	54
Over Beams, Under Stone	Templar Lair	83
Shipwrecked	Templar Lair	103
Paying Respects	Assassin Tomb (available through Uplay website)	55

SEQUENCE 14

▮ MEMORIES 01 & 02 ▮

X MARKS THE SPOT: You must have all 30 Codex pieces to play this Memory – see page 104 for guidance if you do not have them all. With this task accomplished, visit the shops in Monteriggioni to repair armor and replenish your stocks of Medicine, Throwing Knives and Bullets.

Now enter Mario's office to meet with the assembled Brotherhood members (Fig. 1) and follow instructions. To continue, you must activate Eagle Vision and rearrange each square on the Codex Wall to form a specific picture. Feel free to solve it for yourself if you like; see "Codex Wall Solution" if you require assistance. Once satisfied with the result, approach and interact with the Piece of Eden on its pedestal to trigger a cutscene.

IN BOCCA AL LUPO: Ezio's final objective is to infiltrate the Sistine Chapel in Rome and assassinate Rodrigo Borgia. You can find a full walkthrough on the page to your right.

01

02

PRESENT 03

▮ EPILOGUE ▮

After Desmond is ejected from Ezio's world, follow Lucy down to the lower warehouse level to fight the Abstergo invaders. Desmond now has full command of his ancestor's abilities, so the baton-wielding henchmen will pose no threat at all. Desmond fights with his fists by default, so you can use Disarm to grab a weapon, but you can also tap up on the Quick Inventory Buttons to equip the Hidden Blade if deadly Counter Kills seem more appropriate (Fig. 2). There is no way to fail or "die" in this short epilogue, but be sure to continue listening as the screen fades to black. If you are curious to hear hints on what the future may hold in Assassin's Creed III (or, indeed, learn what Minerva's cryptic apocalyptic prediction might entail), the closing dialogue sequence may furnish you with tantalizing clues.

CODEX WALL SOLUTION

The first step to solving the Codex Wall is to notice that the drawing has a thin border that surrounds its outer edge. Rearrange these pieces to form a continuous line, and the rest of the puzzle will soon fall into place (Fig. 4).

04

USER INSTRUCTIONS

MAP: FLORENCE

PRESENT 01

SEQUENCE 01

SEQUENCE 02

MAP: TUSCANY

SEQUENCE 03

SEQUENCE 04

SEQUENCE 05

MAP: ROMAGNA

SEQUENCE 06

PRESENT 02

MAP: VENICE

SEQUENCE 07

SEQUENCE 08

SEQUENCE 09

SEQUENCE 10

SEQUENCE 11

SEQUENCE 14

PRESENT 03

STEP BY STEP: IN BOCCA AL LUPO

Your first task on arrival in Rome is to scale the wall. Make your way up to the hanging platform, then leap across to the hand-holds on the south face of the wall tower. At the top of these, jump to the right to grab the wooden beam (Fig. 3). Wall run to the ledge above, then traverse all the way to the left. Perform a climb leap to reach a final small hand-hold, then continue upward. You can leap over and engage the soldiers straight away, or reduce their numbers with the Assassinate from Ledge technique.

03

Pull the lever to open the gate. In the next area, the necessary lever is on a balcony in the northeast corner – but you'll need to fight your way to it. Once through the second gate, defeat the guards before you climb the tower to the west. After Ezio leaps onto the horse, gallop over the small obstacles to avoid the guards until you reach a gap in the wall. You can either dispatch the guards from horseback, or jump off and free run over to the opposite side. Either way, it may be wise to defeat all adversaries to ensure an uninterrupted climb once you reach the next tower.

The following gameplay section, encompassing several wall sections and towers, provides opportunities to use Ezio's many assassination techniques. After leaping from the final tower, you will be confronted by a large group of combatants, including Brutes and Seekers. The fight will become immeasurably easier if you Disarm and disable the guards wielding two-handed weapons first, though players who have mastered Double Hidden Blade fighting will doubtlessly achieve the same end result with well-timed Counter Kills. Climb up to the waypoint and pull the lever to open the way forward.

The next section marks a brief change in pace; Blend with the robed figures to avoid the guards in the two corridors as you make your way to the two levers. Killing the sentries is fine but it will help if Ezio isn't caught in the act.

Once inside the Sistine Chapel the easiest solution is to free run to a platform above Borgia, then perform an Air Assassination – though you could also choose to climb down to the ground and assassinate your target from behind, or even with the Pistol. This, naturally, is not the end – as the following cutscene soon confirms. Ezio uses the power of his appropriated Piece of Eden to create doppelgangers to distract the Templar leader during the fight, replicating the trick used by Al Mualim against Altaïr at the conclusion of the first Assassin's Creed. This provides opportunities to strike Borgia from behind while his attention is elsewhere. The staff he wields is a two-handed weapon, so avoid Counter Kills – and, for that matter, Disarm attempts, as neither will work. One sneaky trick is to wait until he is facing elsewhere, then unleash a quick flurry of Throwing Knives.

Once Borgia's Health Meter is depleted, a cutscene will begin. When it ends, use Eagle Vision to detect two switches, then activate both to open the way forward. In the final climatic battle between the two adversaries, follow the onscreen prompts to end the confrontation.

05

GAME COMPLETION

After the credits end, play resumes inside the Animus with Ezio standing in the attic room of the Villa Auditore (Fig. 5). You are now free to complete all Secondary Memories, find all collectibles, and obtain any Achievements or Trophies that you have yet to unlock. Consult the Extras chapter for a checklist of optional activities and accomplishments, a complete guide to Feathers and Glyphs, and a special section that recaps and analyzes the Assassin's Creed story to date.

REFERENCE & ANALYSIS | 03

THE PATH OF THE ASSASSIN IS ONE OF CONSTANT LEARNING, TRAINING, SELF-IMPROVEMENT AND ADAPTATION. IN THIS SECTION WE PROVIDE PLAYERS WITH A REFERENCE WORK OF THE GAME'S ITEMS AND ACTIONS, OFFERING IN-DEPTH ANALYSIS ON THEIR USE. WEAPONS AND EQUIPMENT HAVE BEEN TESTED FOR THEIR BEST POSSIBLE DEPLOYMENT. ENEMIES ARE REVEALED BY THEIR ARCHETYPES AND BEHAVIORS. SPECIAL MOVES ARE EXPLORED THROUGH THEIR AVAILABILITY AND POTENTIAL, WITH ADVICE ON HOW TO PERFORM THEM EFFECTIVELY. IF YOU NEED TO KNOW MORE ABOUT THE TOOLS OF THE TRADE, YOU'LL FIND THE ANSWERS HERE.

MOVES

Ezio discovers his potential over the course of the game, honing his skills with constant training. For this reason, don't be surprised if you try out moves from the list and find they don't work – yet. Some may need to be unlocked or upgraded through progression. Others may depend on having the right tools for the job.

▌MOVES OVERVIEW

CATEGORY	MOVE	XBOX 360	PS3	GUIDE DESCRIPTION	AVAILABILITY
Basic Moves	Walk / Move Character	🕹L	🕹L	Movement Stick	Sequence 01
	Look / Control Camera	🕹R	🕹R	Camera Stick	Sequence 01
	Run	Hold 🕹L + RT	Hold 🕹L + R1	Hold Movement Stick + High Profile Button	Sequence 01
	Sprint / Free Run / Jump	Hold 🕹L + RT + Ⓐ	Hold 🕹L + R1 + Ⓧ	Hold Movement Stick + High Profile Button + Legs Button	Sequence 01
	Jump Up	Hold RT, press Ⓐ	Hold R1, press Ⓧ	Hold High Profile Button, press Legs Button	Sequence 01
	Breaking A Fall (Roll On Touchdown)	Hold 🕹L forwards + RT	Hold 🕹L forwards + R1	Hold Movement Stick forwards + High Profile Button	Sequence 01
	Target Lock	LT	L1	Target Lock Button	Sequence 01
	Eagle Vision (Toggle On/Off)	Hold Ⓨ	Hold △	Hold Head Button	Sequence 01
	Speak / Hire	Ⓨ	△	Head Button	Sequence 01
	Interact (With Environment)	Ⓑ	◯	Empty Hand Button	Sequence 01
	Steal / Pickpocket	Press/hold Ⓐ	Press/hold Ⓧ	Press/hold Legs Button	Sequence 02
	Loot	Hold Ⓑ	Hold ◯	Hold Empty Hand Button	Sequence 01
	Pick Up Weapon	Ⓑ	◯	Empty Hand Button	Sequence 01
	Pick Up / Drop Dead Body	Ⓑ	◯	Empty Hand Button	Sequence 01
	Gentle Push	Hold 🕹L, press/hold Ⓑ	Hold 🕹L, press/hold ◯	Hold Movement Stick, press/hold Empty Hand Button	Sequence 01
	Shove / Tackle	Hold 🕹L + RT, press/hold Ⓑ	Hold 🕹L + R1, press/hold ◯	Hold Movement Stick + High Profile Button, press/hold Empty Hand Button	Sequence 01
	Throw Money	Ⓧ	☐	Weapon Hand Button	Sequence 01
	Quick Inventory	✛	✛	Quick Inventory Buttons	Sequence 01
	Weapon Selector	Hold RB, select with 🕹L	Hold R2, select with 🕹L	Hold Weapon Selector Button, select with Movement Stick	Sequence 01
Climbing Moves	Start Climbing	Hold 🕹L + RT + Ⓐ	Hold 🕹L + R1 + Ⓧ	Hold Movement Stick + High Profile Button + Legs Button	Sequence 01
	Climb	🕹L	🕹L	Movement Stick	Sequence 01
	Drop / Let Go	Ⓑ	◯	Empty Hand Button	Sequence 01
	Grasp (When Falling)	Ⓑ	◯	Empty Hand Button	Sequence 01
	Climb Leap / Jump From Ledge	Hold 🕹L + RT + Ⓐ	Hold 🕹L + R1 + Ⓧ	Hold Movement Stick + High Profile Button + Legs Button	Sequence 01
	Synchronize Map	Ⓨ	△	Head Button	Sequence 01
	Leap of Faith	🕹L + RT + Ⓐ	🕹L + R1 + Ⓧ	Movement Stick + High Profile Button + Legs Button	Sequence 01
Combat Moves	Enter / Exit Fight Mode	LT	L1	Target Lock Button	Sequence 01
	Attack (Fistfight / Melee Weapon)	Ⓧ	☐	Weapon Hand Button	Sequence 01
	Combo	Ⓧ, then Ⓧ again as the previous attack is about to make contact with the enemy	☐, then ☐ again as the previous attack is about to make contact with the enemy	Weapon Hand Button, then Weapon Hand Button again as the previous attack is about to make contact with the enemy	Sequence 01
	Attack (Ranged Weapon)	Tap Ⓧ (Throwing Knife) / Hold, then release Ⓧ (Pistol)	Tap ☐ (Throwing Knife) / Hold, then release ☐ (Pistol)	Tap Weapon Hand Button (Throwing Knife) / Hold, then release Weapon Hand Button (Pistol)	Throwing Knife: Sequence 03 / Pistol: Sequence 09
	Special Techniques	Hold, then release Ⓧ	Hold, then release ☐	Hold, then release Weapon Hand Button	Throw Sand: Sequence 01; other special techniques: Training Ground
	Block / Deflect	Hold RT	Hold R1	Hold High Profile Button	Sequence 01
	Dodge	Ⓐ	Ⓧ	Legs Button	Sequence 03
	Counter Kill (With Weapon Equipped)	Hold RT, press Ⓧ when the enemy attacks	Hold R1, press ☐ when the enemy attacks	Hold High Profile Button, press Weapon Hand Button when the enemy attacks	Sequence 03
	Disarm (With No Weapon Equipped)	Hold RT, press Ⓧ when the enemy attacks	Hold R1, press ☐ when the enemy attacks	Hold High Profile Button, press Weapon Hand Button when the enemy attacks	Sequence 03
	Deflect Counter	Hold and immediately release RT, press Ⓧ as the deflect sparks appear	Hold and immediately release R1, press ☐ as the deflect sparks appear	Hold and immediately release High Profile Button, press Weapon Hand Button as the deflect sparks appear	Sequence 01

HOW TO PLAY

WALKTHROUGH

REFERENCE & ANALYSIS

EXTRAS

MOVES

WEAPONS

EQUIPMENT

SHOPS

ENEMIES

CATEGORY	MOVE	XBOX 360	PS3	GUIDE DESCRIPTION	AVAILABILITY
Combat Moves	Grab Opponent	B	O	Empty Hand Button	Sequence 01
	Taunt	Y	△	Head Button	Sequence 01
	Throw (While Holding Opponent)	B	O	Empty Hand Button	Sequence 01
	Headbutt (While Unarmed and Holding Opponent)	Y	△	Head Button	Sequence 01
	Knee (While Unarmed and Holding Opponent)	A	✕	Legs Button	Sequence 01
	Kill (While Holding Opponent, Weapon Equipped)	X	□	Weapon Hand Button	Sequence 01
	Finish Off Enemy On Ground (With Weapon Equipped)	X	□	Weapon Hand Button	Sequence 01
	Escape Fight	Hold L + RT + A	Hold L + R1 + ✕	Hold Movement Stick + High Profile Button + Legs Button	Sequence 01
Assassination Moves	Assassinate	X	□	Weapon Hand Button	Sequence 01
	Assassinate With Throwing Knife	Hold LT, press X	Hold L1, press □	Hold Target Lock Button, press Weapon Hand Button	Sequence 03
	Assassinate With Pistol	Hold LT, hold and release X (the longer the press, the more precise the aiming)	Hold L1, hold and release □ (the longer the press, the more precise the aiming)	Hold Target Lock Button, hold and release Weapon Hand Button (the longer the press, the more precise the aiming)	Sequence 03
	Assassinate From Ledge	X	□	Weapon Hand Button	Sequence 04
	Assassinate From Hiding	Hold LT, press X	Hold L1, press □	Hold Target Lock Button, press Weapon Hand Button	Sequence 04
	Air Assassinate	X	□	Weapon Hand Button	Sequence 04
	Assassinate With Poison	X	□	Weapon Hand Button	Sequence 05
Swimming Moves	Swim	L	L	Movement Stick	Sequence 01
	Swim The Crawl	Hold L + RT	Hold L + R1	Hold Movement Stick + High Profile Button	Sequence 01
	Fast Swim	Hold L + RT + A	Hold L + R1 + ✕	Hold Movement Stick + High Profile Button + Legs Button	Sequence 01
	Submerge	Hold A	Hold ✕	Hold Legs Button	Sequence 01
	Dive	Hold L + RT + A to jump, then press A	Hold L + R1 + ✕ to jump, then press ✕	Hold Movement Stick + High Profile Button + Legs Button, then press Legs Button	Sequence 01
	Climb Out Of Water	L + RT + A	L + R1 + ✕	Movement Stick + High Profile Button + Legs Button	Sequence 01
Horse Controls	Mount	L	L	Movement Stick	Sequence 01
	Dismount	B	O	Empty Hand Button	Sequence 01
	Trot	L	L	Movement Stick	Sequence 01
	Walk	L + A	L + ✕	Movement Stick + Legs Button	Sequence 01
	Gallop	L + RT	L + R1	Movement Stick + High Profile Button	Sequence 01
	Fast Gallop / Jump	L + RT + A	L + R1 + ✕	Movement Stick + High Profile Button + Legs Button	Sequence 01
	Rear (In Trot Or Walk Speed)	X	□	Weapon Hand Button	Sequence 01
	Use Weapon	X	□	Weapon Hand Button	Sequence 01
Carriage Controls	Steer	L	L	Movement Stick	Sequence 06
	Escape From Enemy Grab	Rapidly tap B	Rapidly tap O	Rapidly tap Empty Hand Button	Sequence 06
Gondola Controls	Enter Rowing Position	B	O	Empty Hand Button	Sequence 06
	Exit Rowing Position	A	✕	Legs Button	Sequence 06
	Steer	L	L	Movement Stick	Sequence 06
	Row	B (repeatedly)	O (repeatedly)	Empty Hand Button (repeatedly)	Sequence 06
Flying Machine Controls	Steer	← L →	← L →	← Movement Stick →	Sequence 08
	Gain Altitude / Nose Up	L ↓	L ↓	Movement Stick Down	Sequence 08
	Dive / Nose Down	L ↑	L ↑	Movement Stick Up	Sequence 08
	Kick	Hold LT	Hold L1	Hold Target Lock Button	Sequence 08
Camera & Interface	Center Camera	R (press)	R3	Center Camera Button	Sequence 01
	First-Person Camera	R (press)	L3	First-Person Button	Sequence 01
	Contextual Camera (Point Of Interest)	Hold LB	Hold L2	Hold Contextual Camera Button	Sequence 01
	Display Map / Access Database	BACK	SELECT	Map Button	Sequence 01
	Pause Menu	START	START	Pause Button	Sequence 01

111

■ SPECIAL MOVES ■

Surviving against tougher opponents requires skill and finesse. This section details some of the most noteworthy abilities listed on the previous double page that Ezio will need to utilize to follow in his father's footsteps.

DIVING

To dive, the player must make a jump over a large body of water. Once in the air, another press of the Legs Button will turn the jump into a dive (Fig. 1). This action only becomes available when Ezio is over water.

If you keep the Legs Button held rather than tap it to go into a dive, Ezio will stay under the water once submerged and can swim concealed for a short distance until he needs to catch breath.

01

LOOTING

To Loot is to search a dead body for florins. It also covers the act of opening a Treasure Chest to take the contents. Once in position, you must keep the Empty Hand Button held until the Looting is successful. This action takes five seconds, and if you are interrupted before the Looting icon fills then you will need to start again. Bodies and chests will surrender their entire inventory when searched and cannot be looted again.

STEALING

As long as he is in low profile and not in Fight Mode, Ezio can pick the pockets of other citizens by bumping into them. Aim to brush past your target, during which you will grab their purse. You'll receive instant onscreen notification of the number of florins stolen. Once you have relieved somebody of their purse, further successful attempts will not find any more money on their person.

◆ Victims will check their pockets and raise the alarm after a short period, causing a commotion.

◆ There are two classes of victims. The poor carry less florins and react slowly to being robbed (eight seconds). The rich, generally worth more, will only take three seconds to notice that they are missing such a heavy purse.

THROW MONEY

By selecting his purse as the Weapon Hand item, Ezio can throw his money to cause a distraction among the city's poor. While citizens scramble for coins, blocking the streets, the line of sight of enemy guards is reduced by 50% and is directed toward the crowd.

◆ Each throw costs 10 florins and draws citizens from within 15 meters.

◆ Harassers are influenced by the money, making this a good way to get rid of them.

◆ Coins can be thrown from above into the streets below.

◆ The crowd drawn can be used to blend in.

◆ Workers will drop their tools, including a broom that you can pick up and brandish as a weapon.

LEAP OF FAITH

Viewpoints aside, you'll be alerted to the location of a new Leap of Faith by the cooing of the pigeons that flock to them. Thereafter, the spot will remain marked by bird droppings. Performing the move itself cues a fearless diving animation and it serves three excellent functions:

◆ A quick return from high viewpoints to ground level without manual descent.

◆ Instant access to a hiding spot when being pursued.

◆ Dropping you into an ambush location when stalking a target below.

HOW TO PLAY

WALKTHROUGH

REFERENCE &
ANALYSIS

EXTRAS

MOVES

WEAPONS

EQUIPMENT

SHOPS

ENEMIES

DISARM

While unarmed and blocking, Ezio can disarm enemies and steal their weapon (Fig. 2) by timing a press of the Weapon Hand button when the enemy tries to attack (in other words before their attack actually hits you). The disarmed opponent is severely disadvantaged thereafter.

◆ The timing is the same as the Counter Kill (see below).

◆ The window of opportunity to perform this move is shorter against enemy leaders.

◆ The weapon is set to the unarmed slot in Ezio's inventory. A small or medium weapon can be kept and sheathed if Ezio doesn't already have one.

02

COUNTER KILL

When the enemy attacks with a melee weapon, Ezio can counter from a blocking stance by timing a press of the Weapon Hand button just before the blocking actually occurs.

◆ This move and its timing is the same as Disarm but using a weapon.

◆ Success depends on the rank and stamina of the opponent.

◆ Only Long and Heavy weapons (and the Hidden Blade) can counter Long and Heavy weapons. Counter Kill is the technique to learn if you're to take on higher level enemies whose blocking abilities rival Ezio's. You can draw out a defensive fighter with a Taunt and be ready with this move.

DEFLECT COUNTER

The Deflect Counter allows you to break through an opponent's defense a fraction of a second after successfully blocking an attack. As soon as sparks appear to register that a hit has made contact with Ezio's weapon, immediately release the High Profile Button and tap the Weapon Hand Button to perform a swift (and often unblockable) riposte.

The Deflect Counter can only be performed while Ezio is holding a weapon. The timing is delicate, but is easy to predict with a little practice.

The blow landed is not especially powerful, but it's effective when employed to wear down stronger opponents in large brawls. It can also be used to create an opening for combos against highly defensive enemies.

DODGE

Ezio darts away from an attack in the direction determined by the Movement Stick (Fig. 3). Once locked on, hold the High Profile Button to enter a blocking stance and hit the Legs Button when the enemy attacks.

◆ Like a Counter Kill, this is another move which must be timed to respond to the enemy's attack.

◆ Use the Movement Stick to jump backward or forward, or sidestep left or right. Up close, the sidestep can put you beside the enemy at an angle they can't block.

◆ If you don't block, pressing the Legs button will perform a Strafe evasion instead. This can be done at any time but Ezio may not avoid the hit.

03

TAUNT

The Taunt prompts the targeted enemy into immediate aggressive attack, breaking their defense and creating opportunities for a counter or block. It can be used repeatedly throughout a fight. There are two tips you need to know:

◆ You can initiate a Taunt while holding the High Profile Button, meaning a quicker transition to a Counter Kill when the injured party retaliates.

◆ You may cancel a Taunt by attacking.

DOUBLE ASSASSINATE

Double Assassination is enabled when Ezio takes possession of the Double Hidden Blades during Sequence 04.

◆ The targets must be within two meters of each other.

◆ Both must meet the criteria for assassination. If only one can be slain, a different assassination move will be used.

◆ This devastating technique relies on the player's positioning and ability to get in close – instantly taking out guards on either side of a door, for instance (Fig. 4). A disadvantage is that you can easily slay civilians caught up in the fray.

04

ASSASSINATE FROM HIDING

This assassination technique uses the Hidden Blade and will work for a locked or unlocked target. You will need to find a hiding spot from the following:

◆ A well.

◆ A pile of straw, herbs or leaves (both inside carts and loose on the ground).

◆ A rooftop shelter.

◆ A bench.

A low profile attack stabs the target and pulls them into the hiding spot (Fig. 5). In a high profile attack, Ezio will leap out of hiding and deliver a swift, bloody stab.

05

ASSASSINATE WITH POISON

Having equipped your Poison Blade, this special move must be performed in low profile to count as a Poison assassination. The toxin prevents the victim reacting instantly, so the assassination will not be spotted unless it is in the line of sight of a witness within three meters. This makes it possible for you to leave the scene before your crime is discovered (Fig. 6). In any case, the crowd's attention will be diverted by the victim going berserk and finally collapsing. It's not a pleasant or merciful death but it creates a useful commotion.

After the attempt, you will automatically equip your Hidden Blade in place of your Poison Blade. Every assassination attempt, even a failed one, consumes one dose of Poison. For more information on the acquisition and effects of Poison, turn to page 121.

06

ASSASSINATE FROM LEDGE

This assassination technique uses the Hidden Blade and requires Ezio to be clinging to the wall below the ledge where the target stands. You do not need to lock on to the target to use this move, so it can be tagged smoothly and instantly onto the end of a free run, leap or climb.

A low profile attack pulls the target over the ledge, so that they plummet to the ground below (Fig. 7). If there are crowds around, they will react to the dead body. Enemy guards in the vicinity will investigate.

In a high profile attack, Ezio will leap up onto the ledge to strike the target dead on the spot. Crowds will flee the commotion and nearby enemy guards will enter Fight Mode.

Tactically, this technique proves its worth in areas guarded by rooftop archers. Observe their patrols, pick a wall from which to ambush them and choose between high and low profile to place the body where it will attract the least attention.

07

AIR ASSASSINATE

This technique requires the Hidden Blade to be equipped, and will work on a locked or unlocked target. With the Double Hidden Blades, it is possible to air assassinate two close targets in one strike.

To perform an air assassination, Ezio must be on a ledge or perch overlooking the target. On pressing the Weapon Hand Button, he will leap into the air above this victim before dropping like a hawk, pinning them to the ground (Fig. 8). If the move does not work then you are likely to be either too close or too high for the jump. Even so, it doubles as an effective way to reach the ground instantly from a considerable height and without taking damage, ready to surprise surviving enemies.

08

ASSASSINATE ENEMY ON GROUND

Ezio will deliver an instant kill if he attacks an enemy on the ground with any weapon (Fig. 9). For the purpose of this death blow, an enemy is considered to be on the ground when either lying down or just starting to get up. In any other position, normal damage will be inflicted.

This is extremely useful against armored foes who would otherwise put up a long fight. And what if your opponent isn't on the ground? Try using the Grab and Throw moves if in Fight Mode. You could also attempt a running Tackle at them and hit the Empty Hand Button to wrestle them to the floor.

09

ASSASSINATE WITH PISTOL

The Pistol isn't a quick-draw dueling weapon but it does have a one-shot kill and a superior range, only limited by your ability to lock on. While aiming the shot, during which the line of fire slowly focuses on the target (Fig. 10), you will not be able to move. So you should really think of it as a Renaissance gadget: plan with it, as you would with a sniper rifle in other games, to take down guards who might easily raise the alert before you can get in close.

10

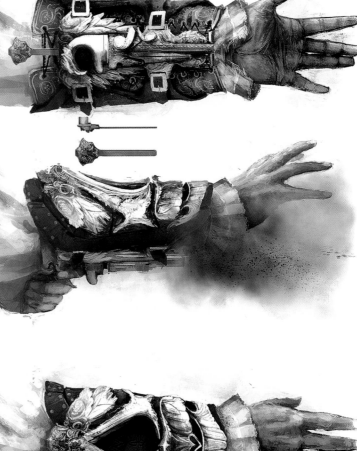

HOW TO PLAY

WALKTHROUGH

REFERENCE & ANALYSIS

EXTRAS

MOVES

WEAPONS

EQUIPMENT

SHOPS

ENEMIES

WEAPONS

While it is desirable for the Assassin to travel light and unencumbered, there may be instances when Ezio will need to use the weapons of his enemies against them. This section covers myriad means of permanent dispatch, also noting how they might best be countered by those who must face them.

▌MELEE WEAPONS

From the thief's dagger to the soldier's polearm, every weapon has three determining characteristics – Damage, Speed and Deflect. These attributes will influence the interaction between combatants and the consequence of each attack. The nature of the wielders themselves will also play a part in determining attack strength and speed.

◆ **Damage:** A weapon's Damage attribute acts as a multiplier for the attack strength.

◆ **Speed:** Determines the attack speed. The higher the value, the faster the attack.

◆ **Deflect:** Affects the recovery time of the enemy whose attack is deflected by Ezio. The higher the value, the longer the enemy will take to recover.

Special Techniques: Note that training (at Villa Auditore's Training Ground) in the advanced aspects of the different weapon categories will grant Ezio the power to make use of special techniques. These are charged moves that will take time to prepare but which have powerful and devastating consequences when unleashed.

FISTS

For those who enjoy a good brawl, Ezio's fist fighting techniques remain effective throughout the game. Unarmed combat is surprisingly effective even against the toughest enemies. Sacrificing a weapon's defensiveness for the speed and proximity of the martial artist is the best way to tackle wielders of Long and Heavy weapons.

FISTS ATTRIBUTES

NAME	DAMAGE	SPEED	DEFLECT	AVAILABILITY
Fists	✱	✱✱✱✱✱	✱	–

Special Technique: Throw Sand

While in Fight Mode, unarmed and standing on the ground, hold the Weapon Hand Button to bend down and pick up a fistful of dirt. Keep it held until the foe is close enough, then release to throw sand in their face and break their defense (Fig. 1). You can't move until you've thrown but you can temporarily blind more than one aggressor.

◆ Combine this with the Quick Inventory Buttons for a speedy weapon assassination by arming yourself immediately after the throw.

◆ Alternatively, step in closer and use the unarmed finishing moves.

HIDDEN BLADE

Your father's secret weapon and evidence of his true nature, repaired and upgraded by Leonardo da Vinci from a series of Codex design documents. The device consists of an arm mounting, like a bracer, from which the assassin can extend a double-edged blade for stabbing and slashing. When not in use it remains hidden inside the sleeve.

The Hidden Blade is required to perform many Assassination techniques, as it enables Ezio to strike invisibly and to hold or pin his enemies in place.

HIDDEN BLADE PROPERTIES

	NAME	DESCRIPTION	AVAILABILITY
	Hidden Blade	Enables Assassination techniques.	Sequence 02, Memory 03
	Hidden Blade Armor Plate	Deflect weapons with the Weapon Hand.	Sequence 03, Memory 02
	Double Blade	Hidden Blades in both hands. Enables Double Assassination techniques.	Sequence 04, Memory 01
	Poison Blade	Second blade for the Empty Hand. Enables Assassination by Poison.	Sequence 05, Memory 07
	Pistol	Firearm added to the Empty Hand.	Sequence 09, Memory 01

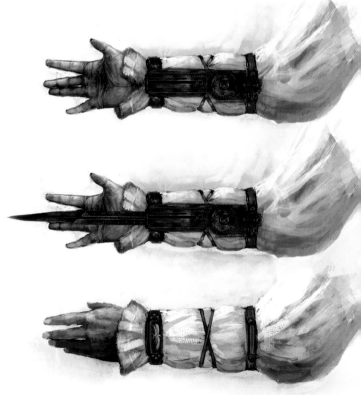

HOW TO PLAY

WALKTHROUGH

REFERENCE & ANALYSIS

EXTRAS

MOVES

WEAPONS

EQUIPMENT

SHOPS

ENEMIES

SMALL WEAPON ATTRIBUTES

	NAME	DAMAGE	SPEED	DEFLECT	PRICE (f)	AVAILABILITY
	Dagger	*	*	**	500	Sequence 03
	Knife	*	**	***	1,300	Sequence 03
	Stilleto	**	****	*	2,200	Sequence 04
	Channeled Cinquedea	***	***	****	4,100	Sequence 05
	Sultan's Knife	***	*****	***	4,300	Sequence 06
	Butcher Knife	****	***	*****	6,400	Sequence 07
	Notched Cinquedea	*****	*****	****	9,300	Sequence 08
	Metal Cestus	***	*****	*	2,000	Sequence 06

<table>
<tr><td>

SMALL WEAPONS
</td></tr>
</table>

The short blade demonstrates that weapon length does matter. A Counter Kill with a small weapon against a sword will frequently see the enemy jump clear of the return blow. But what's lost in range is gained in speed, with the dagger able to move fastest against other weapons.

MEDIUM WEAPON ATTRIBUTES

	NAME	DAMAGE	SPEED	DEFLECT	PRICE (f)	AVAILABILITY
	Common Sword	*	**	**	-	Sequence 03
	Venetian Falchion	*	***	*	1,900	Sequence 03
	Mercenario War Hammer	*	*	***	1,900	Sequence 03
	Old Syrian Sword	*	**	***	2,300	Sequence 03
	Maul	**	*	**	3,600	Sequence 04
	Captain's Sword	**	****	***	5,200	Sequence 05
	Florentine Falchion	**	***	****	5,200	Sequence 05
	Flanged Mace	***	***	***	10,500	Sequence 06
	Scimitar	***	***	*****	11,300	Sequence 06
	Milanese Sword	***	*****	***	11,300	Sequence 07
	Cavalieri Mace	****	**	**	20,800	Sequence 07
	Schiavona	****	*****	****	25,000	Sequence 08
	Sword of Altaïr	*****	*****	*****	50,000	Sequence 09 (Villa, see page 94)
	Condottiero War Hammer	*****	***	****	35,000	Collect 50 Feathers (see page 148)

MEDIUM WEAPONS

The most common sidearms equipped by the city guard are the swords and maces that fall into this category. Bludgeoning weapons are especially effective at breaking through an enemy's defense and will make short work of Agiles wielding Small weapons.

HEAVY WEAPONS

These are edged weapons that rely more on their size and sheer force to inflict bone-breaking damage. When swung with sufficient strength they smash through attempts to parry them with smaller weapons. Opponents caught under the full weight of the blow may collapse and even drop their weapons. Heavy weapons can only be countered by Long or Heavy weapons (with the Hidden Blade being an exception, as it can counter any weapon, though the timing involved makes the maneuver more difficult and thus risky). Counters with these powerful weapons are always lethal to the target, but you will leave the weapon in the victim's body (so use this on the most dangerous enemies only to maximize the effect).

HEAVY WEAPON ATTRIBUTES

NAME	DAMAGE	SPEED	DEFLECT	AVAILABILITY
Bastard Sword	★★★	★★★★	★★★	Obtained from enemies wielding them
Bearded Axe	★★★★	★★★	★★★★	
Labrys	★★★★★	★★★	★★★	

Special Technique: Smash Skill

The Smash Skill is acquired from Training and enables the Smash Attack when a Heavy weapon is equipped. A Smash takes a long time to build up, during which the player is vulnerable to interruption by attacks that will cancel the move. But when a fully charged Smash connects, it breaks through enemy defenses to cause a large amount of damage and further effects (Fig. 2). It cannot be parried, and the victim will be disarmed, knocked to the ground, or may have a Long weapon broken.

The Smash is activated when the Weapon Hand Button is released. Ezio can thus hold a charged Smash until sure that the enemy is in range.

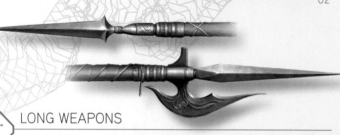

02

LONG WEAPONS

This covers the category of Spears and Halberds. The length of the haft keeps enemies at bay and makes it very difficult to evade. Dodging maneuvers against Halbardiers frequently fail to make sufficient distance, while blocks are overpowered. Long weapons can only be countered by Long or Heavy weapons (again with the Hidden Blade being an exception, as it can counter any weapon, though the timing involved makes the maneuver more difficult and thus risky).

LONG WEAPON ATTRIBUTES

NAME	DAMAGE	SPEED	DEFLECT	AVAILABILITY
Spear	★★★	★★★★★	★★★	Obtained from enemies wielding them
Halberd	★★★★	★★★	★★★★	

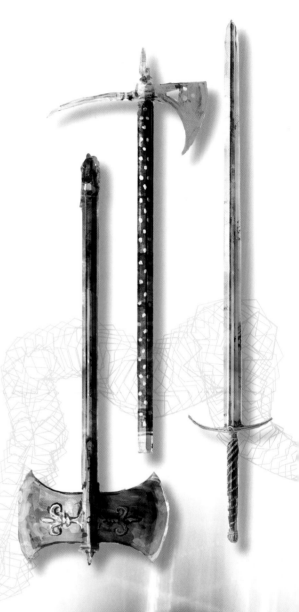

Special Technique: Sweep Attack

The Sweep is another charged move that can be interrupted, but one that can be unleashed at any time during the charge. The longer the Sweep is charged, the greater the arc it will affect. Acquired from Training, it is an attack that requires a Long weapon.

A brief hold of the Weapon Hand Button performs a quick short Sweep. Keep it held and Ezio will turn with the Long shaft over his shoulder, changing stance in readiness to perform a long Sweep spin when released (Fig. 3). Enemies in front of him will trip and fall to the ground, while those behind are knocked over by a blow to the head. Sweeping more than three times with the same Long weapon will cause it to break.

03

Special Technique: Long Weapon Breaking

It is possible to block a Smash attack with a Long weapon. The defender will avoid all damage but the parrying weapon will shatter in two. When a Long weapon breaks, the owner may continue to wield the remaining half as if it were a bladed Medium weapon (Fig. 4).

04

COMBOS

To build a Combo of moves instead of making single attacks, you need to time your button presses so that each attack begins as the last is concluding. Every weapon has a maximum chain or Combo length determined by its type. A successful, uninterrupted perfect Combo attack will stun the recipient on the final strike: this will leave them defenceless and open to an instant kill (Fig. 5).

05

COMBO ATTRIBUTES

WEAPON TYPE	MAXIMUM COMBO
Fists	5 Hits
Small	5 Hits
Medium	4 Hits
Heavy	3 Hits
Long	3 Hits
Ranged	No Combo

HOW TO PLAY

WALKTHROUGH

REFERENCE & ANALYSIS

EXTRAS

MOVES

WEAPONS

EQUIPMENT

SHOPS

ENEMIES

RANGED WEAPONS

The Assassin is never shy of innovation and the profession willingly experiments with the new discoveries of the age in the interests of enhancing its capabilities. Ezio will call upon several such devices in the pursuit of his extraordinary destiny.

Many items are one-shot in nature, consumed when used or requiring refills, and the player must purchase each round or refill individually. Carrying capacity may be increased by purchasing bigger Belts and Pouches from the storekeepers.

SMOKE BOMBS

The Smoke Bomb is a weapon of confusion and a means of escape (Fig. 6). The sound of the exploding charge causes a 15 meter audible commotion among the citizens that will redirect the attention of guards. The smoke expands rapidly to a four meter radius and lasts eight seconds, granting Ezio a chance to flee or perform some other act.

06

Those caught in the cloud will experience detrimental effects:

◆ Anyone inside or entering the cloud will be dazed until it clears.
◆ Dazed guards are considered to be blind, stunned and unable to move or fight.
◆ Guards will recover if knocked outside the cloud by the player.

Any guard who sees Ezio throwing a Smoke Bomb will consider it a reprehensible act and pursue. And while citizens will avoid the smoke, guards will enter it if their patrol route or their sense of duty demands it.

Ezio receives this weapon during Sequence 05, and can carry a maximum of three Smoke Bombs at the same time.

THROWING KNIVES

Throwing Knives are held in a concealed belt, which they can be flicked from very quickly. However, the proper way to use this weapon is to lock on to a target and take aim slowly (Fig. 7): this will cause an instant kill in the first half of the game; two to three Knives will be necessary afterwards. Maximum useful locking distance for the Throwing Knife is 20 meters – you can't throw any further than that.

07

Over the course of the game, you may upgrade to bigger belts from the Tailor to increase the number of Throwing Knives you can carry, up to a maximum of 25.

KNIFE BELT UPGRADES

NAME	CAPACITY	PRICE (f)	AVAILABILITY
Small Knife Belt	10	–	Sequence 03
Medium Knife Belt	+5	3,000	Sequence 06
Large Knife Belt	+5	6,000	Sequence 09
Extra-Large Knife Belt	+5	–	Uplay website

Special Technique: Flying Knives Skill

This skill is learned through Training and becomes available when the character is equipped with Throwing Knives. Holding down the Weapon Hand Button prepares a special technique that grants Ezio the power to simultaneously hurl up to five Knives at multiple targets with deadly accuracy (Fig. 8). Charging the move for longer increases the number of enemies targeted and extends the accurate distance within which targets can be included.

Like all charging techniques, the Flying Knives Skill leaves Ezio open to attacks and interruptions that will abort the move before it is ready to execute.

08

PISTOL

This discreet addition to your Hidden Blade arm is a far cry from the heavy hand-cannons that would be carried by Florentine *archibusieri* in major military campaigns. Leonardo's stealthy interpretation of the design is aimed from the wrist and requires three seconds to reload. Its bullet capacity cannot be upgraded.

PISTOL ATTRIBUTES

NAME	CAPACITY	AVAILABILITY
Pistol	6	Sequence 09

To fire the Pistol, you must first lock on to a target within 20 meters and keep the Weapon Hand Button held until the line-of-sight indicator is focused as a single beam (Fig. 9). The longer it is aimed, the more accurate the shot, though obstacles will block it. The probability of a successful strike decreases over distance but a hit will result in an instant kill.

09

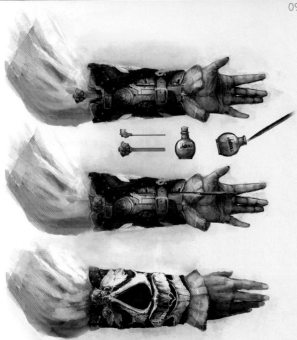

Special Technique: Intimidate

This ability is only available when the Pistol is equipped. If the player is locked on and keeps the Weapon Hand Button held, he will continue to point his gun at the enemy without firing. This will gradually decrease the enemy's morale until they turn and flee, although the shootist will be completely vulnerable to interruption and attack during this stand-off. Actually firing the Pistol will also lower the morale of every fighter present.

POISON

Poison must be used with the Poison Blade acquired in Sequence 05, Memory 07. It can be acquired from any Doctor for 250 florins. To increase the number of doses that you can carry, you can purchase up to two upgrades.

POISON VIAL UPGRADES

NAME	CAPACITY	PRICE (*f*)	AVAILABILITY
Small Poison Vial	3	-	Sequence 05
Medium Poison Vial	6	3,000	Sequence 07
Large Poison Vial	9	6,000	Sequence 10

The symptoms of Poison are as dramatic as they are unpleasant. The victim stumbles around uncontrollably at first, clutching at passing strangers, as the insinuative dose quickly passes through the bloodstream. After 15 seconds they will shout and flail their arms crazily and attack anyone in the vicinity (Fig. 10), brandishing a weapon if they have one. At this point they will attract the attention of the crowd and the guards, but another 15 seconds later they will collapse and die.

10

Poisoned enemies are oblivious to their environment and may spare themselves a longer death by walking off rooftops or bridges in their delirium. Because their demise is often witnessed by many, the public sight of the fallen corpse does not generate a suspicious reaction afterwards.

MEDICINE

The city's street Doctor provides on-the-spot healing for a base price of 50 florins, but he is also a pharmacist of sorts. He will sell healing Medicine under the category of Apothecary Supplies. Each dose will cure your injuries but is consumed in the process.

To use your Medicine, all you have to do is press left with the Quick Inventory Buttons. This will automatically use the item without changing your equipped weapon.

You can carry more Medicine by purchasing larger Pouches over the course of the game. These are available from the Tailor.

MEDICINE POUCH UPGRADES

NAME	CAPACITY	PRICE (*f*)	AVAILABILITY
Small Medicine Pouch	5	-	Sequence 01
Medium Medicine Pouch	10	3,000	Sequence 01
Large Medicine Pouch	15	6,000	Sequence 01

HOW TO PLAY

WALKTHROUGH

REFERENCE & ANALYSIS

EXTRAS

MOVES

WEAPONS

EQUIPMENT

SHOPS

ENEMIES

EQUIPMENT

Your initial expenses are likely to include precautionary Medicine from the local Doctors, as any worthwhile attempt at exploration and experimentation will involve a few hard knocks. Progression will involve purchases of weapons, but more importantly for this section, armor and upgrades that soon start demanding further expenditure through their need of regular Repair at a Blacksmith's.

To be able to afford such spending, you will naturally need to secure yourself a steady source of income. This can be achieved through the following ways:

◆ **Mission Rewards:** You can earn a cash reward by successfully completing missions (main Memories) and performing the free mission side-quests (Secondary Memories). The amount on offer varies according to the challenge or even as an aspect of the storyline. See page 144 in the Extras chapter for complete free missions checklists.

◆ **Looting:** You are swiftly introduced to the concept of looting bodies in Sequence 01, following the first street fight. Once Ezio begins to ply his father's trade, there will be countless opportunities to remind the dead that they can't take it with them.

◆ **Stealing:** Paola, the Madame of the Florentine brothel, will teach you how to pick pockets in Sequence 02. A keen eye for fashion will also be an advantage in identifying those with heavier purses and florins to spare. Indeed there are two classes of victims, poor and rich, who carry amounts of money that reflect their social status.

◆ **Treasures:** You will find chests hidden throughout the city. If you don't want to bother looking for them, Art Merchants sell Treasure Maps that ultimately lead to

01

most of these cash rewards. Some of the largest finds are kept inside the houses of the nobility and are well guarded.

◆ **Borgia Messengers:** Throughout the game, both in the cities and on the road, the player will encounter messengers running errands for the Borgias. Although they can be easily missed in a crowd, these agents may be identified by their Social Status Indicator (Fig. 1). More importantly, they will be transporting taxes and fees in the pursuit of commerce and other, more conspiratorial interests. Ezio may choose to interrupt this business by performing his own. Looting the body will reveal a tidy sum of 1,500 florins, plus whatever small change belonged to the messenger personally.

◆ **Villa Auditore:** The family Villa at Monteriggioni may have fallen into disrepair but investment in the local economy will yield income over time. Ezio may then return to the Villa to claim a regular stipend for his efforts. Turn to page 43 for more information.

HEALTH AND EQUIPMENT

The Health Meter in the top left of your HUD comprises a string of white Health Squares that indicate Ezio's current health. Ezio starts with five Health Squares. He will receive a permanent extra Health Square as a reward every time he deciphers four "Philosophical" Codex Pages (see page 34 for more information). However, wearing armor also adds to the Health Meter, representing the protection it provides.

Armor is rated by the number of Health Squares it adds to the Health Meter, from one to six. Equipping the best armor that you can purchase from the Blacksmith will thus result in a significant increase of your Health Meter.

Each piece of armor also has a Resistance value that indicates how much damage it can soak up. This is represented in the game's inventory screens by a certain number of stars, but our tables reveal the underlying Hit Point values.

Every blow endured affects every piece of armor worn. For every Hit Point of damage Ezio suffers, each of his pieces of armor will take a point of damage. When the damage reaches or exceeds the Resistance value, the armor will be broken. Once broken, the Health Squares provided by a given piece of armor appear on the Health Meter as red blocks (Fig. 2); it then requires the Repair services of a Blacksmith (for more on this, see page 128).

HOW TO PLAY

WALKTHROUGH

REFERENCE & ANALYSIS

EXTRAS

MOVES

WEAPONS

EQUIPMENT

SHOPS

ENEMIES

HEALTH SQUARE STATUS

ICON	SYMPTOM	REMEDY
◇	Health Square: full	-
◈	Health Square: half-empty	Avoid taking further damage for eight seconds.
◆	Health Square: empty	Have a Doctor heal you, or use Medicine.
◆	Health Square: damaged armor	Have the corresponding piece of Armor repaired by a Blacksmith.

INJURY AND DEATH

Each Health Square represents a certain amount of Hit Points in the underlying combat system. A Health Square can thus be only partially emptied by a weak attack such as a punch, for instance. If the player avoids taking further damage for eight seconds, the last block that is incomplete but not fully empty will regenerate to a full white Health Square.

Ezio can also be injured by falling. His agility allows him to drop distances of under eight meters safely, and pushing forward on the Movement Stick will prompt him to roll on touchdown for a safe landing from 12 meters. Otherwise, he will sustain damage based on the height of the fall:

◆ 30% of total Health lost when falling over 8 meters.

◆ 50% of total Health lost when falling over 12 meters.

◆ 75% of total Health lost when falling over 16 meters.

◆ Death occurs after falling 20 meters or more.

Ezio cannot die unless he is hurt further after being reduced to zero Hit Points, where he enters a Critical State indicated by the screen flashing red and white. An injury in this condition will kill him, but if he manages to avoid further damage for five seconds then one Health Square will be restored to his bar.

02

ARMOR TYPES

Ezio starts out in ordinary clothes of the period but he will get the chance to equip pieces of contemporary armor as the game progresses. There are four slots for armor, covering the arms, legs, shoulders and chest (Fig. 3). There are also four levels of upgrade that relate to the materials from which the armor is wrought, each surpassing the previous type, plus one secret bonus armor that cannot be purchased from merchants.

Levels 2 and 4 are named after famous historical families of armorers, the Helmschmieds and the Missaglias, to underline their craftsmanship. Note that there is no calculation of hit location when determining damage to Ezio or his armor, so the four slots should really be thought of as a chance to collect up to four pieces of armor for a cumulative Health Meter bonus. This means it is generally advantageous to fill an empty slot before replacing or upgrading an existing piece.

ARMOR UPGRADE TYPES

LEVEL	NAME
Level 1	Leather Armor
Level 2	Helmschmied Armor
Level 3	Metal Armor
Level 4	Missaglias Armor
Level 5	Armor of Altaïr

03

ARMS

Vambraces cover the forearms but leave the elbows and hands free for climbing, lock-picking, knife-throwing, pickpocketing and other acts of dexterity in a way that metal gauntlets would hinder. They are thus the ideal choice for the Assassin.

ARMS ARMOR

NAME	HEALTH SQUARES	RESISTANCE	HIT POINTS	AVAILABILITY
Leather Vambraces	◇	✹✹	200	Sequence 04
Helmschmied Vambraces	◇	✹✹✹	300	Sequence 05
Metal Vambraces	◇◇	✹✹✹✹	400	Sequence 06
Missaglias Vambraces	◇◇◇	✹✹✹✹✹✹	600	Sequence 09

LEGS ARMOR

NAME	HEALTH SQUARES	RESISTANCE	HIT POINTS	AVAILABILITY
Leather Greaves	◇	✹✹◗	250	Sequence 03
Helmschmied Greaves	◇◇	✹✹✹◗	350	Sequence 03
Metal Greaves	◇◇	✹✹✹✹◗	450	Sequence 07
Missaglias Greaves	◇◇◇	✹✹✹✹✹◗	650	Sequence 08

LEGS

As with the arms, these greaves provide a light armor protection to the shins without impeding running speed or climbing action. They are incorporated into Ezio's footwear for a more discreet and integrated appearance.

SHOULDERS

Spaulders and Pauldrons are armored plates or metal bands designed to protect the shoulders by deflecting the downward blows of blades and maces. They also prevent injury to Assassins who like to barge through crowds or run their prey to the ground with a flying tackle.

SHOULDER ARMOR

NAME	HEALTH SQUARES	RESISTANCE	HIT POINTS	AVAILABILITY
Leather Spaulders	◇	✹✹✹	300	Sequence 01
Helmschmied Spaulders	◇◇	✹✹✹✹◗	450	Sequence 04
Metal Pauldrons	◇◇◇	✹✹✹✹✹◗	550	Sequence 07
Missaglias Pauldrons	◇◇◇◇	✹✹✹✹✹✹	700	Sequence 10

CHEST

The quickest way to a man's heart, as they say, is between the fourth and fifth rib on the left side. A smart Assassin takes precautions against the very things he would strive to use against others. This upper torso armor extends around the back to ward off rocks and arrows while climbing.

CHEST ARMOR

	NAME	HEALTH SQUARES	RESISTANCE	HIT POINTS	AVAILABILITY
	Leather Chest Guard	◇◇	✸✸✸✸	400	Sequence 03
	Helmschmied Chest Guard	◇◇◇	✸✸✸✸✸	500	Sequence 05
	Metal Chest Guard	◇◇◇◇	✸✸✸✸✸✸	600	Sequence 07
	Missaglias Chest Guard	◇◇◇◇◇	✸✸✸✸✸✸✸✸	800	Sequence 09

COMPLETE SET

The Armor of Altaïr is a complete suit that cannot be separated or merged with other pieces of armor. It not only boosts the Health Meter to a potential maximum of 25 Health Squares but it offers protection that never needs repairing. For more details about this reward, see page 147 in the Extras chapter.

ARMOR OF ALTAÏR

	NAME	HEALTH SQUARES	RESISTANCE	HIT POINTS	AVAILABILITY
	Vambraces of Altaïr	◇◇	∞	∞	See page 147
	Greaves of Altaïr	◇◇◇	∞	∞	See page 147
	Pauldrons of Altaïr	◇◇◇◇	∞	∞	See page 147
	Chest Guard of Altaïr	◇◇◇◇◇◇	∞	∞	See page 147

CAPES

It would be wrong to think of capes as disguises. More accurately, they serve as highly visible badges of office, signifiers of family connections and political favor. Consequently, you can adopt any cape you have been awarded and enjoy the benefits of the privilege that it confers.

There is no hostility or rivalry invited by any of the capes, so wearing a Medici Cape in Venice will have no adverse result. Being outside of its sphere of influence, it will simply have no effect at all.

You can examine and swap capes in the Inventory section of the game menu by selecting the Outfits option.

PLAIN CAPE

Your standard cape is neutral in effect, so you are subject to the full range of the effects of Notoriety. Your actions, when witnessed, will stick to you.

Ezio receives the Plain Cape after he discovers his father's equipment locker in Sequence 01.

MEDICI CAPE

The Medici Cape prevents the wearer becoming Notorious in Florence and Tuscany. Ezio's Notoriety is fixed at zero and he will always be treated as Anonymous by city guards. Of course, they will still respond to any illegal or reprehensible act that requires them to enter Fight Mode immediately, such as a physical attack.

The Medici Cape becomes available in Sequence 06.

VENETIAN CAPE

The Venetian Cape marks you out as a man of no concern to the loyal guards of Venice and Romagna. Just like the Medici Cape, this emblem means you will enjoy the protection and anonymity of being favored by the ruling family. You will only have to answer to the local yeomanry if you commit a gross act warranting a physical intervention.

The Venetian Cape becomes available in Sequence 09.

AUDITORE CAPE

The Auditore Cape guarantees permanent 100% Notoriety. The player can do nothing to affect or reduce their public profile while it is worn. On removing the cape, the player will be restored to the Notoriety they had before putting it on.

This is immensely useful if you make efforts to start from a position of low Notoriety. You may commit acts of infamy while wearing the cape and they will all be attributed to the name of Auditore. You may then slip back into obscurity by removing it, thereafter untouched by the family reputation.

To acquire the Auditore Cape, you must complete the Feathers Secondary Memory. See page 148 in the Extras chapter for more information.

CARNEVALE MASK

The Carnevale Mask renders you permanently Anonymous during the Carnival. As you slip in and out of the crowds, the local guards will be unable to tell you from any of the other revelers out to enjoy the festivities. These items will be automatically equipped and removed in accordance with the missions of the game. However, the effect is also subject to any plot requirements in the missions.

The Carnevale Mask becomes available in Sequence 09. There is also a Golden Mask to acquire as a plot item by fulfilling three game challenges during that same Sequence (see page 91).

HOW TO PLAY

WALKTHROUGH

REFERENCE & ANALYSIS

EXTRAS

MOVES

WEAPONS

EQUIPMENT

SHOPS

ENEMIES

EZIO'S APPEARANCE

Ezio can dye his clothes at the Tailor's establishment. There are 15 color options in total, though each Tailor will offer a smaller choice that includes local varieties. This is a purely cosmetic touch, offering no game advantage or disguise, but presents the player with the chance to use those excess florins in customizing Ezio's appearance. You will also notice that Ezio's robes look darker when wet after he emerges from the water, their color being restored as he dries out.

Ezio's facial appearance also changes to reflect the passage of time within the game. Although he resembles Desmond for reasons of ancestry, the likeness is altered by the events of a life in harder days. Over time he will age, develop a scar and grow a beard (Fig. 4-6).

04

05

06

SHOPS

With commerce establishing the fortunes of a merchant class and new trade routes importing fine wares, there is no shortage of opportunity for Ezio to begin squandering his florins on material goods.

⚔ BLACKSMITHS

The Blacksmith will be your most frequent shopping venue. Thankfully it is also the most common, as you'll find at least one in every city district.

ARTICLE SELECTION

Supplying and upgrading Ezio's equipment will be the primary purpose of the Blacksmith until you have acquired everything there is to own, and after each mission you will still need his further skills in the maintenance and restoration of dulled blades and dented armor.

The following table reveals where each article can be bought, and for what price. Note that the items in Monterrigioni can be sold for lower prices. The discounts applied by shop owners depend on the investments you already made to restore Monteriggioni. Turn to page 44 in the Walkthrough chapter for more information on this topic.

BLACKSMITHS: SHOP SELECTIONS

CATEGORY	NAME	PRICE (f)	AVAILABILITY
Armor	Leather Vambraces	1,100	Sequence 04
	Helmschmied Vambraces	2,900	Sequence 05
	Metal Vambraces	6,300	Sequence 06
	Missaglias Vambraces	12,000	Sequence 09
	Leather Greaves	1,200	Sequence 03
	Helmschmied Greaves	5,200	Sequence 03
	Metal Greaves	7,200	Sequence 07
	Missaglias Greaves	14,600	Sequence 08
	Leather Spaulders	2,300	Sequence 01
	Helmschmied Spaulders	6,200	Sequence 04
	Metal Pauldrons	12,000	Sequence 07
	Missaglias Pauldrons	21,300	Sequence 10
	Leather Chest Guard	4,600	Sequence 03
	Helmschmied Chest Guard	10,800	Sequence 05
	Metal Chest Guard	17,200	Sequence 07
	Missaglias Chest Guard	27,900	Sequence 09
Weapons	Venetian Falchion	1,900	Sequence 03
	Mercenario War Hammer	1,900	Sequence 03
	Old Syrian Sword	2,300	Sequence 03
	Maul	3,600	Sequence 04
	Captain's Sword	5,200	Sequence 05
	Florentine Falchion	5,200	Sequence 06
	Flanged Mace	10,500	Sequence 06
	Scimitar	11,300	Sequence 06
	Milanese Sword	11,300	Sequence 07
	Cavalieri Mace	20,800	Sequence 07
	Schiavona	25,000	Sequence 08
	Condottiero War Hammer	35,000	Collect 50 Feathers (Monteriggioni only, see page 148)
	Sword of Altaïr	50,000	Sequence 09 (Monteriggioni only)
Small Weapons	Dagger	500	Sequence 03
	Knife	1,300	Sequence 03
	Stilleto	2,200	Sequence 04
	Channeled Cinquedea	4,100	Sequence 05
	Sultan's Knife	4,300	Sequence 06
	Metal Cestus	2,000	Sequence 06
	Butcher Knife	6,400	Sequence 07
	Notched Cinquedea	9,300	Sequence 08
Ammunition	Smoke Bomb	350	Sequence 05
	Throwing Knife	50	Sequence 03
	Pistol Bullet	175	Sequence 09

REPAIR

When standard Health Squares are replaced with red squares on your Health Meter, you have broken armor that needs repairing. Checking your Inventory will show you the status of each element and the damage it has so far sustained. Repair will restore your armor to its full Resistance, and if you have the funds then the Repair All shortcut will take care of all of your broken armor. For a complete explanation of the system behind armor Resistance, turn to page 123.

Repairs costs depend on the type of the armor concerned, as shown in the following table.

REPAIR COSTS

ARMOR TYPE	COST (f)
Leather	30
Helmschmied	60
Metal	100
Missaglias	150

HOW TO PLAY

WALKTHROUGH

REFERENCE & ANALYSIS

EXTRAS

MOVES

WEAPONS

EQUIPMENT

SHOPS

ENEMIES

POUCHES, BELTS & VIALS

The amount of consumable one-use items that Ezio can carry is determined by the quality and size of his Smoke Bomb or Medicine Pouches, Poison Vials and Knife Belts. The Tailor will sell improved versions that permanently increase total Inventory capacity. Each purchase replaces the currently worn item.

POUCHES AND BELTS UPGRADES

NAME	CAPACITY	PRICE (f)	AVAILABILITY
Medium Medicine Pouch	10	3,000	Sequence 01
Large Medicine Pouch	15	6,000	Sequence 01
Medium Knife Belt	+5	3,000	Sequence 06
Large Knife Belt	+5	6,000	Sequence 09
Medium Poison Vial	10	3,000	Sequence 04
Large Poison Vial	15	6,000	Sequence 10

⚏ TAILORS

There is at least one Tailor in every city district. With new trade and commerce making richer materials available, Ezio can afford to amend his wardrobe and purchase superior accessories.

DYE CLOTHES

The Tailor will dye the Assassin's robes and hood that Ezio inherited from his father. There are 15 color schemes to choose throughout the game, though each Tailor offers a smaller selection that includes the exclusive local style. Each dye costs 500 florins.

DYE COLORS: LOCATION

COLOR	TAILOR
Assassin White	All
Florentine Mahogany	Florence
Florentine Scarlet	Florence
Florentine Crimson	Florence
Tuscan Ember	Tuscany
Tuscan Emerald	Tuscany
Tuscan Copper	Tuscany
Tuscan Ochre	Tuscany
Wetlands Auburn	Romagna
Wetlands Steele	Romagna
Wetlands Ivory	Romagna
Wetlands Ebony	Romagna
Venetian Wine	Venice
Venetian Azure	Venice
Venetian Teal	Venice

ART MERCHANTS

PAINTINGS

There is at least one Art Merchant per city district. Note that all of the 30 Paintings in the game are genuine historical works of art.

For all the famous cultural and artistic achievements of the age, the painters of the Renaissance were still heavily dependent on the whim of wealthy patrons to fund their endeavors. Ezio will play his part by purchasing the latest works to display in the family gallery from Sequence 03 onwards. These ultimately priceless acquisitions will enhance Monteriggioni's value.

PAINTINGS LIST

NAME	PRICE (f)	AVAILABILITY
The Birth of Venus	14,800	Romagna
Jupiter and Io	6,969	Romagna
La Fornarina	32	Romagna
Leda and the Swan	200	Romagna
Three Graces	500	Romagna
Eve	800	Romagna
Venus Rising	7,220	Tuscany
Sleeping Venus	9,175	Tuscany
Venus and the mirror	1,035	Tuscany
Portrait of Simonetta Vespucci	125	Tuscany
Portrait of a Lady (Ambrogio de Predis)	525	Tuscany
Federico da Montefeltro	325	Tuscany
St-Jerome	53	Venice
Adoration of the Magi	1,290	Venice
San Sebastian	163	Venice
St-Jerome in his study	4,300	Venice
Sacred and Profane Love	6,295	Venice
Saint Chrysogonus	3,290	Monteriggioni
St. Francis in Ecstasy	581	Monteriggioni
Ideal City	2,850	Monteriggioni
Battista and Federico	1,238	Monteriggioni
Lady with an Ermine	85	Monteriggioni
Saint Jean Baptiste	1,608	Florence
Portrait of a musician	20	Florence
Portrait of Francesco delle Opere	1,492	Florence
Madonna and Child	320	Florence
Baptism of Christ	280	Florence
Primavera	2,950	Florence
Pallas and the Centaur	3,050	Florence
Annunciation	429	Florence

TREASURE MAPS

The second service offered by Art Merchants is the collection and sale of maps that lead to hidden Treasure Chests. Each of the 14 Treasure Maps in the game displays the location of all of the Treasure Chests in the district or region where the map is bought.

TREASURE MAPS LIST

LOCATION	PRICE (f)	AVAILABILITY
Florence: San Giovanni District	395	Sequence 01
Florence: San Marco District	150	Sequence 02
Monteriggioni	285	Sequence 03
Tuscany: San Gimignano	245	Sequence 03
Tuscany: Countryside	175	Sequence 03
Florence: Santa Maria Novella District	160	Sequence 04
Apennine Mountains	150	Sequence 06
Romagna: Forlì	260	Sequence 06
Romagna: Countryside	235	Sequence 06
Venice: San Polo District	550	Sequence 07
Venice: San Marco District	500	Sequence 08
Venice: Dorsoduro District	495	Sequence 09
Venice: Castello District	485	Sequence 10
Venice: Cannaregio District	995	Sequence 11

HOW TO PLAY

WALKTHROUGH

REFERENCE &
ANALYSIS

EXTRAS

MOVES

WEAPONS

EQUIPMENT

SHOPS

ENEMIES

✚ DOCTORS

Not all of the Doctors you meet will be wearing the distinctive bird-mask, but they will be dressed in black robes and standing beside their green handcart of glass jars and preparations. You can employ a Doctor for two types of services (but never during a fight).

HEALING: You pay 50 florins to restore your Health. Except for those blocks relating to broken armor, your Health Meter will be completely refilled.

APOTHECARY SUPPLIES: You can buy doses of consumable items.

NAME	PRICE (f)	AVAILABILITY
Medicine	75	Sequence 01
Poison	175	Sequence 07

To increase the amount of Medicine and Poison you can carry, consult the entry for the Tailor.

⬌ FAST TRAVEL STATIONS

Fast Travel offers a shortcut to the many different regions in the game, though you may only travel to places you have already visited through progression in your current game.

When you need to find a Fast Travel Station, climb up to a viewpoint and look for the city walls or boundaries. They are frequently placed by the city gates or stables, so following the perimeter to an exit road will usually locate one.

Fast Travel is immensely useful when you start tracking down free missions and using your money to restore Monteriggioni as a base of operations. Travel costs to and from Monteriggioni are kept agreeably low at a 100 florin limit for any other region. In all other instances, the cost of Fast Travel corresponds to the distance travelled.

FAST TRAVEL PRICES (f)	STARTING POINT				
DESTINATION		Tuscany	Florence	Romagna	Venice	Monterrigioni
	Tuscany	-	100	200	300	100
	Florence	100	-	150	200	100
	Romagna	200	150	-	100	100
	Venice	300	200	100	-	100
	Monterrigioni	100	100	100	100	-

ENEMIES

Knowing your enemy is the first step to beating him. Being a true Assassin means understanding your enemy's behavior and knowing just how to exploit it to put him at a disadvantage.

BASIC GUARDS

GENERAL BEHAVIOR

Guards patrol or investigate at brisk walking pace. They will hit running speed when seeing Ezio fleeing from them. Patrol routes are fixed and repeated so that you may observe every point of the route before acting. In pursuit, basic guards can perform some free running maneuvers but cannot climb sheer walls. If Ezio attempts to take any route that the guards cannot follow, they will holster their weapons and begin throwing rocks in an effort to make him fall. Guards cannot swim, and they can be pushed over low walls by a determined hand.

Sentries will remain at their posts unless prompted to move by the detection system. Their placement will relate to a particular area that they regard as out of bounds – a yard, or a door – and they will push Ezio away if he comes too close (Fig. 1); trespass will be treated as an illegal act. Bodyguards are simply sentries who have been assigned to an object or character in the same fashion.

Note that every guard you encounter holds one of three ranks: Militia (weakest), Elite or Leader (strongest). A guard's rank is revealed by his helmet. No matter the uniform, Militia wear caps, Elites favor open-faced helmets, while Leaders have headgear with additional facial protection (see page 81).

01

LINE OF SIGHT

Each guard has a Line of Sight that determines what he can see. This means that Ezio can remain hidden from a guard, even close by, if he is:

◆ Behind the guard, beyond visual range, sufficiently far to one side, or higher/lower than the guard can see.

◆ Hidden by a wall, a column, or some other solid obstacle that provides complete cover.

◆ Concealed in a hiding spot.

◆ Blended into a crowd.

◆ In the Line of Sight but too far away for the guard to notice.

Use the camera controls to observe guards around corners, while out of sight, and time your open moves while they are facing away. If you can't find a route past them, you may need to conjure up a distraction: thrown money, a dead body or some poor victim going berserk under the effects of Poison will all attract the attention of the guards. Even stationary sentries will change their Line of Sight to look at such a commotion. Observe their body orientation to see where they are looking. Courtesans and Thieves can also provide lures and distractions to physically remove guards from their posts.

THE DETECTION SYSTEM

Once a guard has spotted something suspicious, he will start paying attention and his Line of Sight will be attracted to the target. This will be indicated in his Social Status Indicator (SSI), which will start to fill as a yellow bar during the Detection phase. Removing yourself from Line of Sight will cause the bar to recede at the same rate, so you may take immediate action to escape attention. Blending with the crowd, entering a hiding spot or simply walking away and around a corner, out of sight, will be sufficient. But running, performing suspicious and anti-social acts and any High Profile activity in this phase will cause the bar to fill more quickly. Proximity to the guard will also increase the rate of Detection.

Once the Detection SSI is fully yellow, the Investigation phase will begin. This is indicated by the yellow bar filling with red. The guards will draw their weapons, break from their post or their patrol and approach to make a positive identification. During the Investigation phase you *still* have a chance to escape attention by hiding, blending or casually walking out of view in Low Profile. Again, suspicious or illegal activity will prompt the bar to fill rapidly. When it is 100% red, the guard will enter open conflict and initiate combat.

BLOCKING AND PURSUIT

If the player flees open conflict, the guards will give chase by finding the quickest route to his current or suspected location. This is represented on the Mini-Map by a yellow circle (Fig. 2) that the player must escape to shake off the guards and end the chase. The center of the circle is updated by any guard with Line of Sight on the fugitive, creating a last known position at which he was seen.

During open conflict pursuits, guards can also choose to block a road or entrance. On approach, you will see them hold a line with weapons raised above their heads (Fig. 3), ready to stop you if you come close.

02

03

ENEMY ARCHETYPES

The Archetypes are guards with specific roles that introduce a further challenge. They follow the general behavior patterns of basic guards, but have additional features that make them clearly distinct from all others. Although they are often used sparingly, they can drastically change the threat posed by any sentry or patrol. Being able to recognize the different elements that make up an enemy squad will prevent any unpleasant surprises.

HOW TO PLAY

WALKTHROUGH

REFERENCE & ANALYSIS

EXTRAS

MOVES

WEAPONS

EQUIPMENT

SHOPS

ENEMIES

AGILES

Fast and lightly armed, Agiles are trackers and pursuers. They can imitate the Assassin's free running skills with the exception of grasping and climbing sheer surfaces, swimming, and the Leap of Faith. Their tactic is to catch up with Ezio, knock him to the ground and engage him long enough for their tougher cohorts to arrive in support. As a group they will try to surround you, delivering quick stinging attacks like a swarm of insects.

The pay-off for this speed is that the Agile is the weakest of the guards and most easily defeated. They exhibit low morale and are most likely to flee when colleagues fall. Combat also tests their stamina — they will be exhausted after dodging a few attacks and require ten seconds to recover.

In group combat, the Agile is the quickest to beat and so a useful strategy is to target them first to rapidly reduce the number of opponents. But if you have the advantage on them, a better idea is to assassinate the strongest guard in the group and greatly reduce the morale of the Agiles, with further kills making the remainder more likely to turn tail and flee.

BRUTES

The armor-plated Brutes are immediately identified by their stature. Favoring Heavy weapons, they are skilled in the Smash Attack special technique and will use it to disarm and beat down the player. Their self-confidence gives them the strongest morale of any opponent you will face: once engaged, they will never flee a battle.

The threat posed by the Brute is multiplied when in company. Dodging and strafing is essential unless you have already picked up a Long or Heavy weapon to deflect and counter.

The Brute takes no damage when deflecting a Small or Medium weapon and does not tire from it either. Instead try dodging or strafing to the side, to get around the Brute, and land direct hits outside his blocking arc. Incidentally you may find that unarmed combat lands hits where weapons fail.

The Brute is disadvantaged by low speed, moving at only 75% of the pace of a normal guard, so you can outrun them. They cannot use ladders, free run or climb, so you can escape vertically too. From a vantage point above, it is possible to use ranged weapons to reduce the number of Brutes below.

SEEKERS

Smarter than the average guard, the Seeker will investigate hiding spots in search of criminals. He will do this as part of his patrol routine, even when Ezio is Incognito. You can often identify Seekers from a distance by their favored carrying of a Long weapon. They use this to prod haystacks and wells, forcing you out of cover if you happen to be inside. If Ezio is Notorious, the Seeker will also stop at benches and ask the seated citizens to rise. This will instantly break your blending if you were hiding here.

Seekers tend to stay on the outside of a combat skirmish and use the full reach of their weapon while you are tackling their colleagues. They will also perform Sweep Attack special techniques to knock you to the floor. A good solution is to disarm them, though this may take a few attempts.

To get rid of a Seeker, a daring approach is to lurk in a hiding place on the patrol route, ready to ambush your enemy when he approaches. Use the Assassinate from Hiding move to eliminate him first, watching your Controls HUD in the top right of the screen in order to strike at the first opportunity. This will cause the rest of his patrol to enter open conflict, but it will remove both the Seeker and that irksome Long weapon from play instantly.

Note that Seekers can climb ladders and ledges but they need to sheath their weapons to do so: you can catch them with a well-timed blow as they reach the top.

FIGHT STRATEGIES

If too many aggressors are drawn to the vicinity of the player in open conflict then the group will divide into an inner and outer circle, one feeding the other (Fig. 4).

Although the fights will vary greatly in different scenarios, especially when the missions demand specific and urgent goals, there is a set of rules that the player can learn to survive and conquer in any skirmish with a large group of opponents.

04

◆ If you have the advantage on your enemy before combat begins, assassinate as many as you can first. Start with Low Profile silent kills, then make sure any High Profile assassination takes down the strongest enemy first – a Brute or a Seeker for instance. You will then be left with the weakest and most likely to flee.

◆ Once combat begins, quickly reduce the enemy numbers by picking on the weakest first. They will try to circle you to strike from behind, and you will be forced to use the Movement Stick with the Deflect move to keep parrying attacks from all sides.

◆ Keep your guard raised and the High Profile Button held by default until you are ready to perform an attack. Keep in mind that you can instantly initiate a Dodge, a Disarm or a Counter Kill while deflecting.

◆ You can try Counter Kills from the outset against the weakest enemies. Counters grow less likely against strong and defensive foes, though, and the chance of success will only rise again once they start to lose stamina and tire out toward the end of a long fight.

◆ If your Counters are failing, feint backwards or sideways and immediately follow up with an attack to thrust forward again, making only one or two hits before deflecting again. The purpose of these small strikes is to whittle away the health, stamina and morale of your opponent while you stay untouched. This greatly increases the chances of further attempted Counter Kills. Full combos would invite interrupting attacks from other opponents anyway.

◆ Another really effective strategy is the "Grab and Throw" technique. When fighting multiple enemies, Grab any rank-and-file guard, but instead of killing him right away, Throw him as a projectile at your toughest opponent. As soon as the latter is down, run to him and quickly finish him off to make the rest of the battle much easier.

◆ Enemies can hurt each other (Fig. 5). That includes wide strikes from Brutes and arrows fired from a distance, if you are able to put an enemy between you and the attack.

◆ By briefly dropping your guard and strafing at speed, you can manipulate the group to a favored location or get yourself out of a corner. Strafing is also better than dodging when used up *very* close to circle around the side or rear of an attacking enemy, where they cannot deflect: from here you can deliver an automatic hit and, often, an instant finishing kill.

ARCHERS

Archers are assigned to defend towers and rooftops, where they can spot Ezio instantly. During open conflict, they will immediately open fire using their bows. If Ezio is within close range, the Archer will switch to his sidearm and become a basic guard.

Archers patrol more slowly than Ezio walks, so he can catch them at walking speed if he approaches stealthily from behind. High Profile running or sprinting will break stealth and cause them to enter Detection phase.

Note that the Assassinate from Ledge technique is especially useful for ambushes on rooftop guards, but you will want to choose carefully between High and Low Profile assault to conceal the body. At range, a single Throwing Knife will take out an Archer and you will appreciate carrying a large Knife Belt full of them later in the game.

05

ENEMIES: MORALE

Morale is the factor that determines the bravery or cowardice of your enemies. Each unit starts with a personal morale value.

MORALE VALUES

UNIT	MORALE
Basic guards	20
Archers	30
Agiles	40
Seekers	80
Brutes	1,000

The morale of all enemies is then constantly adjusted by the events that unfold in combat, as shown in the nearby table. You may thus strive to intimidate enemies through your prowess in combat. If you can establish your superiority over your strongest foes through successful techniques then the rest will reconsider their odds and their propensity to attack. You may even get a visual clue in their behavior as they shake their heads and look beaten (Fig. 6).

ENEMY MORALE ADJUSTMENTS

EVENTS DURING COMBAT	VARIATIONS
Death of a Brute	- 30
Death of a Seeker	- 20
Assassinate with Pistol	- 20
Kill with weapon acquired through Disarm	- 10
Death of a basic guard	- 5
Death of an Archer	- 5
Death of an Agile	- 5
Disarm	- 5
Assassinate enemy on ground	- 5
Counter Kill	- 5
Ezio injured	+ 10
Ezio escapes from combat	+ 20
Ezio enters Critical State	+ 25

Fleeing enemies will first freeze briefly to the spot, dropping their weapon, before running away at maximum speed. Unless pursued, they will keep running until they are either caught or else make sufficient distance to be permanently removed from play.

06

HOW TO PLAY

WALKTHROUGH

REFERENCE & ANALYSIS

EXTRAS

MOVES

WEAPONS

EQUIPMENT

SHOPS

ENEMIES

NOTORIETY & ENEMIES

Notoriety is the degree to which Ezio is known, and will be recognized in public, by both the local people and the guards. When Ezio is "Incognito", he may walk freely through the streets without being noticed. However, committing spectacular and infamous acts will inevitably stick to the perpetrator and raise his profile over time. Once "Notorious", guard reactions will be quicker and more aggressive toward a known felon.

The Notoriety meter in the top left of the HUD increases with every such act. Ezio will be considered Incognito until the bar fills completely, at which point the icon will turn red – Ezio is then Notorious. The bar must be fully emptied to restore the icon to gray, making Ezio anonymous again. In essence, your status remains constant until it flips at 0% or 100%.

If you want to lower your Notoriety, there are actions you may take as detailed in our walkthrough on page 33. Their availability rests on your Notoriety level. Note that these may also incur some Notoriety unless undertaken discreetly.

NOTORIETY ADJUSTMENTS

ACTION	VARIATIONS
Killing a Borgia Messenger	+ 50%
Every guard fleeing from a fight	+ 10%
Every five enemies killed in one continuous open conflict	+ 10%
Double Air Assassinate	+ 7.5%
Air Assassinate	+ 7.5%
Assassinate with Pistol	+ 7.5%
Any High Profile Assassination	+ 7.5%
Double Assassinate	+ 5%
Serenaded by a Harasser	+ 5%
Tearing down a Poster	- 25%
Bribing a Herald	- 50%
Killing a corrupt Official	- 75%

EXTRAS | 04

SPOILER WARNING: IF YOU HAVE YET TO FINISH SEQUENCE 14, *DO NOT READ THIS CHAPTER*. IT CONTAINS STORY AND GAMEPLAY SPOILERS OF THE MOST CATASTROPHIC VARIETY.

YOU MAY HAVE COMPLETED ASSASSIN'S CREED II, BUT WE CAN CONFIDENTLY WAGER THAT YOU HAVE YET TO SEE EVERYTHING IT HAS TO OFFER. IN THIS FINAL CHAPTER WE EXPOSE ALL REMAINING SECRETS, INCLUDING COLLECTIBLES AND UNIQUE REWARDS, AND TAKE A SPECIAL LOOK AT THE STORY SO FAR.

ACHIEVEMENTS & TROPHIES

Though many will have acquired the majority of possible Achievements and Trophies during their first playthrough, this section will help readers to complete any that they are missing. If you are an anxious Trophy or Gamerscore addict stealing an early glance at the requirements, we can reassure you that practically all can be unlocked when you are ready to tackle each task. The only exception to this rule is clearly mentioned in the relevant section of the Walkthrough.

▮MILESTONES ▮

These accomplishments are recognized by completing plot-specific Memories, and cannot be missed. If you have already completed Assassin's Creed II – and, given the stern spoiler warnings at the start of this chapter, we would certainly hope so – then you will already have these.

	NAME	Ⓖ	TROPHY	UNLOCKED BY...
	The Birth of an Assassin	20	Bronze	...witnessing Ezio Auditore's birth.
	Arrivederci Abstergo	20	Bronze	...escaping the Abstergo building.
	Welcome to the Animus 2.0	20	Silver	...entering the Animus in the Assassin's Hideout.
	The Pain of Betrayal	30	Silver	...completing Sequence 01.
	Vengeance	30	Silver	...completing Sequence 02.
	Exit the Son	30	Silver	...completing Sequence 03.
	Bloody Sunday	30	Silver	...completing Sequence 04.
	Undertaker	20	Silver	...finding the Assassin Tomb beneath Santa Maria Novella during Sequence 04.
	The Conspirators	30	Silver	...completing Sequence 05.
	An Unexpected Journey	30	Silver	...completing Sequence 06.
	Bleeding Effect	30	Silver	... trying out Desmond's new abilities in the warehouse before returning to the Animus (Present 02).
	The Merchant of Venice	30	Silver	...completing Sequence 07.
	The Impenetrable Palazzo	30	Silver	...completing Sequence 08.
	Masquerade	30	Silver	...completing Sequence 09.
	Bianca's Man	30	Silver	...completing Sequence 10.
	The Prophet	30	Silver	...completing Sequence 11.
	The Vault	30	Silver	...completing Sequence 14.
	An Old Friend Returns	100	Gold	...escaping the hideout (Present 03).

SECONDARY MEMORIES & ASSASSIN TOMBS

Though not linked to mandatory gameplay sections, we expect that most readers will also have collected these accomplishments during their first playthrough. If you find any that you have missed, follow the provided page references for more information.

	NAME	G	TROPHY	REQUIREMENTS
	Macho Man	10	Bronze	Complete a Beat-Up free mission. See page 34.
	Steal Home	10	Bronze	Win a Race free mission. See page 34.
	Assassin For Hire	10	Bronze	Complete an assassination for Lorenzo Il Magnifico. See page 62.
	I like the view	10	Bronze	Synchronize at a total of 10 viewpoints. You should almost certainly have this by the end of the story, but consult the Walkthrough maps if you are (rather surprisingly) short of a few.
	Venetian Gladiator	20	Silver	Locate and enter the Assassin Tomb at Santa Maria della Visitazione and complete the objectives. See page 95.
	I can see your house from here!	20	Silver	Locate and enter the Assassin Tomb at Torre Grossa, then complete the objectives. See page 65.
	Hallowed be thy name	20	Silver	Locate and enter the Assassin Tomb at Basilica di San Marco and complete the objectives. See page 89.
	Prison Escape	20	Silver	Locate and enter the Assassin Tomb at the Rocca di Ravaldino fortress and complete the objectives. See page 73.
	Choir Boy	20	Silver	Locate and enter the Assassin Tomb at Santa Maria del Fiore and complete the objectives. See page 53.

ITEM COLLECTION & MONTERIGGIONI TASKS

Like its predecessor, Assassin's Creed II is filled with collectibles. Finding every last one is no trivial endeavor, so you should regard some of these as the hardest Achievements or Trophies to unlock. As certain collectible items are connected to the Villa Auditore sub-game, we've also included accomplishments specific to Monteriggioni in this section.

	NAME	G	TROPHY	REQUIREMENTS
	Art Connoisseur	10	Bronze	Buy two paintings: one from an art dealer in Florence, and another from Venice.
	Handy Man	10	Bronze	Upgrade a single building in Monteriggioni. See page 44.
	Podestà of Monteriggioni	30	Silver	As you invest money in Monteriggioni, its value increases. Reach 80% of the potential maximum to unlock this. See page 44 if you would like to learn more about the underlying mechanics.
	Myth Maker	5	Bronze	Collect all eight Statuettes hidden around Monteriggioni. See page 46.
	In Memory of Petruccio	30	Silver	Collect all collectible Feathers hidden throughout the game world. See page 148 for a comprehensive guide to their locations.
	Victory lies in preparation	10	Bronze	You must complete three sub-objectives to unlock this: obtain all Hidden Blade enhancements (page 116) and all Pouches and their respective upgrades (page 120), and purchase every available piece of armor (page 123). Note that the Uplay "bonus" Pouch for throwing knives is not required.
	Tip of the Iceberg	10	Bronze	Locate a hidden Glyph, then use Eagle Vision to read it. See page 148.
	A Piece of the Puzzle	10	Bronze	After finding and reading your first Glyph, you can visit the Database page to decode the data it contains by solving a puzzle. You unlock this by completing the first.
	Vitruvian Man	20	Silver	Beat all 20 Glyph puzzles. You can find solutions on page 170.

HOW TO PLAY

WALKTHROUGH

REFERENCE & ANALYSIS

EXTRAS

ACHIEVEMENTS & TROPHIES

FREE MISSIONS

SECRETS

AC1: STORY RECAP

AC2: STORY RECAP

■ SPECIAL FEATS

The remaining accomplishments are all designed to encourage players to have a little fun with the Assassin's Creed II game world. Some offer specific challenges, others reward exploration. Florence is a great place to work on combat-oriented goals, as wearing the Medici Cape removes all potential Notoriety penalties.

"LIGHTNING STRIKE"

	G	TROPHY
	10	Bronze

Run at full speed for at least 100 meters. Attempt this on the bustling streets of Florence or Venice, and you may experience difficulties. Smarter sprinters, however, will chose an uninterrupted stretch of countryside to unlock this.

"MESSER SANDMAN"

	G	TROPHY
	10	Bronze

Stun four opponents simultaneously with the Throw Sand ability; remember to hold the button down to increase the effect radius. See page 116 for tips on using this move.

Blinding four opponents is obviously easier when you are surrounded by several enemies at once, but doing so increases the risk of having the necessary charge period interrupted. This is especially likely when you face Seekers, who have an uncanny knack of interrupting special attacks. Your best bet is to kick up a fuss in Florence in an area with a suitably high concentration of static guards and patrols.

"STREET CLEANER"

	G	TROPHY
	10	Bronze

Hide five dead bodies in a pile of hay or leaves, either loose on the ground or in a cart. The square in front of the Palazzo Della Signoria in Florence is a happy hunting ground for this task. There are sufficient patrols to get the numbers you require, but they're not so numerous that there's any danger of being overwhelmed or disturbed come the time to conceal your victims.

"DOCTOR"

	G	TROPHY
	20	Bronze

This one is fun. The objective is to stick a target with the Poison Blade, then climb to a higher ledge and perform an Air Assassination on your ailing plaything before he collapses. Find an alleyway or sparsely populated street surrounded by fairly low roofs on at least one side, confirm the presence of a guard patrol, then go about your (rather cruel) business.

"NO-HITTER"

	G	TROPHY
	20	Bronze

The brief is simple: defeat ten opponents in one continuous combat sequence without sustaining a single blow in return. In practice, it's not nearly as straightforward as you might think. Because the hidden morale system will cause less dedicated soldiers to flee if you systematically slaughter their associates, attempting this during an earlier Sequence (where opponents are weaker) is not really a viable option. The indomitable Brute is the key to completing this. Find one in a well-guarded area of Venice, then aim to keep him alive and focused on Ezio until you can engage and kill ten enemies.

"SWEEPER"

	G	TROPHY
	10	Bronze

Once you've learned the Sweep Attack special technique from the Training Ground at Monteriggioni, find a Long weapon (a common Spear will do), then perform a charged Sweep Attack that hits five opponents in quick succession. If the group you are fighting includes Seekers or Agiles, it may be a good idea to dispatch them before you try this: the former will attempt to hit you during the charge period, while the latter have a tendency to stand outside the attack range.

"MAILMAN"

	G	TROPHY
	10	Bronze

Intercept and rob a Borgia courier. You can learn more about these on page 35.

HOW TO PLAY

WALKTHROUGH

REFERENCE & ANALYSIS

EXTRAS

ACHIEVEMENTS & TROPHIES

FREE MISSIONS

SECRETS

AC1: STORY RECAP

AC2: STORY RECAP

"KLEPTOMANIAC"

	ⓖ		TROPHY
	10		Bronze

Pickpocket a total of 1,000 florins; see page 112 for tips on pilfering from civilians. The best strategy is to equip the Medici Cape and find an area of Florence with few or no guard patrols. If you steal indiscriminately, it should take you no more than five minutes to accrue the specified sum.

"HIGH DIVE"

	ⓖ		TROPHY
	10		Bronze

Perform a Leap of Faith from the top of Giotto's Campanile, the large tower that stands next to Santa Maria del Fiore in Florence. This is actually the highest building in Assassin's Creed II. You'll need to make a running leap from the roof of the adjacent cathedral to begin climbing it, as there are no viable routes from its base. Once you've reached the top, note before taking the plunge that there's only one pile of hay for you to land in, so make sure you jump in the right direction.

"RED LIGHT ADDICT"

	G		TROPHY
	10		Bronze

Spend a total of 5,000 florins on acquiring the services of Courtesans. This works out at 34 transactions. Most players will reach a number close to this during the course of their first playthrough, so it shouldn't take long to reach the specified amount.

"MAN OF THE PEOPLE"

	G		TROPHY
	10		Bronze

Use the Throw Coins ability to disperse a lifetime total of 300 florins. Most players will have unlocked this through their interactions with Harassers during plot missions. If you don't have it yet, find a quiet spot outside the Florence city gates before you start.

"PERFECT HARMONY"

	G		TROPHY
	10		Bronze

Dye Ezio's clothes with two particular colors: Wetlands Ebony and Wetlands Ivory. These can be purchased from a Tailor in the center of Forlì; the stall is located a short walk southwest from the cathedral.

"FLY SWATTER"

	G		TROPHY
	5		Bronze

While piloting Da Vinci's wondrous invention in the last Memory of Sequence 08, swoop over a guard to kick him.

"SHOW YOUR COLORS"

	G		TROPHY
	10		Bronze

Before you can attempt this, you must first collect all Feathers to unlock the Auditore Cape: a uniquely provocative garment that places Ezio in a constant state of maximum Notoriety. Wear it during visits to every town and city in the game world to unlock this Achievement or Trophy.

"MASTER ASSASSIN" (PS3 ONLY)

	G		TROPHY
	–		Platinum

Unlock all other Trophies to obtain this final accolade.

HOW TO PLAY

WALKTHROUGH

REFERENCE & ANALYSIS

EXTRAS

ACHIEVEMENTS & TROPHIES

FREE MISSIONS

SECRETS

AC1: STORY RECAP

AC2: STORY RECAP

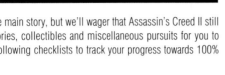

FREE MISSIONS

You may have finished the main story, but we'll wager that Assassin's Creed II still has many optional Memories, collectibles and miscellaneous pursuits for you to spend time on. Use the following checklists to track your progress towards 100% completion.

 ## FLORENCE

COLLECTIBLES

ICON	CATEGORY	TOTAL	EARLIEST COMPLETION
	Viewpoints	20	Sequence 04
	Codex Pages	5	Sequence 04
	Glyphs	5	Sequence 04
	Feathers	27	Sequence 04
	Treasure Chests	71	Sequence 04

SECONDARY MEMORIES

MISSION	MAP ICON	TYPE	SEQUENCE	REWARD (f)	PAGE
A Woman Scorned		Beat Up Event	Sequence 01	200	34
Casanova		Courier Assignment	Sequence 01	100	34
Florentine Sprint		Race	Sequence 01	100	34
San Marco Scuttle		Race	Sequence 04	1,500	52
Il Dumo's Secret		Assassin Tomb	Sequence 04	Seal of Iltani	53
Home Invasion		Templar Lair*	Sequence 04	–	54
Day At The Market		Assassination Contract	Sequence 05	1,000	62
Fallen Archers		Assassination Contract	Sequence 05	2,000	62
Political Suicide		Assassination Contract	Sequence 05	2,000	62
Caveat Emptor		Assassination Contract	Sequence 05	2,000	62
Meeting Adjourned		Assassination Contract	Sequence 05	2,000	63
Needle In A Haystack		Assassination Contract	Sequence 05	2,000	63
Peacekeeper		Assassination Contract	Sequence 05	2,000	63
Leader Of The Pack		Assassination Contract	Sequence 05	2,000	63

* ASSASSIN'S CREED II BLACK EDITION ONLY

MONTERIGGIONI

COLLECTIBLES

ICON	CATEGORY	TOTAL	EARLIEST COMPLETION
	Viewpoints	1	Sequence 03
	Codex Pages	–	–
	Glyphs	1	Sequence 03
	Feathers	4	Sequence 03
	Treasure Chests	27	Sequence 03
	Statuettes	8	Sequence 03 (see page 46)

SECONDARY MEMORIES

MISSION	MAP ICON	TYPE	SEQUENCE	REWARD	PAGE
Paying Respects		Assassin Tomb*	Sequence 04	–	55

* UPLAY ACCOUNT REQUIRED. THERE IS NO SEAL FOR THIS ASSASSIN TOMB.

VILLA COLLECTIONS

CATEGORY	EARLIEST COMPLETION	NOTES
Weapons	Sequence 11	You will need to collect 50 Feathers to unlock the Condottiero War Hammer for purchase in Monteriggioni.
Armor	Sequence 10	The Missaglias Pauldrons are the last piece of armor collected; you can actually unlock the superior Armor of Altair beforehand in Sequence 09.
Models	Sequence 08	The Carriage and Flying Machine are awarded automatically on completion of their associated Memories.
Codex Pages	Sequence 11	Collecting them all is mandatory to proceed in Sequence 14.
Paintings	Sequence 07	You can finish the collection once you reach Venice – but only if you have sufficient florins to afford each painting.
Portraits	Game complete	Displayed in the attic study, the gallery of Ezio's most notable assassination targets will be complete when play resumes after the final credits.
Feathers	Sequence 11	Can be completed once the final district of Venice is unlocked. We would suggest that you wait until at least early Sequence 14, though, when you have the Venetian Cape to prevent Notoriety increases for all the archers you slay in the process of collecting them.
Seals	Sequence 09	The final Assassin Tomb is unlocked when you reach the Dorsoduro district in Venice.

HOW TO PLAY

WALKTHROUGH

REFERENCE &
ANALYSIS

EXTRAS

ACHIEVEMENTS
& TROPHIES

FREE MISSIONS

SECRETS

AC1:
STORY RECAP

AC2:
STORY RECAP

TUSCANY & SAN GIMIGNANO

COLLECTIBLES

ICON	CATEGORY	TOTAL	EARLIEST COMPLETION
	Viewpoints	9	Sequence 03
	Codex Pages	2	Sequence 03
	Glyphs	5	Sequence 03
	Feathers	11	Sequence 03
	Treasure Chests	46	Sequence 03

SECONDARY MEMORIES

MISSION	MAP ICON	TYPE	SEQUENCE	REWARD (ƒ)	PAGE
Wedding Bells Are Ringing		Courier Assignment	Sequence 03	1,000	42
San Gimignano Dash		Race	Sequence 03	1,000	42
Torre Grossa's Secret		Assassin Tomb	Sequence 04	Seal of Wei Yu	65
Spear of Infidelity		Beat Up Event	Sequence 05	2,000	63
Speedy Delivery		Courier Assignment	Sequence 05	2,500	63
Reap What You Sow		Assassination Contract	Sequence 05	2,000	64
Don't Get Your Hands Dirty		Assassination Contract	Sequence 05	2,000	64
Supply In Demand		Assassination Contract	Sequence 05	2,000	64
Flee Market		Assassination Contract	Sequence 05	2,000	64
Vertical Slice		Assassination Contract	Sequence 05	2,000	64
No Camping		Assassination Contract	Sequence 05	2,000	64
Showtime		Assassination Contract	Sequence 05	2,500	64

ROMAGNA & FORLÌ

COLLECTIBLES

ICON	CATEGORY	TOTAL	EARLIEST COMPLETION
	Viewpoints	9	Sequence 06
	Codex Pages	3	Sequence 06
	Glyphs	2	Sequence 06
	Feathers	12	Sequence 06
	Treasure Chests (Romagna)	45	Sequence 06
	Treasure Chests (Apennine Mountains)	16	Sequence 06

SECONDARY MEMORIES

MISSION	MAP ICON	TYPE	SEQUENCE	REWARD (ƒ)	PAGE
Wanton Hubby		Beat Up Event	Sequence 06	2,500	72
Promiscuity Knocks		Beat Up Event	Sequence 06	2,500	72
The Messenger's Burden		Courier Assignment	Sequence 06	2,500	72
Romagna Hustle		Race	Sequence 06	2,500	72
Horseplay		Race	Sequence 06	2,500	72
Thin The Ranks		Assassination Contract	Sequence 06	2,500	70
Beginnings Of A Conspiracy		Assassination Contract	Sequence 06	2,500	70
Arch Enemies		Assassination Contract	Sequence 06	2,500	70
Wet Work		Assassination Contract	Sequence 06	2,500	70
Dead On Arrival		Assassination Contract	Sequence 06	2,500	71
Go Towards The Light		Assassination Contract	Sequence 06	2,500	71
Mark And Execute		Assassination Contract	Sequence 06	2,500	71
Ravaldino's Secret		Assassin Tomb	Sequence 06	Seal of Qulan Gal	73

VENICE

COLLECTIBLES

ICON	CATEGORY	TOTAL	EARLIEST COMPLETION
	Viewpoints	27	Sequence 11
	Codex Pages	6	Sequence 11
	Glyphs	7	Sequence 10
	Feathers	46	Sequence 11
	Treasure Chests	125	Sequence 11

SECONDARY MEMORIES

MISSION	MAP ICON	TYPE	SEQUENCE	REWARD (f)	PAGE
Thicker Than Water		Assassination Contract	Sequence 07	2,500	82
Zero Tolerance		Assassination Contract	Sequence 07	2,500	82
Over Beams, Under Stone		Templar Lair*	Sequence 07	–	83
Blade In The Crowd		Assassination Contract	Sequence 08	3,000	88
Honorable Thief		Assassination Contract	Sequence 08	3,000	88
San Marco's Secret		Assassin Tomb	Sequence 08	Seal of Amunet	89
No Laughing Matter		Assassination Contract	Sequence 09	3,000	94
Crash A Party		Assassination Contract	Sequence 09	3,000	94
False Legacy		Assassination Contract	Sequence 09	3,000	94
Visitazione's Secret		Assassin Tomb	Sequence 09	Seal of Leonius	95
Shipwrecked		Templar Lair*	Sequence 09	–	103
Hunting The Hunter		Assassination Contract	Sequence 10	4,500	102
Venetian Rush		Race	Sequence 10	3,500	102
Philanderer On The Roof		Beat Up Event	Sequence 11	3,500	102
The Perfect Marriage		Courier Assignment	Sequence 11	3,500	102

* ASSASSIN'S CREED II BLACK EDITION ONLY

HOW TO PLAY

WALKTHROUGH

REFERENCE &
ANALYSIS

EXTRAS

ACHIEVEMENTS
& TROPHIES

FREE MISSIONS

SECRETS

AC1:
STORY RECAP

AC2:
STORY RECAP

SECRETS

For players seeking 100% Synchronization, this section covers all hidden items and unlockable bonuses.

▌UNLOCKABLES ▌

SUBJECT 16'S VIDEO

Collect all the hidden Glyphs (see "Feathers & Glyphs"), and solve each puzzle to view Subject 16's video in its entirety. You can find solutions on page 170.

CONDOTTIERO WAR HAMMER & AUDITORE CAPE

After you place 50 Feathers in the chest in Maria's room at the Villa Auditore, a short cutscene takes place where Mario informs Ezio that he can now buy the powerful Condottiero War Hammer from the town Blacksmith. The base price is a hefty 33,250*f*, but this is reduced to 29,750*f* if you have implemented the two shop upgrades.

After collecting and storing all 100 Feathers in the Villa Auditore, Mario awards Ezio with the Auditore Cape. This special garment places Ezio in a permanent state of maximum Notoriety, which makes it a great tool for post-credits troublemaking. See the Reference & Analysis chapter for more details on these two items.

ALTAÏR'S ARMOR

You must collect six Seals from Assassin Tombs hidden throughout the game world to open the locked compartment in the Assassin Sanctuary beneath Villa Auditore. The table below provides page references to appropriate guidance for each one in the Walkthrough chapter. The attributes of Altaïr's armor are detailed on page 125.

SEAL	PAGE
Seal of Iltani	53
Seal of Qulan Gal	73
Seal of Amunet	89
Seal of Leonius	95
Seal of Wei Yu	65
Seal of Darius	51

PS3 EXCLUSIVE BONUSES

Players who own both Assassin's Creed II on PS3 and Assassin's Creed: Bloodlines on PSP can take advantage of unique connectivity between the two games to obtain special rewards. The first of these provides an opportunity to gain florins. Each Templar Coin collected in Bloodlines unlocks money in Assassin's Creed II at an exchange rate of 10*f* for Bronze, 100*f* for Silver, and 500*f* for Gold.

Once you collect them in Assassin's Creed: Bloodlines, six weapons can be transferred from your PSP to a special display rack at Villa Auditore. This process takes place automatically. Note that these do not count towards the value of the Monteriggioni settlement in the Villa minigame.

PSP TO PS3 WEAPON LIST

	NAME	DAMAGE	SPEED	DEFLECT
	Mace of the Bull	**	*****	**
	Maria Thorpe's Longsword	*	***	***
	Fredrick's Hammer	**	**	**
	Twins' Rapier	**	***	*****
	Bouchart's Blade	**	*****	*****
	Dark Oracle's Bone Dagger	**	****	****

FEATHERS & GLYPHS ■■■■

The 22 pages that follow reveal the locations of every last Feather and Glyph. With each annotated map accompanied by screenshots and helpful captions, we've tried to make the process of acquiring all 120 of these collectibles as painless as possible. Before we begin, a few valuable hunting tips:

◆ It's a good idea to have all Throwing Knife Belt upgrades before you start (see page 120). You'll encounter dozens of rooftop archers during your search, so these are essential tools. Replenish your supply at regular intervals, especially when you reach the more heavily guarded regions of Venice.

◆ Use the Medici and Venetian capes (see page 126) in the appropriate regions to avoid Notoriety-related complications.

◆ You must stand (or hang) close to Glyphs to scan them with Eagle Vision. Their puzzles start automatically, but you can access them again later via the Database/The Truth menu.

On the west face of Leonardo Da Vinci's workshop.

On a crane positioned on a rooftop north of Casa di Vespucci.

On top of a wooden crane positioned on a rooftop.

In front of a small window; there is a viewpoint tower just to the north of it.

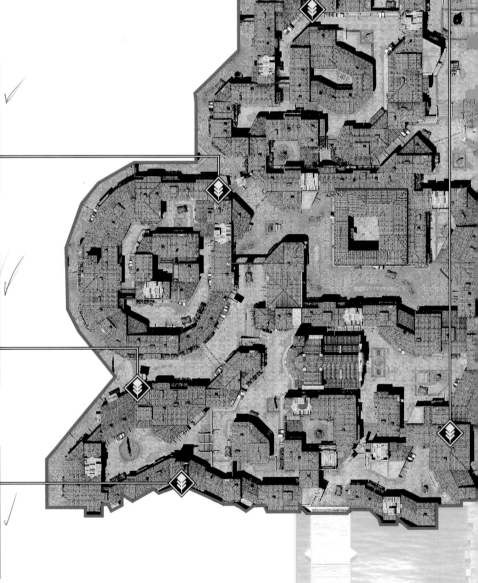

HOW TO PLAY

WALKTHROUGH

REFERENCE & ANALYSIS

EXTRAS

ACHIEVEMENTS & TROPHIES

FREE MISSIONS

SECRETS

AC1: STORY RECAP

AC2: STORY RECAP

On top of a chimney a short distance to the north of the Ponte Vecchio.

Climb up to the cross above the huge dome at Santa Maria Del Fiore.

East side of the Palazzo Della Signoria – the back end of the building you climb for the Jailbird mission.

On a wooden beam protruding from a building overlooking the river.

On top of a wooden beam, east side of the Ponte Vecchio.

On a wooden beam on the east side of a building not far south of the city gate.

Just outside a window above a small courtyard. Easy to spot if you approach via the surrounding rooftops.

On top of a derelict building.

On the southern rooftop of La Rosa Colta.

On a rooftop crane west of the Palazzo Della Signoria.

At the end of a beam on a wall above a Tailor's shop.

HOW TO PLAY

WALKTHROUGH

REFERENCE &
ANALYSIS

EXTRAS

ACHIEVEMENTS
& TROPHIES

FREE MISSIONS

SECRETS

AC1:
STORY RECAP

AC2:
STORY RECAP

Above a door, street level, at the northwest corner
of the Ospedale Degli Innocenti.

On the eastern rooftop at the Ospedale Degli
Innocenti.

On top of a partially derelict building north of
Santa Croce.

On top of Santa Croce — check the northern edge
of the roof.

On a beam extending from the top of an
abandoned building.

On the north side of Santa Croce, lower roof
section.

On a wooden beam on the city's north wall – easy to spot from the nearby rooftops.

On a wooden beam extending from the city wall. After climbing the first of the three beams, you'll twice need to perform a vertical wall run before jumping left to reach the Feather.

Just outside a small window situated just beneath the building's roof, with a Leap of Faith position above it.

Artfully disguised against decorative embellishments found high on the south face of Santa Maria Novella.

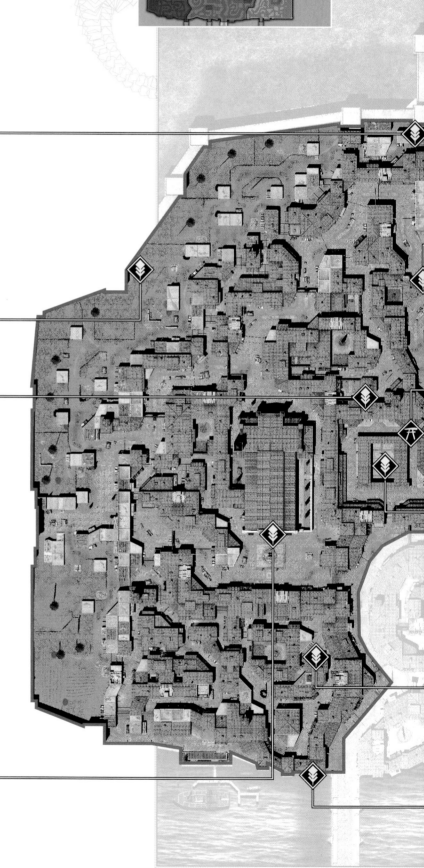

Situated between the dome and a bell tower at the northern edge of the San Lorenzo church.

HOW TO PLAY

WALKTHROUGH

REFERENCE &
ANALYSIS

EXTRAS

ACHIEVEMENTS
& TROPHIES

FREE MISSIONS

SECRETS

AC1:
STORY RECAP

AC2:
STORY RECAP

On a rooftop just a little to the east of the San Lorenzo dome.

Above two decorative archways.

On top of a statue partially covered by a white sheet at the center of the Mercato Vecchio.

Stand on the roof at the northeast corner of the Mercato Vecchio, then look down.

In front of a small window; should be easy to spot from on top of the building just across the street to the east (the one with three chimneys).

On a beam high on the wall of a building next to the river. Identify it from the nearby bridge, then climb up and drop down to it from the rooftop above.

On the roof of the cottage.

On the front face of Villa Auditore, close to the southwest corner.

On the roof of a house, just above a pile of hay.

On a rooftop near the center of the town; it's at the highest point of the building complex that includes the Bank.

On a Leap of Faith position halfway up the tower above the town entrance.

HOW TO PLAY

WALKTHROUGH

REFERENCE &
ANALYSIS

EXTRAS

ACHIEVEMENTS
& TROPHIES

FREE MISSIONS

SECRETS

AC1:
STORY RECAP

AC2:
STORY RECAP

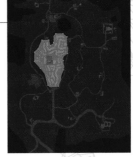

Behind the bell on top of the church.

Check the main entrance at the front of the Monte Oliveto Maggiore; facing it, the Feather is above and slightly to the right.

On the east face of the tower at the Monte Oliveto Maggiore.

On top of a pillar on the west side of the Antico Teatro Romano.

Inside a covered "tunnel" section on the east side of the Antico Teatro Romano.

On a beam extending from the north face of the tower.

On top of a tower north of Santa Maria Assunta (note: not the one with the belfry).

Facing the front of the Santa Maria Assunta, go through the archway to the left of the main entrance.

On the east face of the tower, positioned on a beam. While scaling the walls (start on the south face), drop down from the hand-holds above to reach it.

On a beam extending from a tower; you will pass it en route to the viewpoint above.

HOW TO PLAY

WALKTHROUGH

REFERENCE &
ANALYSIS

EXTRAS

ACHIEVEMENTS
& TROPHIES

FREE MISSIONS

SECRETS

AC1:
STORY RECAP

AC2:
STORY RECAP

On a wooden beam, north face of the tower.

At the top of the Torre del Diavolo.

On a beam extending from the northern tower of
the Torri dei Salvucci – look right from the Leap of
Faith position to see it.

Visible from a rooftop between the two towers of
the Torri dei Salvucci.

On the outer wall of the town; it's above a herald.

Above the south entrance to San Gimignano.

On a beam at the back of the church; drop from the platform above to reach it.

On top of a building; easy to see from any one of the surrounding rooftops.

Situated above the colonnade on the west side of San Mercuriale.

On top of a wall tower; like others in a similar position here in Forlì, you can reach it via a rope that connects it to nearby buildings.

On a wooden beam on the west side of a building, easy to spot if you look up from street level. Drop down from the platform above to reach it.

On top of wooden beams that link two separate buildings just across the street from the west side of San Mercuriale.

On a wooden beam high on a building to your left as you enter Forlì's south gate

HOW TO PLAY

WALKTHROUGH

REFERENCE &
ANALYSIS

EXTRAS

ACHIEVEMENTS
& TROPHIES

FREE MISSIONS

SECRETS

AC1:
STORY RECAP

AC2:
STORY RECAP

Behind a large abandoned building not far from
a viewpoint tower in the northeast corner of the
map; drop from the platform above to reach it.

On the outside of a lighthouse tower (with a
viewpoint above) situated in the far northeast
corner of the map.

On top of a wooden pole in the water; it looks like
a mooring point.

On a wooden beam that extends from the outer
wall that surrounds the town; climb the building
to the west to cross the ropes.

On a pole that extends from the wall above the
south entrance of San Mercuriale.

On top of the city walls; reach it via ropes
that link it to buildings to the west.

On a beam that extends from the east face
of the tower.

On a rooftop just north of the entrance to the main office at the Gilda dei Ladri di Venezi.

On top of wooden beams above a canal that connect two separate buildings.

On a wooden beam overlooking the sea, south face of the buildings.

On a wooden beam above a Blacksmith.

On a wooden beam above a bridge.

Between two sets of wooden planks and beams that link two buildings; almost directly above a bridge.

On top of a blue and white mooring pole in a canal, not far west of a bridge.

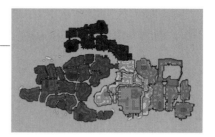

HOW TO PLAY

WALKTHROUGH

REFERENCE & ANALYSIS

EXTRAS

ACHIEVEMENTS & TROPHIES

FREE MISSIONS

SECRETS

AC1: STORY RECAP

AC2: STORY RECAP

On top of a wooden pole on the Ponte di Rialto.

Beneath the east side of the Ponte di Rialto – it's clearly visible as you swim under the bridge.

Between the dome and bell tower on top of San Giacomo di Rialto.

On top of a sign on the west face of a building; easy to see from the street below.

On a beam extending from the west face of a building overlooking a canal; below, there are two bridges to either side of it.

On a balcony – easy to see if you approach via the surrounding rooftops.

On top of a mooring pole in the canal.

On the side of a house overlooking the water; there is a wharf slightly north of it.

On the side of a building directly above an arch; can be seen from the bridge.

On a balcony overlooking a canal; there are two bridges to either side of it.

HOW TO PLAY

WALKTHROUGH

REFERENCE &
ANALYSIS

EXTRAS

ACHIEVEMENTS
& TROPHIES

FREE MISSIONS

SECRETS

AC1:
STORY RECAP

AC2:
STORY RECAP

On a wooden beam above a narrow alleyway.

On the south wall of a building, near the roof;
there is a hiding spot above it.

On a crane situated on a rooftop south of the
domes at the Basilica di San Marco.

On the roof of the Torre dell'Orologio, directly
above the clock.

On the side of a building; there is a Blacksmith
directly below.

On the floor of an open section near the top of the
Campanile di San Marco.

Above a basket of flowers hanging from the corner of a building that overlooks the water.

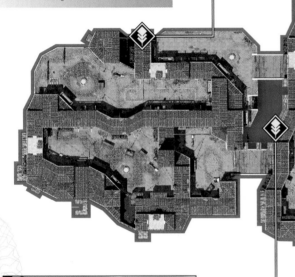

On the west face of a building, above a canal; there is a bridge just south of its position.

On the east face of a building, with a canal below; there is a bridge to the south.

On a wooden beam that connects two houses high above a street; it's easier to see from the rooftops.

HOW TO PLAY

WALKTHROUGH

REFERENCE &
ANALYSIS

EXTRAS

ACHIEVEMENTS
& TROPHIES

FREE MISSIONS

SECRETS

AC1:
STORY RECAP

AC2:
STORY RECAP

On a beam that connects two buildings; it's a short walk southwest from a nearby rooftop shelter.

On the north face of a building overlooking a canal.

On the windowless west face of a building, just above an enclosed garden area.

On the ship – more specifically, on top of a yardarm.

On the east face of a building; it's directly above an archway.

On a wooden beam linking two houses in the
northwest corner of the Arsenale di Venezia
compound.

On top of the Scuola Grande di San Marco.

On a wooden beam above a small courtyard;
there is a crane on the rooftop opposite.

On a wooden beam that extends from the roof
of the last house in a row of buildings; there are
three cranes nearby.

On the west face of the Quartier Generale di
Bartolomeo D'Alviano; a ladder on the east side
of the building offers easy access to the rooftop.

On the east face of a building next to a canal.

On a wooden framework above a bridge.

HOW TO PLAY

WALKTHROUGH

REFERENCE &
ANALYSIS

EXTRAS

ACHIEVEMENTS
& TROPHIES

FREE MISSIONS

SECRETS

AC1:
STORY RECAP

AC2:
STORY RECAP

On a wooden beam extending from a guard tower; to reach it, scale the buildings in the northeast corner of the compound to get on top of the outer wall.

On the east face of a building; there is a Tailor a short distance south of it.

On a wooden beam just west of a rooftop hiding spot; it's visible from the nearby bridge if you approach it from street level.

On the east side of San Pietro di Castello.

Above a Blacksmith east of San Pietro di Castello.

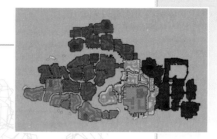

On the north face of a building with a glorious sea view; there is a wooden balcony to the west of it.

On a wooden beam in a narrow alleyway; it's directly above a boarded-up door and three barrels.

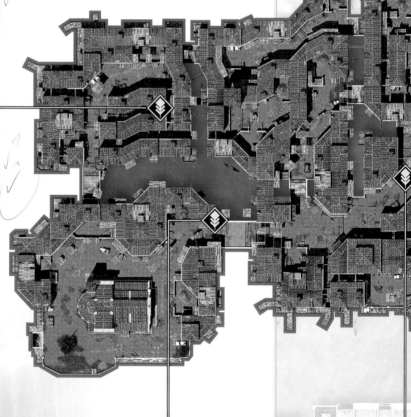

On a wooden platform on the south face of a house, above a bridge.

On top of a crane; it's much easier to see from one of the surrounding rooftops.

HOW TO PLAY

WALKTHROUGH

REFERENCE &
ANALYSIS

EXTRAS

ACHIEVEMENTS
& TROPHIES

FREE MISSIONS

SECRETS

AC1:
STORY RECAP

AC2:
STORY RECAP

High on the north face of a building; there is a wharf directly below it.

On a wooden beam above a narrow alleyway; face east from the entrance beside the Blacksmith store to see it.

On top of a mooring pole; easy to spot from the bridge just south of its position.

On the wall of a building opposite an Art Merchant.

A little west from a rooftop hiding spot, on top of stonework linking two buildings.

Finding all 20 Glyphs is only half of the challenge: to view Subject 16's secret video, you must first solve his puzzles using the Database/The Truth menu. Each type has its own interface, with relevant button commands displayed onscreen. The four most common varieties warrant a brief introduction.

◆ **Observation puzzles:** highlight and select an obscure point of interest on the displayed photograph or illustration.

◆ **Picture identification puzzles:** challenge you to discover a theme that connects five pictures out of ten, then select them.

◆ **Combination lock puzzles:** present a circular picture divided into five rings with a fixed point at the center. You must rotate these rings to display the correct image. The first you encounter are ridiculously simple, but they become far more complicated when certain rings are connected to others. Our solutions refer to the innermost ring as Ring 1 and the outermost as Ring 5, with an obvious progression in between.

◆ **Password puzzles:** require players to find a cipher key hidden somewhere on the screen, then use a codewheel to learn a three-digit code.

Note that it doesn't matter what Glyphs you find first: you will always have to solve the puzzles in the same order.

Before you continue, a warning: the solutions we offer in this section are *very* direct. If you're keen to work on the puzzles yourself, read no further.

Puzzle	1: In the Beginning
Description	

A gentle start: choose the paintings that contain apples.

Solution

Puzzle	2: Sixty-Four Squares
Description	

Rotate the wheels to complete pictures of Queen Elizabeth I, Napoleon and George Washington.

Solution

These first examples of the combination lock puzzle type are extremely simple – just start with the inner ring, using the central point as a "key", then work your way outwards.

Puzzle	3: Descendants
Description	

Locate a Piece of Eden in three pictures.

Solution

The first is on the left edge of Roosevelt's desk, the second is just below Houdini (on the right-hand side of the water tank), and the third on top of Gandhi's walking stick (left-hand side of his body).

Puzzle	4: Infinite Knowledge
Description	

-

Solution

First, locate a hidden image in three pictures. With the Burning Viet Cong Base Camp, it's in the barrel of the weapon carried by the soldier; in the second picture, it's the helmet of the crouching soldier on the far side of the street; for the third, it's on a bayonet in the center. For the final picture, select the apple held by a figure near the top right-hand corner.

Puzzle	5: Instruments of Power
Description	

Puzzle #1: Pick the pictures where figures are carrying swords.

Solution

Description

Puzzle #2: Choose the five paintings where a person is carrying a staff.

Solution

Puzzle	6: Brothers
Description	
Picture #1	
Solution	

◆ Move Ring 1 two notches left.
◆ Move Ring 2 three notches left.
◆ Move Ring 4 (linked to Ring 3) one notch to the right.
◆ Move Ring 5 (linked to Ring 4) three notches to the right.
◆ Rotate Ring 3 to complete the puzzle.

Description
Picture #2
Solution

◆ Rotate Ring 1 three notches to the left.
◆ Rotate Ring 3 one notch to the left
◆ Rotate Ring 4 (linked to Ring 2) four notches to the left.
◆ Rotate Ring 5 one notch to the right.
◆ Rotate Ring 2 to complete the puzzle.

Description
Picture #3
Solution

◆ Rotate Ring 1 three notches left.
◆ Rotate Ring 3 one notch to the right.
◆ Rotate Ring 4 five notches to the left.
◆ Rotate Ring 5 one notch to the left.
◆ Rotate Ring 2 to complete the puzzle.

Description
Picture #4
Solution

◆ Rotate Ring 3 one notch to the right.
◆ Rotate Ring 5 (linked to Ring 4) two notches left
◆ Rotate Ring 4 (linked to Ring 2) two notches left
◆ Rotate Ring 2 (linked to Ring 1) six notches to the right.
◆ Rotate Ring 1 to complete the puzzle.

Puzzle	7: Keep On Seeking, And You Shall Find
Description	

Puzzle #1: You need to pick four pictures that contain red cloth, and a fifth where a snake is entwined around a tree beside a golden fleece.

Solution

Description
Puzzle #2
Solution

Select the "shroud" Piece of Eden to the right of Jesus.

Puzzle	8: Martyrs
Description	

-

Solution

Select the staff in the first picture, then the sword in the second. Let the sound effects guide you to the precise positions. On the final screen, move the pointer into the flame and carry it to Joan of Arc, then combine the final two images.

Puzzle	9: Hat Trick
Description	

-

Solution

Select the Piece of Eden on Houdini's body and on Gandhi's chest by following the heartbeat signal. At the password puzzle, the solution is "312".

Puzzle	10: Apollo
Description	
Puzzle #1	
Solution	

Select the hidden lunar lander near the bottom of the screen, just to the left of the moon.

Description
Puzzle #2
Solution

◆ Rotate Ring 5 (linked to Ring 1) six notches to the left.
◆ Rotate Ring 2 (linked to Ring 4) four notches to the left.
◆ Rotate Ring 4 (linked to Ring 3) three notches to the right.
◆ Rotate Ring 3 (linked to Ring 1) five notches to the left.
◆ Rotate Ring 1 to complete the puzzle.

Description
Puzzle #3
Solution

The Piece of Eden is located in the shadow to the left of the astronaut.

Puzzle	11: The Inventor
Description	
Puzzle #1	
Solution	

Before you can begin the puzzles, move the pointer into each light bulb to continue. Now select the hidden picture directly above the main door, between the small windows.

Description
Puzzle #2
Solution

The Piece of Eden is on Tesla's lap.

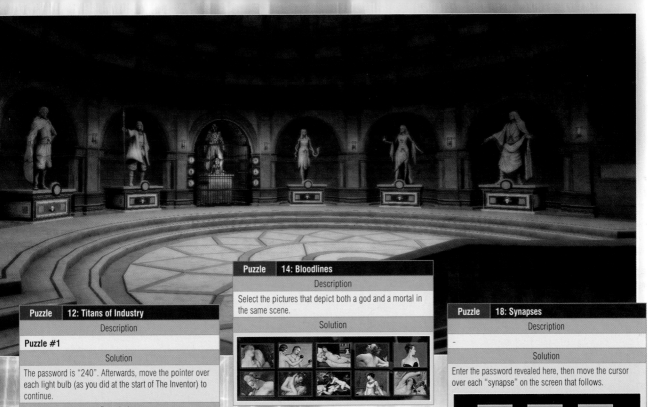

HOW TO PLAY

WALKTHROUGH

REFERENCE & ANALYSIS

EXTRAS

ACHIEVEMENTS & TROPHIES

FREE MISSIONS

SECRETS

AC1: STORY RECAP

AC2: STORY RECAP

Puzzle 14: Bloodlines

Description

Select the pictures that depict both a god and a mortal in the same scene.

Solution

Puzzle 15: Guardians

Description

This is a tricky combination lock. After you complete it, highlight the red markers on the following screen to continue.

Solution

- Rotate Ring 5 (linked to Ring 2) five notches to the right.
- Rotate Ring 3 (linked to Ring 4) two notches to the right.
- Rotate Ring 4 (linked to Ring 1) five notches to the right.
- Rotate Ring 2 five notches to the left.
- Rotate Ring 1 (linked to Ring 5) one notch to the left.

Puzzle 16: The Cavalry

Description

-

Solution

Carefully move the cursor to select Alaska without touching any other names, then direct the pointer to Tunguska at the top of the screen. Collect the staff, then move it onto Tesla's picture.

Puzzle 17: The Bunker

Puzzle #1

Solution

The solution is:

Description

Puzzle #2

Solution

Select the Assassins Brotherhood logo. It's just below the roof of the building in the top right-hand corner of the image.

Puzzle 12: Titans of Industry

Description

Puzzle #1

Solution

The password is "240". Afterwards, move the pointer over each light bulb (as you did at the start of The Inventor) to continue.

Description

Puzzle #2

Solution

The Piece of Eden is clearly visible in the middle of the image.

Description

Puzzle #3

Solution

The password is as follows:

Puzzle 13: "I Am Become Death, the Destroyer of Worlds"

Description

Puzzle #1

Solution

The solution is:

Description

Puzzle #2

Solution

Press the button.

Description

Puzzle #3

Solution

Use the sound effects as a cue to locate the code at the bottom of the screen.

Puzzle 18: Synapses

Description

-

Solution

Enter the password revealed here, then move the cursor over each "synapse" on the screen that follows.

Puzzle 19: The Fourth Day

Description

Select the pictures that contain depictions of the sun, then scour the surface of the sun to find the Earth.

Puzzle 20: The Origin of the Species

Description

Puzzle #1

Solution

- Rotate Ring 5 (linked to Ring 3) two notches to the left.
- Rotate Ring 4 two notches to the left.
- Rotate Ring 3 (linked to Ring 1) two notches to the right.
- Rotate Ring 2 five notches to the right.
- Rotate Ring 1 (linked to Ring 5) three notches to the left.

Description

Puzzle #2

Solution

Use the sound effects as a cue to locate the icon of the Vitruvian Man at the top of the screen.

Description

Puzzle #3

Solution

Notice the phrase: "Nothing is true, everything is permitted." Therefore, all possible choices in the cipher keypad are correct: simply select any three glyph symbols. Finally move the pointer over all of the skeleton bones.

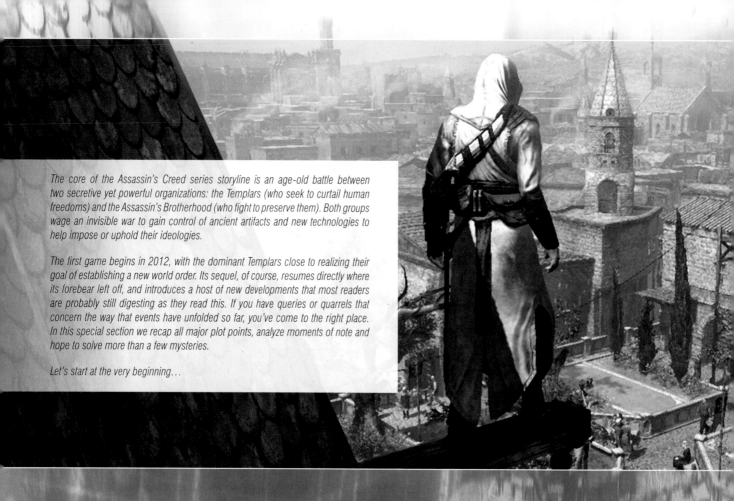

The core of the Assassin's Creed series storyline is an age-old battle between two secretive yet powerful organizations: the Templars (who seek to curtail human freedoms) and the Assassin's Brotherhood (who fight to preserve them). Both groups wage an invisible war to gain control of ancient artifacts and new technologies to help impose or uphold their ideologies.

The first game begins in 2012, with the dominant Templars close to realizing their goal of establishing a new world order. Its sequel, of course, resumes directly where its forebear left off, and introduces a host of new developments that most readers are probably still digesting as they read this. If you have queries or quarrels that concern the way that events have unfolded so far, you've come to the right place. In this special section we recap all major plot points, analyze moments of note and hope to solve more than a few mysteries.

Let's start at the very beginning…

ASSASSIN'S CREED: STORY RECAP

Assassin's Creed features two parallel yet intertwined tales. In one, Desmond Miles is a barman inexplicably kidnapped by Abstergo, a pharmaceutical company. Designated as "Subject 17", Desmond is forced to interact with a machine called "the Animus" (Latin for "soul"). This phenomenally advanced technology immerses its subject in a form of virtual reality where they can experience hereditary memories that are stored in DNA. This information, the story postulates, is responsible for what might traditionally be regarded as instinct in animals. By interpreting this data, the Animus user can conceivably relive past lives with a startling degree of authenticity.

The second (and dominant) plot strand concerns the experiences that Desmond has of a direct-line ancestor through his interaction with the Abstergo machine. Though the company seeks a very specific memory, the Animus cannot simply pluck it directly from a subject's body or mind. Instead, Desmond must live through several days in the life of a distant antecedent: Altaïr, a trained assassin.

Both narratives dovetail to form a cliffhanger ending that fascinated and frustrated players in equal measure, with particular attention focused on its post-credits mystery (where Desmond is left to ponder cryptic messages left for him by Subject 16, a former prisoner in the Abstergo laboratory). After rampant speculation from fans worldwide, we hope to finally answer many of the questions that have haunted Assassin's Creed players since its original release. We'll begin with a recap of the two main stories.

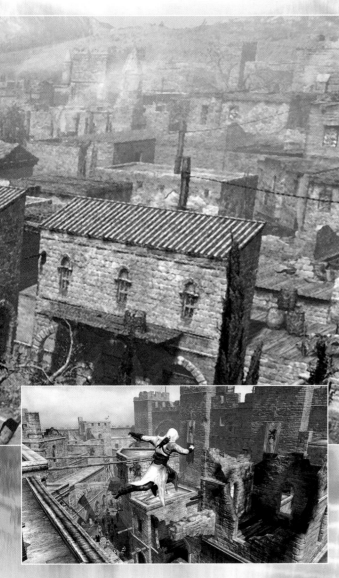

same object – Altaïr is thrown aside by de Sablé, cut off from the melee that ensues by a collapsing wall, and escapes alone.

On his return to the Brotherhood stronghold at Masyaf, Altaïr meets with faction leader Al Mualim ("The Teacher"), and is shamed by the account offered by his surviving accomplice, who successfully retrieved the strange golden object. Despite Altaïr's bravery during a subsequent Templar siege of the fortress, he is subjected to a mock execution. He awakes to learn that he has been demoted to a mere Initiate, losing all weapons and privileges unique to his previous high rank. Al Mualim castigates Altaïr savagely, but offers a path to redemption: assassinate nine targets in the cities of Damascus, Acre and Jerusalem, and be restored to his former standing.

HOW TO PLAY

WALKTHROUGH

REFERENCE & ANALYSIS

EXTRAS

ACHIEVEMENTS & TROPHIES

FREE MISSIONS

SECRETS

AC1: STORY RECAP

AC2: STORY RECAP

▌1191: ALTAÏR ▐

While installed in the Animus, Desmond relives key moments in the life of Altaïr Ibn La-Ahad ("Son of None"). Altaïr, we learn, is a senior member of the Assassin's Brotherhood during the Third Crusade. The memory begins with the assassin, joined by two accomplices, attempting to secure an artifact from the Temple of Solomon.

We soon learn that Altaïr is a flawed character, defined (at least at first) by his arrogance and an almost contemptuous disregard for the central tenets of the Brotherhood. When he rashly confronts Robert de Sablé – Grand Master of the Knights Templar, sworn enemies of the Brotherhood, who are also seeking the

As Altaïr tracks down each target in turn, he begins to question the motivation for the killings. Though the majority of the nine are ostensibly guilty of great cruelty or venality, many of them insist (during ethereal post-mortem dialogue sequences that follow each assassination) that their actions were necessary to achieve a higher purpose. Altaïr learns that the object retrieved from the Temple of Solomon is a "Piece of Eden", a mystical device that enables its holder to manipulate the minds of others. The Templars, it transpires, would use it to bring peace to the region and, ultimately, the world, but at a questionable moral price: the enforced sacrifice of free will by all who fall under its spell.

The ninth Templar, Robert de Sablé, reveals to Altaïr that the device's power is now known only to one other: Al Mualim, who seeks to possess it exclusively for his own ends. The assassin, finally comprehending the full import of his tutor's manipulation, returns to Masyaf to confront him. Altaïr is less susceptible to the Piece of Eden than others, Al Mualim reveals, yet he still struggles to overcome its illusions during their climatic battle. Once Al Mualim falls to Altaïr's blade, the Assassin watches in wonder as the Piece of Eden opens, projecting the location of other devices throughout the world.

Though Altaïr's story ends abruptly as Desmond is ejected from the Animus, it is possible to re-enter the assassin's world after the final credits to replay various moments. Inquisitive players who explored the text summaries for each Sequence were rewarded with an epilogue written by Altaïr, attached to the final Al-Mualim fight. In it, he reflects on the purpose of the Piece of Eden and his decision not to destroy it, and appears to be resolved to leading the surviving members of the Brotherhood.

HISTORICAL INFLUENCES

The Assassin's Brotherhood is based loosely on the Hashshashin, a faction of **Nizārī Ismāʻīlī Shīʻa Islam** defined by political, social and philosophical goals too complex to summarize in a satisfactory manner here. Hashshashin (or, some believe, the Arabic word "**haššāšīn**", "Followers of Hassan-i Sabbah", an important figure in the Hashshashin) is thought to be the source of the word "Assassin".

Rather than raise a conventional army, the Hashshashin trained sleeper agents (known as Fedayeen) to infiltrate the ranks of their enemies. When Nizari interests or civilians were threatened, the Fedayeen would take necessary steps to remedy the situation. This did not always necessarily involve the murder of a specific target; instead, an individual might awake to find a dagger placed on their pillow in a chilling statement designed to curtail further antagonism. One unverified but thrilling account relates that when Saladin besieged the Hashshashin fortress of Musyaf in 1176, an assassin stole into his tent in the dead of night and left a poisoned cake and a note on his chest as he slept. The message read, simply: "You are in our power." Saladin, the tale ends, immediately entered into parley and maintained a respectful relationship with the Hashshashin thereafter.

The Templars are clearly inspired by The Knights Templar, who should be familiar to most readers through their appearances in literature, cinema and conspiracy theories. The devoted soldiers of this Christian military order were both iconic and effective during the Crusades, while the wider infrastructure of the organization is said to have made important innovations in the nascent field of banking. When the war to claim the Holy Land ended, however, charitable donations and popular support dwindled. Later persecuted by Philip IV in France in 1307 (where senior Templars were arrested, tortured and executed), the order was officially disbanded by Pope Clement V in 1314.

This abrupt dissolution, along with the appropriation of Templar imagery by later Masonic orders and an association with the Grail legend in fiction, is perhaps why the Knights Templar remain the subject of enthusiastic speculation to this day. According to one legend, Jacques de Molay, the last recognized Grand Master, cursed Philip IV and Clement V during his execution, claiming that both would be summoned to face God within a year. Though the authenticity of the tale is obviously uncertain, it's true that both king and Pope died before this portentous deadline.

2012: ABSTERGO LABORATORY

HOW TO PLAY

WALKTHROUGH

REFERENCE & ANALYSIS

EXTRAS

ACHIEVEMENTS & TROPHIES

FREE MISSIONS

SECRETS

AC1: STORY RECAP

AC2: STORY RECAP

Despite his initial protestations and bewilderment at his abduction, Desmond Miles is not accurately characterized as simply a barman: he is an estranged member of the modern-day Assassin's Brotherhood. After escaping from a secret Brotherhood compound at age 16, he attempted to live anonymously under an assumed name, avoiding all contact with technology or agencies that might reveal his identify or location. His sole mistake was to acquire a license for a motorcycle (a "guilty pleasure", he admits) that united a photo and fingerprint. This was all that his captors needed to locate him.

Abstergo is a corporation run by modern-day Templars, who still wage a secret crusade to protect mankind by restricting free will, while the Brotherhood still fight to preserve humanity's right to self-determination. Through the exploration of Desmond's ancestral memories of Altaïr, the Templars hope to discover the location of all existing Pieces of Eden. By subsequently launching one of these artifacts into orbit on board a satellite, they plan to broadcast its power worldwide, enslaving (though they would doubtlessly argue "saving") all but the few with innate resistance to the control each device exerts. It is perhaps telling that "abstergo" is a Latin word that means to "cleanse", or "wipe away".

In the sterile confines of the Abstergo laboratory, Desmond interacts with only two of the company's employees: Warren Vidic (who, in a broad sense, invented the Animus), and his assistant, Lucy Stillman. Vidic is officious, driven and arrogant; a Templar with little regard for Desmond's wellbeing. Stillman is more pragmatic, and is quick to rebuke Vidic on his treatment of their test subject. The relationship between the two scientists is complex. Stillman reveals to Desmond that Abstergo hired her as a graduate, having taken a special interest

in her studies. Despite her vital contributions to the Animus project, three company employees (presumably Templars) were sent to execute her once the device was complete. Only the timely intervention of Vidic saved her life; for this, she says, tolerating his brusque manner and assorted foibles is a small price. However, like Desmond, she too is a prisoner of the company, unable to leave the premises.

Over the course of several days Desmond enters the Animus for hours at a time, before spending his evenings locked in a suite adjacent to the laboratory. Through conversations with Vidic and Stillman, and his experiences as Altaïr, he gradually learns more of Abstergo's activities and intentions. Following the death of Robert de Sablé, he is abruptly pulled from the Animus due to an unsuccessful (and unseen) attempt by the Brotherhood to storm the facility. At this point, Stillman subtly reveals that she, too, is an Assassin, a sleeper agent sent to infiltrate the Templar ranks.

With the completion of the memory where Altaïr confronts Al Mualim, the Templars obtain the locations of the Pieces of Eden. As Desmond lies on the Animus, he hears Vidic confirm the existence of at least six of these to an unseen male colleague, with teams poised to explore each location to retrieve them. Vidic intends to execute Desmond, but refrains from doing so when Stillman insists that he may yet still be of value. As the two scientists depart, Desmond realizes that something is seriously amiss. His vision is blurred yet augmented in a way that resembles Altaïr's Eagle Vision, his uncanny ability to discern the unseen and differentiate between friend and foe. Vidic appears highlighted in an angry red hue; Stillman, a reassuring blue.

The Abstergo employees exit the laboratory, leaving Desmond to discover that the walls and floors are somehow covered in arcane symbols and coded, cryptic texts apparently written in several languages. As he exclaims his astonishment, the final credits roll…

ABSTERGO ESPIONAGE

During his time in the Abstergo laboratory, Desmond is mysteriously provided with the keycode to his cell, and later acquires passcards that enable him to read emails on the laboratory computers. Some of these make small yet intriguing contributions to the Assassin's Creed backstory, so we'll review the most interesting revelations here.

◆ A Piece of Eden (described as "number two") was recently in the Templar's possession, but was destroyed in an explosion during the launch or construction of a satellite at Denver International Airport. This clearly indicates that the Templars have attempted to put their grand plan into action before the events of Assassin's Creed. An email from a surviving witness alleges that the Abstergo personnel present at the site "went crazy" when a "metal ball" opened. "Shooting. Stabbing. Tore each other to pieces," the writer flatly states, before threatening to blow the whistle on the company's involvement.

◆ Abstergo's pharmaceutical division has been shut down pending a government investigation into the illegal use of an experimental drug (dubbed "New Fluoride") that poisoned the inhabitants of an unspecified town. This scrutiny of the firm's activities means that senior Templars are unequivocal in their insistence that the plan to launch the Piece of Eden into space must proceed on schedule.

◆ Subject 12 was the direct descendant of an individual involved (or subjected to) the Philadelphia Experiment, a popular conspiracy theory where a naval vessel is alleged to have travelled forward in time for 18 minutes. The email claims that the Templars obtained sufficient information to reconstruct the device responsible, but will not continue with development due to concerns about the creation of irreparable time paradoxes.

◆ The Templars believe that the Tunguska Event (a massive explosion that flattened more than 2,000 kilometres of pine forest in what is now Krasnoyarsk Krai in Russia) was the result of a Brotherhood attack on one of their research stations. The real-life event took place in 1908, and is popularly attributed to the airburst explosion of a large meteoroid or cometary fragment.

◆ As not everyone is apparently influenced by the Pieces of Eden, Abstergo are planning to retrieve and recreate technology destroyed in the Tunguska Event as

a tool or weapon to use against "holdouts". The company's Lineage Discovery and Acquisition Division has been tasked to locate descendants of any potential Tunguska survivors.

◆ The Templars have cancelled their search for the Holy Grail, now believing it to be a myth or of no specific value.

◆ "Mitchell-Hedges communicators" are being used to transmit secure messages between Templar facilities, but their numbers are apparently limited. This alludes to a crystal skull allegedly discovered buried inside a temple (located in what is now Belize) by Anna Le Guillon Mitchell-Hedges in 1924. The skull is crafted from a single block of quartz and, Mitchell-Hedges claimed, is both thousands of years old and possesses supernatural powers. The hypothesis that it (and others like it) might enable telepathic communication is one of many strange, wonderful and categorically unproven theories that surround these objects. As an interesting footnote, it's worth knowing that crystal skulls have been associated by aspirant eschatologists with the coming of the thirteenth Baktun of the Mayan calendar on December 21 2012, and the events that will supposedly ensue. (The scientific view, by contrast, is that many of the skulls were manufactured in nineteenth century Germany to capitalize on a profitable trade in fake Mesoamerican artifacts.)

◆ Lucy Stillman has deleted emails that suggest that she was in direct contact with the Brotherhood throughout Desmond's time in captivity. When the attack on the facility fails (apparently instigated at her request), she reassures Desmond by folding a finger out of sight – a gesture taken to mean that she, like Altaïr (who had a digit removed to accommodate his hidden blade) is an assassin.

▌EPILOGUE: SUBJECT 16 ▌

Some fans have argued that the most fascinating developments in the Assassin's Creed story occur during its eerie epilogue sequence, where Desmond is free to explore the laboratory and consider the import of the hidden messages he finds.

The first and easiest mystery to solve is how Desmond comes to acquire the Eagle Vision power. An email on Vidic's computer explains the "Bleeding Effect", a symptom of Animus use that causes a potentially dangerous blending of genetic and real-time memory. Prolonged exposure, it seems, may lead to users being incapable of differentiating between their own memories or personal attributes and those of antecedents, in a manner akin to an exaggerated multiple personality disorder. Though Desmond appears to be spared the deleterious effects that apparently drove previous subjects insane, he has nonetheless experienced a "bleeding" of Altaïr's mind into his own. This explains the Eagle Vision. Attentive players will have noticed that this is foreshadowed on several occasions during the story: every time Desmond fell asleep in his cell, glowing writing could be seen to briefly flash on the wall above his bed.

The same email introduces Desmond's predecessor, Subject 16, who Lucy Stillman believes lost his mind due to aggressive use of the Animus and the damaging consequences of the Bleeding Effect. This individual eventually took his own life – but only after daubing the lab's walls and floors with arcane symbols and messages

written in his own blood. Though naturally scrubbed clean before Desmond's arrival, his Eagle Vision enables him to see them as if freshly painted.

In this final section we will examine each message and picture in turn. Though we can identify *what* they are, and speculate on plausible interpretations, the truth of *why* Subject 16 wrote them will be explained later...

TRIANGLE & BAR CODE

Triangular block of text: Though it seems impenetrable at first glance, this is pretty easy to decipher. Start at the bottom right-hand corner, then read each column from bottom to top. The full message reads: "They drained my soul and made it theirs. I drain my body to show you where I saw it." This is Subject 16's introduction to his dramatic valediction. "They drained my soul," refers to his experience of being forced to use the Animus; "I drain my body to show you where I saw it," starkly attests that he sacrificed his life to write the messages in his own blood.

Lines: Some have suggested that this is a bar code, and therefore an oblique reference to Revelations 13:16-18. In the New International Version this reads: "He also forced everyone, small and great, rich and poor, free and slave, to receive a mark on his right hand or on his forehead, so that no one could buy or sell unless he had the mark, which is the name of the beast or the number of his name. This calls for wisdom. If anyone has insight, let him calculate the number of the beast, for it is man's number. His number is 666."

12212012: This is a date. December 21, 2012 (though some say the 23rd) is believed to be the day that the Mesoamerican Long Count calendar, most notably used by the Maya, reaches its thirteenth Baktun cycle. Though little if any corroborating evidence exists, some believe that the advent of "13.0.0.0.0" in this calendar will mark the beginning of Armageddon, and the end of the human race. Others have posited less radical (but perhaps no less fanciful) claims that it will be a transition to a new age, accompanied by a palpable shift in human consciousness or behavior. In the Assassin's Creed universe, of course, December 21, 2012 is the day that the Templars plan to launch a satellite loaded with a Piece of Eden into Earth orbit.

HOW TO PLAY

WALKTHROUGH

REFERENCE & ANALYSIS

EXTRAS

ACHIEVEMENTS & TROPHIES

FREE MISSIONS

SECRETS

AC1: STORY RECAP

AC2: STORY RECAP

THREE INTERLOCKING CIRCLES/RINGS

Situated at the bottom of the Animus, this drawing could be interpreted as being a biological hazard trefoil, with Subject 16 communicating the dangers of extended exposure to the machine. It is, however, a (very subtle) allusion to the Templars. The interlocking circles resemble trefoils or Borromean rings employed to explain and illustrate the Christian Trinity of Father, Son and Holy Ghost united in one Godhead.

PENTAGRAM

A pentagram with a single point facing downwards is popularly associated with Satanism; interestingly, a solitary prong of this drawing points towards the headrest of the Animus. This is Subject 16 attempting to warn that the work conducted by Asbtergo in the device is "evil". (The fact that the five-pointed star is enclosed within circles means that some might more readily identify it as a pentacle – a symbol associated with Wiccan and neo-Pagan beliefs.)

SQUARE OF WRITING

Like the triangular block of text, this isn't too taxing to decode: just read each column from bottom to top, starting from the right-hand side and moving left. The message is the clearest warning of the Templar's grand plan: "Artefacts sent to the skies to control all nations. To make us obey. A hidden crusade. Do not help them."

HOW TO PLAY

WALKTHROUGH

REFERENCE &
ANALYSIS

EXTRAS

ACHIEVEMENTS
& TROPHIES

FREE MISSIONS

SECRETS

**AC1:
STORY RECAP**

AC2:
STORY RECAP

TRIANGLE & APPLE

Subject 16 knew of the Templar plot to send a Piece of Eden into orbit. This drawing represents the artifact controlling the minds of all who live beneath it.

ANIMAL PICTURES

These are representations of three geoglyphs located in Peru as part of the Nazca Lines. They have been preserved to the modern day by the stable climate of the desert plateau, and are believed to have served a religious purpose. Historians have speculated that they were drawn by the Nazca culture in an attempt to communicate with gods in the sky. This is a clue as to who Subject 16's ancestors were, and where a Piece of Eden may be located.

YONAGUNI

It's easy to discern the Japanese themes here: what appears to be Mount Fuji, the sun, a gate, and a pagoda. Yonaguni is a small Japanese island at the south of the Ryukyu chain that is tied to the Yonaguni Monument: a sizable underwater rock formation that some claim contains significant man-made features. It has been referred to as "the Japanese Atlantis".

RAISED PLATFORM ART

This drawing represents Machu Picchu, the famous Incan city situated on top of a mountain ridge above the Urubamba Valley in Peru. Again, this is a hint from Subject 16 to reveal where he has travelled in the Animus.

PYRAMID

This appears to be a step pyramid of the type most commonly associated with Mesoamerican cultures, with no other distinguishing characteristics. It can be interpreted as Subject 16 underlining the point made by his drawings of the Nazca Lines and Machu Picchu.

EYE IN TRIANGLE

This is the Eye of Providence (or "all-seeing eye"), a symbol traditionally used to represent God looking down upon his subjects. It has been employed by Freemasons as a motif since the eighteenth century and, to the perpetual consternation of many conspiracy theorists, features on the Great Seal of the United States of America (and, therefore, the reverse of the US dollar bill). Though tenuous, it could be that this is an allusion to the launch of a Piece of Eden into space: that it will be akin to a god in the skies above its subjects.

EYE 2

This is the Eye of Horus, an ancient Egyptian symbol used to represent the sky god of the same name. It is likely that this inspired the Eye of Providence and, again, may have been used by Subject 16 to suggest the power of the Piece of Eden in orbit. Then again, it might simply be a way to make the reader's mind leap towards Egypt – clearly a probable location for Subject 16's ancestors. The triangles behind represent the pyramid complex at Giza.

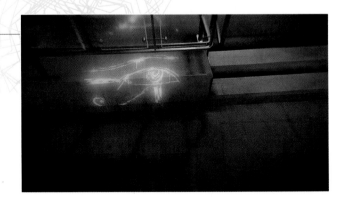

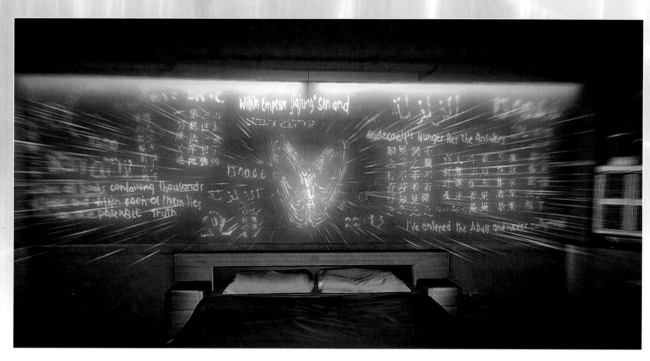

HOW TO PLAY

WALKTHROUGH

REFERENCE & ANALYSIS

EXTRAS

ACHIEVEMENTS & TROPHIES

FREE MISSIONS

SECRETS

AC1: STORY RECAP

AC2: STORY RECAP

BEDROOM WRITINGS

22:13: This hints at Revelations 22:13 in the New Testament: "I am the Alpha and the Omega, the First and the Last, the Beginning and the End." This is written as the words of the post-resurrection Jesus speaking on behalf of the Godhead (the Trinity of God, the Son and the Holy Ghost). Essentially, it's a declaration of God's omniscience, omnipotence and omnipresence – powers that Abstergo's modern-day Templars aspire to possess over mankind.

Hebrew text: This reads "Olam Ha-Ba" in Hebrew, which translates approximately as "The World to Come"; the afterlife.

Arabic text: This Arabic text translates as "Az-Zalzala", which means "the earthquake", but almost certainly refers to the 99th Sura of the Qu'ran, which concerns the Day of Judgment, the end of times – or, in Templar words, the new world order.

Drawing (butterfly wings): This is a plot of a Lorenz Attractor (a fractal generated by very specific equations), named after creator Edward Lorenz, an American mathematician and meteorologist best known for his pioneering work in chaos theory. He coined the term "butterfly effect". Subject 16 may be using this drawing to communicate how actions in past lives have a profound impact on those who live centuries later.

"We are all books containing thousands of pages and within each of them lies an IRREPARABLE truth": This is Subject 16 reflecting that hereditary memories stored in DNA can be read, but not rewritten.

"Within Emperor Jiajing's sin and Quetzcoalt's hunger lies the answers": Jiajing was the eleventh emperor of the Ming dynasty in sixteenth century China. Remembered for his cruelty and contempt for the traditional requirements of his role, he acquired an obsessive interest in alchemy in a vain attempt to extend his life. Quetzcoalt is a misspelling of Quetzalcoatl, a Mesoamerican deity (though a man writing in his own blood can almost certainly be forgiven a few typos). The natural interpretation is alchemy + god = Abstergo.

"I've entered the abyss and never returned": Subject 16 expressing his despair at losing his sanity; perhaps the final lucid lament of a mind broken by the Bleeding Effect.

Mandelbrot Set: This is a Mandelbrot Set. When this fractal is animated (look online for examples), it suggests a sense of endless progression as the pattern is replicated no matter how far you zoom in – like Animus Subjects always going deeper and deeper in their own memories.

Asian text: These messages all have a meaning related to the game and its key protagonists. Here are the corresponding translations.

個人生死個人了，個人業報個人消: Buddhist saying equivalent to "you reap what you sow".

欲知未来果，今生作者是: "One who wants to read into his future simply needs to write his own present."

人無遠慮，必有近憂: "A man without far sight, must have near worries."

不聞不苦聞之，聞之不若見之，見之不若知之，知之不若行之: "Hearing is better than not hearing, observing is better than hearing, knowing is better than observing and doing is better than knowing" – an ancient Chinese saying that is evocative of the assassin's creed.

若人欲了知。三世一切佛。应观法界性，一切唯心造: "As a human being, if you want to know the spiritual realm of Buddha, you have to observe, you have to know that everything you see in the world comes from your own mind."

Although we have now analyzed the source of all these symbols, Subject 16's strange decision to kill himself in order to paint them remains inexplicable. However, Assassin's Creed II bursts this mystery wide open, and the secret truth of Subject 16 is revealed in the following pages.

ASSASSIN'S CREED II: STORY RECAP

In this section we re-examine the plot revelations of Assassin's Creed II, filling in the gaps for those players who missed any telling information or revealing disclosures along the way. It should be clear that this section contains major spoilers for those who haven't yet reached the final sequences.

STORY SUMMARY

As Desmond stands contemplating the ethereal imprint of Subject 16's messages in his cell, a bloodstained and preoccupied Lucy shows up and orders him to enter the Animus. He briefly witnesses the birth of a child, Ezio, in Renaissance Italy before he is abruptly withdrawn. The pair escape the Abstergo complex and travel to a secret hideout where members of the Assassin's Brotherhood and a new Animus 2.0 await. Lucy believes that the Templars are not the only threat to mankind – and that a young Florentine noble is the key to a deeper truth.

Lucy also believes that experiencing the life of an Assassin might confer a significant secondary benefit. With the Templars closing in, their relentless crusade reducing Brotherhood numbers worldwide, she speculates that the Bleeding Effect might enable Desmond to learn his family trade through his ancestor's deeds.

The Ezio Auditore that Desmond encounters in the Animus is a freewheeling, insouciant 17-year-old. His carefree youth comes to an end, however, when his family is falsely accused of conspiracy to commit treason. His father and two brothers are executed after Uberto Alberti, a corrupt magistrate, suppresses evidence of the true perpetrators. Evading capture, Ezio becomes a fugitive. After receiving advice and assistance from Paola, the Madam of a Florentine brothel who

something far larger than simple political corruption. Both the Brotherhood and the Templars seem to be searching for the pages of a mysterious Codex, a book that, once complete, will lead to a powerful secret.

At this point, Lucy invites Desmond into the hideout's warehouse to test out skills acquired during his time in the Animus. Sure enough, he learns that his agility has improved exponentially, his physical ability seemingly equivalent to that of Ezio. Other developments are less heartening. Desmond experiences a sequence of disturbing hallucinations that appear to be brief scenes in the life of both Altaïr and Ezio, a stark reminder that the Bleeding Effect may yet bear terrible consequences. He even undergoes a lengthy "flashback" as he watches Altaïr pursue Maria (a Templar agent spared by the Assassin near the end of the first game). The chase, it transpires, was a playful game; Desmond witnesses the pair make love at the top of a tower before he returns to his senses. Awaking the next morning, having seemingly recovered, he returns to the Animus.

HOW TO PLAY

WALKTHROUGH

REFERENCE & ANALYSIS

EXTRAS

ACHIEVEMENTS & TROPHIES

FREE MISSIONS

SECRETS

AC1: STORY RECAP

AC2: STORY RECAP

is sympathetic to his plight, Ezio slips into a public art exhibition and vengefully slays Alberti before spiriting his mother and sister to safety in the Villa Auditore, in the town of Monteriggioni.

Residing there to receive combat training from his uncle Mario, Ezio discovers that Uberto Alberti did not work alone: the Pazzi family, long at odds with the Auditore, were the true agents of the conspiracy. Ezio also learns that his father was not merely a banker in the Medici bank, and an advisor to Lorenzo de' Medici, but a member of the Assassin's Brotherhood. The Pazzi, in turn, are members of the secretive Templar order: sworn enemies of the Brotherhood who aspire to rule Italy and, ultimately, the world. As Ezio hunts down and dispatches each Pazzi in turn, honing his skills through tuition from Mario and the mysterious La Volpe, he comes to understand that his father had uncovered

Ezio travels to Venice to track down a list of men created by his father, and finds out that they are all members of the Templar order. As he stalks and assassinates each in turn, finding more Codex pages in the process, the purpose of their scheming and maneuvering becomes apparent. Their leader, Rodrigo Borgia ("The Spaniard"), is attempting to locate a hidden Vault that contains some form of astonishing power. The Templars intend to use it to secure dominion over mankind. To open the Vault, one must possess two "Pieces of Eden": ancient artifacts that enable those who wield them to perform astonishing feats. During his attempt to steal one of these from Borgia, Ezio is astounded when several friends from his travels through Italy (including Mario Auditore, Paola and La Volpe) arrive to offer aid and reveal themselves to be members of the Brotherhood. Moreover, we learn that Ezio's role in events was foretold by an ancient prophecy.

After a period of time that corresponds to memories that the Animus cannot access because of a glitch, the story resumes as Ezio completes his collection of the Codex pages. A map hidden in the pages leads to Rome, where he challenges Rodrigo Borgia who, through his expert machinations, now serves in the Vatican as Pope. Borgia holds the second Piece of Eden (the Papal Staff), and the two fight

in the Sistine Chapel for the right to open the Vault hidden beneath. Though the Templar appears to triumph, he rages at the discovery that the secret chamber is resolutely closed to him. The indomitable Ezio, though gravely wounded, confronts him again. After beating him to the ground, Ezio opts to spare Borgia's life.

Entering the chamber, Ezio meets with a holographic projection of a woman who introduces herself as Minerva. Dismissing the Assassin's questions, she instead speaks directly to Desmond. Minerva warns of an imminent catastrophe that could destroy all life on Earth, and explains that this cataclysm occurred once before – annihilating her kind many thousands of years ago. She claims that her people had been developing a way to prevent it, their labors hidden in other secret locations around the world. Desmond (and the modern-day Brotherhood) must visit these Vaults and somehow finish their research.

Desmond is pulled out from the Animus to discover that Templar agents, led by Warren Vidic, have arrived at the hideout to recapture their erstwhile assets. Demonstrating his now awe-inspiring combat skills, Desmond fights alongside Lucy to repel the attack. When Vidic flees, the Assassins make their escape before the closing credits roll…

ANALYSIS & SPECULATION

HOW TO PLAY

WALKTHROUGH

REFERENCE &
ANALYSIS

EXTRAS

ACHIEVEMENTS
& TROPHIES

FREE MISSIONS

SECRETS

AC1:
STORY RECAP

AC2:
STORY RECAP

Many of the mysteries encountered in Assassin's Creed II will only be solved by the future games in the series. This doesn't mean that we cannot bring certain facts to your attention, though, and engage in a little speculation that should set you on a course of discovery for yourself…

What happens to Ezio after the events in the Vault? Does he die from his wounds?

Ezio cannot die at this point, as Desmond's very existence testifies. For the bloodline to continue, Ezio must survive and reproduce; passing on the essential genetic material in which is encoded everything that the Animus reveals. Somehow, whether aided or alone, he must survive his terrible wounds and make a recovery.

Beyond compassion and sheer fatigue, why did Ezio not kill Rodrigo Borgia?

Examine the dialog that occurs between them at the end. This is not just a defeat for Rodrigo Borgia, whose entire existence has been dedicated to a falsehood, a destiny that was not his. It represents something far greater in the struggle for dominion. The Templars do not have a prophet after all, even in their most powerful leader. The Assassins do. As both sides begin to realize the consequences of this outcome, the symbolic result of the battle between the old Pope and the new Assassin shifts the balance of power in a way that has ramifications for the world.

And that is why, we suspect, Ezio concludes with the famous words of Hassan-i Sabbah: "Nothing is true; everything is permitted". By invoking the Brotherhood of the Assassins, Ezio is not just asserting what he represents but demonstrating that he is not bound by any rule to slay an enemy already defeated. He has the power *and* the freedom of will to transcend.

What does the story ending reveal about the true goal of the Templars? And why didn't the Vault open for Borgia?

The Templars are obsessed with First Civilization technology. Their machinations and deceptions, from Al Mualim to Rodrigo Borgia to Abstergo Industries, have all concerned the acquisition of artifacts. They are clearly not seeking this lost technology as mere collectors, but to implement a far greater and more terrible global plan: to acquire power over others where they can, and to eliminate all those they cannot control or make conform. As a means of delivering worldwide peace and security, it is a solution that will be troublingly familiar to scholars of twentieth-century history.

The importance of the artifacts is that they may be the only way the Templars can ever acquire the seemingly divine powers of the First Civilization. Would they use the knowledge to exploit a potential Doomsday rather than prevent it? But even then, as the Borgia plot to open the Vault suggests, there is more to it than simply holding the right keys.

Who is Minerva?

Minerva was one of the last surviving members of the First Civilization, and so it fell to her to shoulder their duties to posterity. She is most certainly long dead, even in Ezio's time, as it is clear that only a holographic simulacrum of her now remains. The Capitoline Triad of Jupiter, Juno and Minerva was a sub-pantheon of supreme deities worshipped in Rome long before the Holy Roman Empire, prior even to the Republic.

What are the images that appear on the wall as Minerva speaks to Desmond?

They show Vault locations: this is the true "data" of Minerva's genetic transmission. For example, you can clearly see step pyramids, so one can assume that there's a Vault in Mesoamerica or perhaps in a ziggurat of Mesopotamia. But what are the other symbols and images?

Looking back to Assassin's Creed, Altaïr encountered a holo-globe indicating the locations of other Pieces of Eden. These may well be the same locations as the Vaults that Minerva describes.

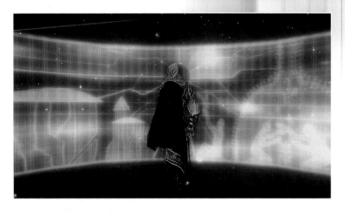

If Ezio is the "Prophet", why does Minerva appear to ignore him and address Desmond directly?

Ezio's role as Prophet is to act as a conduit for Minerva to deliver data to Desmond alone. After all his trials and personal tragedies, we find that Ezio is being used – rather unsentimentally, it must be said – as an answering machine or biological bulletin board. Minerva simply leaves information (including the location of other hidden Vaults) for Desmond to collect in the far future. Consider the sheer import of the message conveyed. Its incalculable worth – and the consequences, should it fall into the wrong hands – means that this is actually an ingenious way of communicating "secure" data from past to future. In justifying this method, Minerva laments that what her people achieved was always misunderstood.

One of the game's recurring motifs is that historical facts have been misinterpreted and misrepresented in the telling down the years, taking on the status of myths and legends. Genuine but extraordinary events are distorted over time, perhaps attributed to a divine cause that is more easily dismissed by rational minds. The controversial twentieth-century author and Catastrophist, Immanuel Velikovsky, proposed that the Ten Plagues described in the Old Testament were evidence of the Earth being

caught in the tail of a comet, with blood-red rivers and fatal diseases explicable by recourse to perfectly natural but cosmic disasters. And though his intention may have been to grant scientific veracity to Biblical accounts, he illustrates the idea that scripture, culture and oral tradition may result in flawed and corrupted attempts to convey knowledge down the ages.

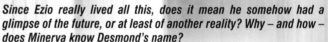

Since Ezio really lived all this, does it mean he somehow had a glimpse of the future, or at least of another reality? Why – and how – does Minerva know Desmond's name?

The Animus tech might actually be appropriated First Civilization science, recreated by Assassins and Templars. Minerva would know that mankind would reach the point of creating such devices, so delivered her message not to Ezio (who is living in the wrong era), but to the first human to access the past through memories. Ezio may, at least, come to appreciate that his life is one thread of a much grander tapestry intended for the eyes of others. Such is the role of a prophet.

Minerva's direct appeal to Desmond might imply that, in knowing his name, the First Civilization had powers to foresee the future. She mentions, cryptically, that her people perceive time "differently". However, another possibility is that the means of communication is so peculiarly intimate that whoever received the message would, by necessity of context, hear themselves addressed by their own name.

The relationship between the First Civilization and Time is not a clear one, but it could be hoped that any capacity for clairvoyance would have at least revealed the catastrophe that befell them. Instead, Time seems to have been their greatest enemy in all things.

What is the link between the First Civilization and Roman gods?

In passing, Minerva mentions the Etruscan etymology of her name. With the other names she gives us, the unavoidable implication is that all faiths and mythologies have derived from her people's manipulations of, or interactions with, humans. It also follows that all known "gods" and "goddesses" were actually members of the First Civilization, local to regions where respective religions first flourished.

How long have Minerva and her companions in the other sarcophagi been dead?

It is possible that they lay dead for millennia before they came to be worshipped as

gods, but just how many thousands of years? 10,000? 50,000 years? Or just 5,000? Entire human civilizations have risen and flourished only to vanish into oblivion. If not for the construction of large stone monuments, our knowledge of myriad cultures from Stonehenge to Easter Island would have been lost to prehistory. Given the cataclysmic event that Minerva describes, and its effectiveness in wiping the slate of the earth, the era of the First Civilization may be closer than we guess.

HOW TO PLAY

WALKTHROUGH

REFERENCE & ANALYSIS

EXTRAS

ACHIEVEMENTS & TROPHIES

FREE MISSIONS

SECRETS

AC1: STORY RECAP

AC2: STORY RECAP

Are the members of the First Civilization human?

They must be mortal, at least, though little more is known. Perhaps they're just human, but with the ability to tap greater potential only latent in mankind. In any case, the First Civilization is clearly tremendously advanced, with incredible technology, but there is no indication of whether they are from another time, or space, or dimension, or simply the true and original indigenous race of Earth. Minerva says that they built humans in their own image, and that they made them to survive. But it appears they may have designed us too well: not content to exist as slaves and inferiors.

Who won the war between the First Civilization and humans?

All we know is that the First Civilization died, and that humans didn't, so we can assume that the latter (and more specifically, we might guess, proto-Templars in their lust for power) won the war. This would explain why Minerva warns Desmond to "guard against the cross - for there are many who will stand in your way".

Are the Vaults shelters where Humans or First Civilization survivors would be safe from the after-effects of disaster?

Desmond's understanding of the catastrophe is of some kind of solar flare of such magnitude that it could reach out to scorch the earth (and would certainly explain how a civilization can be wiped from history). The theory of Geomagnetic Reversal is suggested by Lucy. It would be fair to say that the true nature of the cataclysm is still unknown at this point.

Minerva's message is that the Vaults contain some form of assistance or research which will be useful in staving off a repeat of the catastrophe. Ancient knowledge? Powerful technologies, in the form of artifacts? At the very least, the information sealed within should give some indication of just what kind of threat is on the way.

What is a "Geomagnetic Reversal"? How will this be a catastrophe?

There is a theory that Earth's magnetic field can flip its North-South polarity, and has done so in the past, with reference to petrological anomalies as proof. Scientific opinion is divided and certainly doesn't endorse the wilder speculation that a temporary loss of magnetic field strength could leave the Earth vulnerable to deadly cosmic rays. Nor is this to be confused with the Pole Shift hypothesis of Charles Hapgood, who also denied the existence of plate tectonics in his book *The Earth's Shifting Crust* (1958). Hapgood was pondering catastrophic geological events that could explain the disappearance of Atlantis or the Lost Continent of Mu. However, all of these may be influences on the backstory.

The mention of solar flares in context could refer to Coronal Mass Ejections (CMEs) that scatter life-threatening radiation. Proton storms created by solar flares can inflict biochemical damage and already cause concern for astronauts working outside the protection of the atmosphere, so a synchronous occurrence of cyclical cosmic events could leave the planet prone to bombardment.

Why has Desmond not yet been struck by the worst consequences of the Bleeding Effect?

Because he has only experienced and absorbed the memories of two ancestors to date. The Bleeding Effect is proportional to the number of "personalities" that a Subject explores, and Subject 16 was immersed in the lives of many. Even so, Desmond's condition is deteriorating. The Altaïr flashback came unbidden, of itself, and scenes of the game spent outside the Animus are starting to suggest that other thoughts and memories are already beginning to bubble up to the surface of his mind during ordinary life. If he continues down this path, we have seen what may await him at the end.

What does the Altaïr flashback mean?

On one level, it underlines the detrimental effects of extended Animus use. Experiencing a "lucid dream" while standing in a corridor suggests that Desmond's acquisition of incredible physical prowess (not to mention knowledge) is accompanied by the dangerous consequences of the Bleeding Effect. His time as Ezio is turning him into a truly formidable Assassin – but what purpose could that serve if, like Subject 16, he cannot differentiate between his life and those of his ancestors?

There is another explanation. For Desmond to exist, Altaïr must have sired at least one child – and this short interlude suggests a potential mother. Maria, if you recall, was a young Templar ordered to pose as Robert de Sablé during the events of Assassin's Creed. Altaïr saw no reason to take her life once he discovered the subterfuge. After the defeat of Al Mualim, they became lovers; the scene at the top of the tower alludes to a moment of conception.

HOW TO PLAY

WALKTHROUGH

REFERENCE &
ANALYSIS

EXTRAS

ACHIEVEMENTS
& TROPHIES

FREE MISSIONS

SECRETS

AC1:
STORY RECAP

**AC2:
STORY RECAP**

Why was the Codex created by Altaïr broken up and hidden around Italy?

The answer to this is revealed in the Auditore Family Crypt, though not without relating a sad tale in the process. Another ancestor of Desmond comes by the Codex in his dealings with Marco Polo, being introduced to its secrets by Dante Alighieri. But the prize extorts a sacrifice.

"Cloaked in darkness, the pirates came. I didn't see them until they were already boarding my ship.

I hid with my family in the hold. Pulling out the Codex, I ran the worn leather cover through my hands, then, I broke the spine. The pages slid silently onto the floor. I scattered them into the chests, boxes and containers I was carrying to market."

And so it was dispersed, cheating the Templars of their plunder. What's curious is that the Codex finds its way back to the bloodline, perhaps by the deliberate intentions of the Assassins. The timeline also indicates that this was the account of a close descendent of Altaïr, no more than a few generations past, and so explains how the family tree extends its branches to Europe. Crucial to the maritime spice routes, Venice would have been a ready destination for somebody who needed to escape the Holy Land. With the fabrication of the Auditore nobility and the naturalization of further generations, the genetic continuity is explained.

Who was Altaïr writing the Codex for?

The Codex would appear to be an attempt to encapsulate and share some of the knowledge that Altaïr gained from his Piece of Eden, following the events in Assassin's Creed. Mechanisms, techniques and anachronisms share pages with accounts, beliefs and philosophical reflections, because the Codex is also a diary. And why does anyone write a diary? Perhaps Altaïr himself did not see the hand on his shoulder. The usefulness of the information, which sleeps in opacity for years before suddenly surrendering itself to those with the understanding to make best application of it, may have been disseminated by higher motives. Perhaps it is the Pieces of Eden themselves that guide and impel others to impart their ancient wisdom shrewdly and with an eye on the future.

Who is Subject 16? Why do the Glyphs look like the blood drawings left by Subject 16? How did Subject 16 hide the Glyphs in the Memory Core?

Subject 16 was an Assassin captured by Abstergo Industries, who used him to explore history with the Animus. They kept him inside the Animus for so long that – because of the Bleeding Effect – his mind merged with the minds of his ancestors, making him a super genius lost in the broken timeline within his own head. It is with this viewpoint from ubiquity that Subject 16 was able to discover a startling, shattering truth, though he realized that he must find a way to secretly convey it to the Assassins before death or insanity stole it away. Racing against his own mental breakdown, he hacked into the Animus while the Abstergo scientists were out of the room and planted a video inside the machine's Memory Core for the next user to find. Then, in a final act of desperation and defiance, he cut open a vein and painted the symbols across the room in his blood. Even after they were scrubbed away, he hoped that his successor would be able to spot the markers that would lead to the The Truth video. The doctors were too late to save him.

The transfer of the Memory Core that Lucy took from Abstergo explains how the Glyphs made their way into the Animus 2.0. Incidentally this means Subject 16 assumed that Lucy would take the Core with her when escaping from Abstergo.

What does Subject 16's The Truth video mean?

Strictly speaking, it isn't just a video. It's a memory, as recorded by the Animus. This means that Subject 16 must be a descendent of Adam. Not figuratively, but born of Adam's genetic ancestry.

The memory reveals that the story of Adam and Eve and the Garden of Eden is true – in a fashion. It would appear that they disobeyed their masters and strove to rebel by stealing a Piece of Eden, an Apple, presumably to give themselves some kind of defense or power to resist. This could have been the first act of defiance that led to the conflict described by Minerva. The "innocence" of humankind was lost when we realized how much of their superiority lay in their technology, and a war between the two species – First Civilization and humans – began.

Is this why "Apples" can be used to control humans?

Subject 16's record also shows that the artifacts – the Staff, the Apple, the Pieces of Eden – were tools that the First Civilization used to wield power over humans. Whether the artifacts were made to control humans, or humans were

HOW TO PLAY

WALKTHROUGH

REFERENCE &
ANALYSIS

EXTRAS

ACHIEVEMENTS
& TROPHIES

FREE MISSIONS

SECRETS

AC1:
STORY RECAP

**AC2:
STORY RECAP**

made to obey artifacts, is another matter. Even so, some are immune to their effects.

Moreover, the Glyph puzzles give hints to the involvement of Pieces of Eden in world history. Famous figures and crucial events may have been shaped by the influence that the technology can exert.

Are Desmond, Ezio and Altaïr somehow descended from the members of the First Civilization? Does this explain Eagle Vision, and their resistance to Pieces of Eden?

From Subject 16's The Truth memory, it's also apparent that Adam and Eve demonstrate feats of agility that might ordinarily be ascribed to Assassins. Are they humans? What might be interesting here is to note the text from Subject 16's Glyph puzzle #14, Bloodlines, which reads:

"The seeds were planted as two worlds became one. Behold, the Assassins, the children of two worlds!"

If we were built in their image, is it too much to suggest that Assassins, with their innate abilities, are a product of the union of humans and the First Civilization?

What might the future hold in Assassin's Creed III?

Minerva's warning raises the stakes with a frightening perspective. Where once we glimpsed a power struggle between two arcane enemies, wresting political control from each other down the ages, now we see the future of Earth itself hanging in the balance. With Minerva's assertion that these events are cyclical in nature, we can no longer remain blissfully ignorant of the knowledge that a great disaster, a cosmic catastrophe, could be approaching once again.

But the Vaults of the First Civilization are still out there. Help may be at hand, for those who can track it down. Will Assassin's Creed III take us to new locations in search of old artifacts? It may seem unlikely that the Templars would wish for the end of the world, but if they suspect they could harness the ancient wisdom and use it to protect their own, while nature claims the rest, their New World Order could be ushered in after all.

BEHIND THE SCENES

For this section, we have invited key members of the Ubisoft Montreal development team to talk freely on a selection of topics. Their contributions (and, of course, the concept art that they so thoughtfully provided) offer an illuminating insight into the creative processes behind Assassin's Creed II.

FROM ASSASSIN'S CREED TO ASSASSIN'S CREED II

Altaïr & Ezio

BENOIT LAMBERT – *After the release of AC1 we undertook a lot of market research and listened to the views of both gamers and journalists. We wanted to know not only what we got right with AC1 but also what we got wrong. The feedback told us there were lots of great things about AC1 – the setting, the free running system, the crowd scenes – but it appeared that we had not offered the player a wide enough variety of experiences. So we completely revamped the game's structure, first removing the repetitive "investigation" section that always preceded an assassination mission. The latest game is far more open and fluid as a result, and you are invited to experience many more things than in AC1.*

We don't just have nine assassination missions this time; the game now offers more than 100 missions. We designed 15 modular mission types, building blocks that we could use to create unique assignments. Tailing a target through the crowds might lead to a chase and then to an assassination, for example. Our new system offers a huge range of experiences and altering the sequence varies the pace. I am very proud of what we have achieved here, as I believe that we succeeded in the vital task of ensuring that the story and the gameplay work together – and that each is enhanced by this synergy. This is one of our biggest accomplishments.

But that wasn't all we focused on. The combat now has far more depth and introduces new moves, enemies and weapons. Ezio now has the ability to swim, to pilot a boat. The economic system is another novel addition that renews the experience. There are lots of new ideas in AC2.

GAELEC SIMARD – *In AC1, Altaïr grew more notorious as the story progressed. In AC2 we wanted to give control of that aspect, and its consequences, to the player. You can now choose how to approach a situation, weighing up how it might affect your notoriety, and then perform tasks later to reduce it if necessary.*

For a brand new combat system, the fights in AC1 showed real promise. However, the counter attack move was simply too powerful and ultimately made the brawls seem repetitive. In AC2, we added additional layers of strategy to the fighting and devised many more effective methods for dispatching enemies. We also made sure that, even without a weapon to hand, Ezio remains a force to be reckoned with.

We listened to our fans when they told us they found the investigation loop before each assassination repetitive. We decided to guide the player in a more linear fashion through the story while making sure that every mission would be different and offer new gameplay experiences. I think this also helped us create a stronger narrative.

With AC1 we introduced two innovations to the world of videogames: free running and social stealth. In conjunction with fighting, these constituted the three defining principles of Assassin's Creed. With AC2, we felt that it would be good to have dedicated enemies who specifically tested those three elements – challenging the players who mastered AC1 to change their gaming habits. For example, if you try to hide in a haystack, you now have to be prepared for a suspicious Seeker armed with a spear.

Seeker

Notoriety poster

Charles Randall, Combat Team Leader

CHARLES RANDALL – *For AC2, we wanted to make combat feel as cohesive and complete as possible. So we set out to design everything from the ground up, using AC1 as our foundation. As we knew we wanted disarming and new weapons, we built on what we had, removed what didn't work – defense breakers, combo kills – and replaced them with similar systems which were more entertaining and designed to fit as part of the whole. AC2's combat system has a feeling of being "complete" in a way that was missing in AC1.*

GAELEC SIMARD – *In addition to the increased range of moves and Ezio's extended inventory, we used other ways to reinforce the player's sense of freedom. This includes new means of transportation such as the gondola, the horse, the carriage and the Fast Travel system. The choice of many side missions grants the player the liberty to change the pace of the game and roam freely, but still with a purpose, whenever they wish.*

Minerva concept art

The carriage chase

MOHAMED GAMBOUZ – *AC2 is a sequel, which usually means graphical improvements because the team is used to working on the hardware and the processes are well established. So our main objectives were to bring greater variety and richer environments, visually speaking. Because the setting of the game had changed in both time period and geographical location, we had to rebuild most of the graphic content. But, of course, we used all the things we learned when developing AC1.*

JEFFREY YOHALEM – *It was an exciting and challenging task to write within this rich world. We were able to play with many of our fans' expectations in a way that was not possible in AC1 due to the increased scope of AC2. To match that scope, pieces of the storyline were spread across the game, creating an incredibly deep experience. It was very important to us that all the stories relate to each other, so in addition to continuing with the past and present narratives of AC1, the two storylines of AC2 interlock. Desmond in the present is searching Subject 16's files for a deep and powerful secret, while Ezio is following a prophecy to discover a secret hidden within the Vault. At the end, they discover two different sides of the same mystery, even though they are separated by hundreds of years. This kind of interconnection is part of what makes the Assassin's Creed storyline so strong.*

Inside the vault

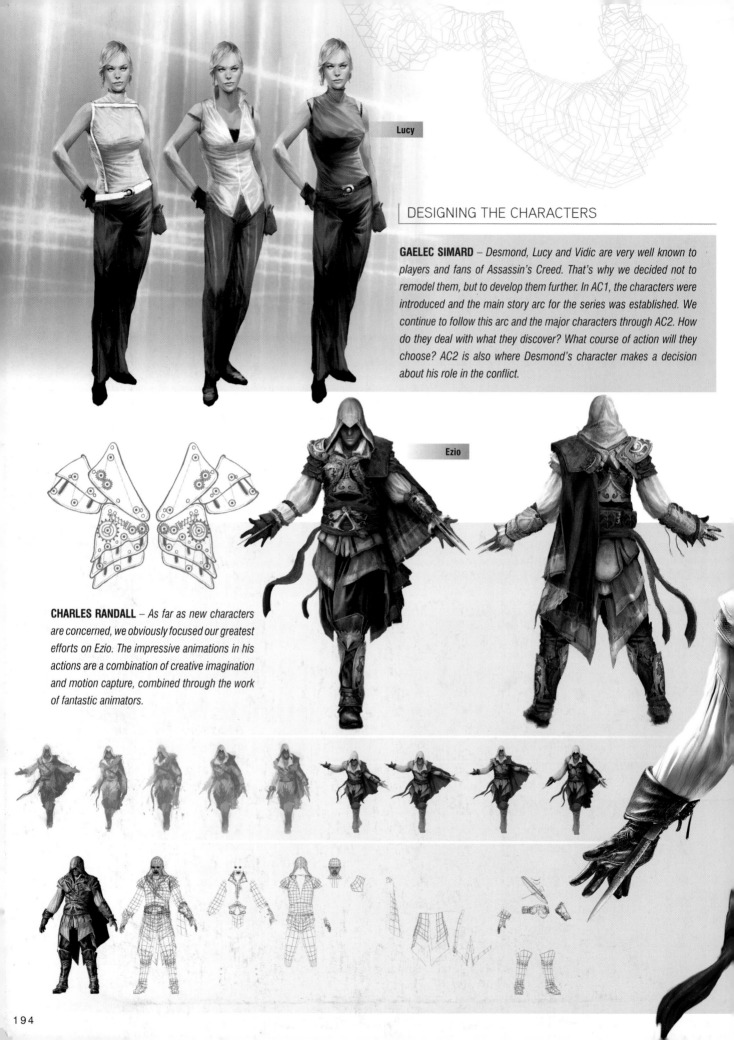

Lucy

Ezio

DESIGNING THE CHARACTERS

GAELEC SIMARD – *Desmond, Lucy and Vidic are very well known to players and fans of Assassin's Creed. That's why we decided not to remodel them, but to develop them further. In AC1, the characters were introduced and the main story arc for the series was established. We continue to follow this arc and the major characters through AC2. How do they deal with what they discover? What course of action will they choose? AC2 is also where Desmond's character makes a decision about his role in the conflict.*

CHARLES RANDALL – *As far as new characters are concerned, we obviously focused our greatest efforts on Ezio. The impressive animations in his actions are a combination of creative imagination and motion capture, combined through the work of fantastic animators.*